THE HISTORY OF
UNDERCLOTHES

C. WILLETT AND PHILLIS CUNNINGTON

DOVER PUBLICATIONS, INC.
New York

This Dover edition, first published in 1992, is an unabridged, slightly corrected republication of the work first published by Michael Joseph Ltd, London, in 1951.

Manufactured in the United States of America
Dover Publications, Inc., 31 East 2nd Street, Mineola, N.Y. 11501

Library of Congress Cataloging-in-Publication Data

Cunnington, C. Willett (Cecil Willett), 1878–1961.
    The history of underclothes / C. Willett and Phillis Cunnington.
       p.   cm.
    Originally published: London : M. Joseph, 1951.
    Includes bibliographical references and index.
    ISBN 0-486-27124-2 (paper)
    1. Underwear—Great Britain—History. I. Cunnington, Phillis
Emily, 1887-   . II. Title.
GT2073.C8   1992
391'.42'0941—dc20
                                          91-48049
                                              CIP

❧ CONTENTS ❧

ILLUSTRATIONS

Fig.

CHAPTER I (*page* 21)

CHAPTER II (*page* 34)

CHAPTER III (*page* 53)

CHAPTER IV (*page* 68)

CHAPTER V (*page* 96)

CHAPTER VI (*page* 120)

ACKNOWLEDGMENTS

FOR permission to examine specimens of garments, trade catalogues and old records, and to obtain photographs; for technical information generously supplied, and for help in our researches, we are specially indebted to:

The British Museum; the Victoria and Albert Museum; the National Museum of Wales; the Belfast Museum; the Castle Museum, York; the Castle Museum, Norwich; the City Museum, Hereford; the Holly Tree Museum, Colchester; the Gallery of English Costume, Manchester; the Whitworth Art Gallery, Manchester; the Wenham Art Society, Massachusetts, U.S.A.; L'Union Française des Arts du Costume, Paris; Nordiska Museet, Stockholm; the Rosenborg Slot Museum, Copenhagen; the Metropolitan Museum of Art, New York; the Dean and Chapter, Westminster Abbey.

The Tailor and Cutter, Men's Wear, The Drapers' Record, The Outfitter, Corsetry and Underwear.

Messrs. Debenham & Freebody, Dickins & Jones, S. Simpson, Austin Reed, Hope Brothers, Welch Margetson & Co., Jaeger & Co., I. & R. Morley, Warner Brothers, Lillywhites, the Kettering Clothing Society, Atkinsons of Dublin, Tootal, Broadhurst Lee & Co., Charnaux Corset Co., Drew & Son of Bath, Newey Brothers of Birmingham.

The Essex Records, Chelmsford.

Messrs. Faber & Faber for permission to reproduce illustrations from *English Women's Clothing in the Nineteenth Century*. Executors of the late Mrs. Esdaile and the Oxford Press, for permission to reproduce an illustration from *The Life and Works of Roubiliac*.

We have also to thank those whose family records have supplied us with valuable information, and we owe much to Miss Phillipson for her drawings, and to our secretary, Miss Coleman, for her careful revision of the text.

Introduction

IN the many books on period costume the subject of under-clothes has seldom been treated adequately, if, indeed, at all. Yet we cannot appreciate the significance of the outer form unless we understand the nature of the supporting garments beneath. The complete costume is a combination of the two, producing, very often, a shape singularly unlike that of the human body.

For this the undergarments may be mainly responsible. The historian must regard it as unfortunate that underclothes are so generally associated with eroticism, often to a pathological extent; and it may well be that writers have hesitated to expand on a topic which might suggest that their interest is of that nature.

It is perhaps sufficient for the authors of the present book to claim, as doctors, that they approach the subject in a scientific spirit, surveying impartially the various aspects of this subsidiary—though important—element in the art of costume.

The book deals with the underclothes worn by both sexes in this country during the last six centuries.

Though for the most part such garments have had a utilitarian function the fact that they may have also served an erotic purpose is frankly recognized as a social phenomenon. It seems strangely prudish to pretend (as some writers appear to do) that various garments have not been so employed; or to shrink from perceiving the influence which the sexual instinct has exerted upon the coverings of the body. We regard it as an obvious commonplace.

Underclothes have had—and still have—an important 'psychological' interest. To understand this aspect we have to view them in the spirit of their epoch. Thus, in the days of Victorian prudery the human body was so concealed that some of its erotic attraction was transferred to its coverings, which became a matter of furtive pre-occupation. When such words as 'trousers' and 'drawers' were thought indelicate because they recalled the fact that men and women had legs, it was inevitable that almost any concealed garment should have acquired erotic properties, though it may be a little difficult to perceive it in specimens of the period now starkly exhibited in a museum case.

In more remote times that kind of transferred eroticism was less common, but to-day we are still in the backwash of Victorian prudery. For though that former reticence, which shrouded the subject in mystery, seems, at first sight, very unlike the modern attitude, there is a psychological affinity.

Feminine underclothing, for instance, now claims to be 'amusing,' and is given playful nicknames—or pet names—with an air of coy audacity which betrays (to a psychologist, at least) an erotic prudery still lurking about them. Such illusions are sufficiently grotesque to be worth recording.

In our survey the sources of information for the earlier centuries are extremely scanty. We have to rely on chance references by contemporary writers, and these, by modern standards, were not always 'refined.' We have, however, preferred to quote textually rather than to bowdlerize this kind of information.

So too, with contemporary illustrations; we reproduce them if informative, however 'vulgar' their original intent. Often enough it is only from such sources that knowledge can be obtained. From about the sixteenth century onwards a number of actual garments have survived with increasing frequency until in the nineteenth century there is almost a superfluity of women's, though not of men's, for examination.

We have aimed at describing the more usual types worn; and though the book deals mainly with English underclothing we have had at times to use foreign sources of information when the two countries were probably wearing much the same kind of garment.

Underclothing includes all such articles, worn by either sex, as were completely or mainly concealed from the spectator by the external costume.

Some occupy an equivocal place, such as stockings; of which man's has been a 'surface' garment while woman's has emerged only in modern times. But inasmuch as stockings are generally well described in works on period costume we have decided to omit

It is perhaps equally illogical to insert in this book the garments worn in bed (nightdress, nightshirt, etc.) but these, on the other hand, are generally omitted from the text-books and so may usefully be included here. Included too are the various mechanical devices, such as hoops and bustles, which, though not exactly 'garments,' belong to the subject of the book, as an essential 'prop to our infirmity.'

In the history of underclothes it has not seldom happened that a particular garment, long submerged, has eventually risen to the surface, becoming, in fact, an integral part of the visible costume. Woman's stockings have been thus transformed in modern times, following the example of man's waistcoat three centuries ago.

Sometimes the reverse process has occurred; the early Saxon breeches were, later, entirely concealed by the tunic, and became drawers. Centuries later the garment rose again to the surface, in the form of pantaloons or breeches in the modern sense of that word.

So, too, a traditional undergarment may be closely imitated by a surface garment; the female 'chemise' appearing as a 'chemise dress,' or the stays becoming a boned bodice laced up across the front.

Such changes had, of course, a definite significance; an undergarment rising to the surface draws attention to that region; the motive may be erotic, or it may be merely an escape from bondage.

This vacillating habit of the two layers of clothing has affected the names of garments: we see how the 'pantaloons' of the early nineteenth century became presently man's 'pants'—synonymous with 'drawers' in this country but with 'trousers' in the U.S.A.

Woman has not hesitated to borrow man's nomenclature for her own underwear; 'chemise' was the Norman word for his shirt, and the modern 'panties' is, of course, but a playful variant of his pantaloons.

It is strange that by a series of complicated changes the name of an early Christian martyr—Saint Pantaleone—should have arrived at this latter end and that the girl of to-day should find a seat on the relics of a saint.

For centuries woman has claimed for her own the name of 'petticoat'; this 'little coat' was man's property in the Middle Ages which, together with his chemise and drawers, has been taken from him.

She has been prone to attach the name of some notable person to particular types of undergarment. The 'Princess' petticoat is a delicate compliment paid to Alexandra when she became Princess of Wales in '63, and the name, if not the memory, still survives.

In the history of woman's underclothing all sorts of eminent names have been attached to one item or another for a brief spell; one only has become immortal, that of the American lady Amelia Jenks, who, by her marriage to Mr. Bloomer, has supplied a poetical name for a prosaic garment.

It is characteristic of man's conservative habits that he has clung to the ancient names of his underwear, while woman has exercised her imagination in devising new ones for hers, with a preference for diminutives—'undies,' 'cami-bocks,' 'cami-knicks,' 'bras,' 'slips'; it scarcely needs a psychologist to point out that thereby her aim is to give them fresh erotic values, especially as they have become 'fine by degrees and beautifully less.'

FUNCTIONS OF UNDERCLOTHES

I. TO PROTECT THE BODY FROM COLD

Until modern times women have usually worn more underclothing than men, partly because their lives were less active and partly because their outer dress was often of flimsier materials. For warmth they have preferred to rely on additional outer garments. There was also the fact that the male leg has always been clothed whereas under the skirt and petticoats woman's thighs were bare, until well into the nineteenth century.

For the upper part of the body, while man has had no objection to adding to the appearance of bulk, woman has always been reluctant to do so; so that for the last six centuries the chief part of her underclothing has covered the lower half of her body; and though woollen textiles are warmer than linen or cotton, she has generally preferred to use this material for the lower rather than for the upper half.

Man, on the other hand, in order to preserve the free use of his legs, has tended to reverse that arrangement.

The amount of underclothing considered necessary for the purpose of warmth has varied but slightly with man but greatly with woman, though with both sexes there has been a considerable reduction since the first world war.

2. TO SUPPORT THE SHAPE OF THE COSTUME

Female costume has assumed far greater varieties of shape than that of the male, and has appeared with almost any outline—except that of a woman. This has been effected, mainly, by the under-clothes, which have therefore been much more important than man's. Those extraordinary shapes compelled speculation as to what lay beneath, and so gave an artificial air of mystery to the structure.

3. FOR CLEANLINESS

Underclothing protects the skin from the outer costume, but the reverse also holds good. Bodily cleanliness was scarcely thought important until less than two hundred years ago. The magnificent materials worn in Elizabethan times, for instance, had to be pro-tected from the filthy skin beneath. Physical cleanliness, an innova-tion started by the Macaronis towards the close of the eighteenth century, became in Victorian times almost a symbol of class dis-tinction and so led to frequent changes of underclothing.

Up to the first world war, the notion that any part of the skin should be in contact with the dress or suit had become abhorrent among the leisured classes. It may be noted that this nicety has lapsed, with both sexes, during the last thirty years, so that in spite of the general habit of the daily bath the modern man and woman cannot claim to be as clean in their habits as were the Edwardians. To-day a considerable portion of a man's skin is in direct contact with his trousers, and a girl will dance in a frock with hardly any underclothing beneath it; a practice which their grandparents would have thought very disgusting.

4. EROTIC USE OF UNDERCLOTHES

To reveal portions of underclothing is, in women, an obviously erotic gesture, symbolizing the act of undressing. Frequently, there-fore, either the top of the chemise has been exposed or simulated, or the hem of the petticoat. Sometimes the bodice of the evening dress has been designed to look like corsets, as though to suggest that the wearer was incompletely clad—a device seen at the very acme of Victorian prudery about 1880.

If the stockings were habitually concealed then occasional glimpses of ankle served the same purpose.

Undergarments designed with erotic symbols (hearts, arrows, etc.),

THE HISTORY OF UNDERCLOTHES

or, of bizarre colours, belong to the same category; so too the semi-transparent nightdress, which, be it observed, the modern young woman, though normally using pyjamas, insists on having for her wedding trousseau. And though man has not required similar aids to his own physical attraction, it is significant that almost the only gay raiment he ventures to wear is peacock-coloured pyjamas and dressing-gown.

The fact that (respectable) women began to wear 'attractive' nightwear only after the introduction, in the early eighties of last century, of the practice of birth-control, has an obvious implication. In the days of unlimited birth-rate the feminine nightdress was markedly unappealing: perhaps a calculated discretion.

Man has never used provocative underclothing; its plain prose has been in singular contrast to the poetical allurements worn by woman, and perhaps the feminine undergarment with the longest history of eroticism is the corset. Its main purpose, indeed, has been to diminish the size of her waist, and to emphasize the contours of the breasts, thus adding to her 'sex attraction.' In those periods when men, too, wore corsets we may suppose the shapely waist thus produced helped to emphasize the breadth of the male shoulder-line.

During these six centuries women have almost continuously employed various kinds of 'undergarments' serving no other purpose than to accentuate, or even to create, those physical features which characterize their sex—mechanical devices such as the bustle (at least six centuries old), artificial breasts, hip hoops and pads, and in modern times the brassière.

The eroticism associated with particular undergarments has varied very much in different epochs. For centuries the word 'petticoats' served poets as a symbol of feminine charm, becoming a refined synonym for the sex, while, paradoxically, to speak of woman as 'a skirt' was a vulgarism.

The nineteenth century endowed the word 'drawers' with extraordinary qualities, and on the comic stage veiled allusions to the garment were greatly appreciated by (masculine) audiences. When in the nineties an actress with a bicycle sang a ditty about:

> Just a little bit of string—such a tiny little thing,
> Not as tightly tied as string should be;
> So in future when I ride, I shall wear things that divide,
> Or things that haven't strings, you see!

the verse was hailed as a daringly witty allusion to a closely guarded secret.

We must infer that the fascination of any undergarment depends mainly on its concealment; its too liberal display, as in the notorious can-can, shocked the prudish nineties by shattering a cherished illusion. The term 'shocking' was then in constant use; it implied a peculiar sensitiveness to erotic symbols—or what seemed to be such—and was characteristic of a generation capable of detecting charm in calico.

5. AS A METHOD OF CLASS DISTINCTION

The sense in which this term is used by us requires some explanation. A large community tends to become separated into groups based in a measure on their economic status. The crudest form of distinction is by wealth, which, however, can be tempered by the cultivation of taste. Culture, indeed, has never been wholly dependent on wealth and is, in fact, rather the expression of a particular attitude of mind, which has its own values and, in spite of extravagancies of wealth or sex-display, sustains standards of beauty.

These niceties may be incomprehensible to those who confuse culture with wealth, and destroy the one in trying to obliterate the other. They imply more than accidents of birth or accumulations of riches. By expressing a quality of taste they have served in the art of costume to control methods of sex attraction. It has been, in the main, the influence of culture which has condemned in fashions the grosser forms of eroticism as well as the more vulgar display of wealth. If the restraint exercised by class distinction were to be removed from costume, there would be little to prevent it from exhibiting sex appeal in the crudest forms.

Men have used underclothes to emphasize class distinction even more than women, and have used the shirt for this purpose to a remarkable extent. Glimpses of it have been revealed ever since the days of the Tudors, either by slashings of the jerkin or by unbuttoning the top of the eighteenth-century waistcoat and subsequently by means of the V opening. In these ways the quality of the material, starched or frilled, was exposed to distinguish the 'gentleman' from the manual worker. The clean white shirt-cuffs were a visible proof that the wearer had no occasion to soil his hands.

Even more conspicuous has been the shirt-front in his evening dress as a symbol of gentility, real or assumed.

Woman has demonstrated class distinction chiefly by the size of the skirt, which has been supported either by abundance of petticoats or by mechanical aids such as hoops. But, unlike men, she has not displayed part of an undergarment to indicate social rank.

MATERIALS

Linen is the oldest, and from the days of Beau Brummel became almost a material of class distinction. The word itself became a Victorian synonym for the underwear of a 'gentleman.' Cotton, which was linen's 'social inferior,' came into general use after the Restoration of 1660.

We must suppose that woollen petticoats were at least as old as the Middle Ages. Men, however, do not seem to have worn woollen undergarments habitually until the close of the eighteenth century or even after. From the sixteenth century woollen waistcoats were occasionally worn for extra warmth by both sexes, and in the Middle Ages there are references to the use of leather for that purpose. It seems curious that such additional outer garments were preferred to the use of genuine 'undergarments' in the modern sense.

Silk was rarely used, except by the leisured classes, until late in Victorian times, and artificial silk belongs, of course, to the present century. Both these materials have been used chiefly by women.

CONSTRUCTION

Until the middle of the last century underclothes were necessarily hand-made, and the absence of fit was noticeable until the introdution of man's drawers, fitting the leg, at the close of the eighteenth century. The notion that a close-fitting garment next the skin gave greater warmth was a Victorian innovation, made possible by improved methods of weaving. However, belief in its efficacy has declined to-day, especially with women.

METHODS OF FASTENING

Strings and ribbons were the fastenings for underclothes until the middle of the seventeenth century, when they were replaced by buttons. The first type was the 'high-top,' shaped like an acorn and made of cotton or silk threads closely radiating from the centre. This type survived well into the nineteenth century.

The 'high-top' was followed about the beginning of the eighteenth century by the 'Dorset thread' button. By contrast the new fashion was flat, an echo of the change in style of metal button at the same period from hemispherical or conical. The 'Dorset thread' button was made on a brass wire ring and lasted on till about 1830, with cotton threads radiating starwise from the centre.

The next fashion was for small mother-o'-pearl buttons, of which the earliest examples known to us are those on George IV's shirt, dated 1827, in the museum at York. The flat calico button did not become common until the 1840's.

These distinctions can be very helpful in dating early specimens of underclothes; but their evidence must be used with care. The buttons may always be replacements—either later or earlier in date than the garment. Again, in the days when undergarments, for example shirts or fine shifts, were inherited from an earlier generation, a later pattern of fastening may have been introduced. The only safe method is 'to examine with a strong glass the thread with which the buttons are attached, to make certain that it appears contemporary with that used on the garment.'[1]

Studs for fastening men's shirts supplanted the button when starching was introduced, and the stud for closing the neckband in front began to appear in the middle of the last century. But it is remarkable how reluctantly the change was accepted, for shirts with a button at the back continued as late as 1860. To-day apparently studs are about to disappear; we are told that collar studs are almost unobtainable in the United States.

Holes for cuff-links do not appear until the nineteenth century, the earliest example known to us being the shirt, dated 1824, in the museum at Hereford. It is probable that the similar holes in the women's habit-shirts of the eighteenth century were not for links but for a ribbon fastening.

The earliest snap-fasteners (late nineteenth century) were of the bird-cage type, with a dome slit by longitudinal perforations and a rigid ring as a socket into which the dome was forced. About the turn of the last century a German firm invented a snap-fastener with

[1] Mrs. Russell Smith: personal letter.

a double S spring made from phosphor bronze wire.[1] Slide fasteners (zip) were produced in the early part of this century in France. The present 'zip,' which probably originated in the U.S.A., did not become practical until after the first war, when I.C.I. took up its manufacture.

Hooks and eyes have seldom been used on undergarments. A rare example can be found on the inner surface of the turned-back collar of Pieter Brueghel's *The Old Shepherd, c.* 1567 (*see figure* 11, p. 36).[2] The collar, with its ruffled border, would have stood up when fastened leaving the hooks and eyes concealed, as we see in the Sture shirts of 1567 (*see* pp. 261–2).

One of the aims of this book is to emphasize the relationship which exists between underclothes and surface garments. It has become customary to regard these two branches of the art of costume as entirely distinct, both in function and meaning, and the distinction is accentuated by the habit of each having its own trade literature, its own department in a store, and its own group of manufacturers. Nor can we ignore that each is popularly associated with its own 'moral significance.' Such distinctions are, however, artificial and unreal. We have come to understand that the influences responsible for surface 'fashions' have, in the main, been responsible also for the changes beneath, though such changes may have taken longer to develop.

Thus, for the last six centuries the two principal influences creating surface 'fashions' have been class distinction and sex attraction, the former mainly responsible for men's fashion, the latter for women's. We can trace the same causes, in similar proportions, affecting the underclothes. More ephemeral impulses ruffling the surface design have been much less prone to disturb the deeper layers, which respond only to profound social upheavals. We can almost measure the intensity of the storm by the depth to which its effect is carried. A revolution or a great war, such events as these, will derange costume to the very skin.

[1] Communicated by Messrs. Newey Brothers Ltd., of Birmingham.
[2] Kunsthistorisches Museum, Vienna.

I

Medieval Period

THROUGHOUT the Middle Ages the underclothing of both sexes possessed a characteristic inherited from earlier times. By tradition it was a part of costume entirely lacking significance. Its function was purely utilitarian. It was not used to express class distinction and only very indirectly to enhance sex attraction. The absence of these features was due to the simple reason that very little of the underclothing was exposed to view. No doubt there was a wide variation in quality and workmanship between the garments of different classes, but as they were not usually perceptible to the spectator this could have created no obvious impression.

Not until after the Renaissance did underclothes develop those two important features, which have in varying degrees become essentials.

Contemporary literature supplies but vague descriptions of such garments, and the illuminated manuscripts only occasionally—and as it were by accident—give glimpses of them. It is true that we can sometimes detect in the female figures a suggestion that they may be wearing something in the nature of corsets to narrow the waist; this would be, then, an undergarment used primarily for sex-attraction. But with that possible exception the underclothes of the period seem to have been—in every sense—insignificant. Even as utilitarian garments they appear to have been cumbersome and ineffective. The material used by the superior classes was linen, and in cold weather warmth was secured by adding to the outer garments, not by warmer underclothing. It is curious that this principle has been revived, especially by women, in modern times.

The purpose, then, of those undergarments was partly to protect the skin from the harsh surface of the outer coverings, and equally to protect the latter from the dirt of the body. We may suppose that the social inferiors were content to wear coarse woollen materials next to the skin. (Cotton was not imported in considerable quantities until 1430.)[1]

The modern conception of 'fashions' in the costume of both sexes began to appear in the second quarter of the fourteenth century, with symbols of class distinction and sex attraction strongly marked; but this only applied to the visible garments. It did not percolate below the surface, where, being invisible, such symbols would have been wasted. Indeed until the close of the epoch the medieval attitude towards underclothing differed enormously from that of later times. So far from developing the symbolism of social rank or sex appeal, the idea of underclothes was associated with the idea that the body was sinful, a source of evil, which needed constant discipline. The wearing of a hair-shirt, for instance, was not only an act of penance but was also a meritorious habit.

> She vowed then a vow to the Father in heaven,
> Her smock to unsow and a hair-shirt to wear,
> To enfeeble her flesh, that was so fierce to sin.[2]

Underclothes could also symbolize the discipline of humility. To appear clad only in underclothes was a voluntary form of self-abasement often practised by pilgrims. The Lord of Joinville records that he went on a pilgrimage 'barefoot in my shirt.'[3] From humility to humiliation is a short step; to appear compulsorily only in under-clothes was a method of punishment. A woman guilty of adultery might have to do penance in church dressed only in her 'shift'; and we read of repentant Lollards abjuring their errors 'in shirt and braies.' The burghers of Calais were ordered by Edward III to surrender (1347) wearing only their shirts—a further humiliation. A supreme example is shown in the account of the Emperor Henry IV who, when seeking absolution from Pope Gregory VII, went to

---

[1] *The Draper's Dictionary.*

[2] *The Vision of Piers Plowman* (1377). Cf. the chaste maiden, Cecile, in the 'Second Nonnes Tale,' who

> Under her robe of gold that sat so fair
> Had next her flesh yclad her in an hair.

[3] *Memoirs of the Crusades*, 1309.

Canossa and there in the bitter winter 'three successive days remained in a woollen shirt and with naked feet.'[1]

The notion that underclothes might express the spirit of the changing times, in sympathy with the outer clothing, did not enter the medieval mind. Consequently it escaped the critical notice of those contemporary writers who were so alert in detecting the sinful impulses responsible for 'fashion.' The fulminations directed at the extravagant modes of the fifteenth century, for instance, were confined to surface warfare, a fact which the student of costume is bound to lament, as he attempts to explore the *terra incognita*.

It is usually stated that neither sex habitually wore nightclothes in bed; nevertheless there are contemporary illustrations showing the contrary, at least for particular occasions such as 'lying-in' and ceremonial visits. The more usual custom of being naked in bed is suggested in the fourteenth-century romance of Lancelot du Lac; there a man is described as going to bed on one occasion 'and took not off his shirt nor his breeches (drawers)'—as though this was a singular omission. So, too, in the instructions to young women on going to bed; the last one in the room to get undressed is advised to extinguish the candle with her finger and thumb, and not 'by throwing her chemise at it.' For which we conclude that she did not stop to put on anything else. On the other hand, in Chaucer's 'The Marchantes Tale' a man is described as sitting up in bed in his shirt and nightcap. The Lord of Joinville (1309), ill with malaria, slept in his tunic.

∽ MEN ∽

I. THE SHIRT

Of all the undergarments worn by either sex this is the one which, if not the most ancient, has certainly preserved longer than any other not only its original name but also its essential design and masculinity. Until a hundred years ago it was always worn next the skin.

The length of the shirt was less than that of the modern garment, especially after the middle of the fourteenth century, but contemporary illustrations suggest that in earlier times it varied a good

[1] Hallam: *View of the State of Europe during the Middle Ages*, 1818.

FIG. I. MEDIEVAL SHIRTS: (a) WITHOUT VENTS, 15TH CENTURY. (b) WITH VENTS, 15TH CENTURY. (c) WITHOUT VENTS, 14TH CENTURY. (d) WITH BRAIES, 15TH CENTURY

deal (*figure* 1). The width increased from above downwards so that the material hung in folds, the front and back pieces being joined by a straight seam across the shoulders. Occasionally, however, the material was gathered at the neck.

The two side vents, a feature which has been so characteristic of the male shirt from the sixteenth century onwards, was by no means invariably seen in the medieval shirt. When present the front and back panels were of the same length (*figure* 1(*b*)). Vents were sometimes not at the side seams but more forward, the front panel being narrower than the back. Sometimes there was also a slit in the centre of the front.

The sleeves were somewhat full, without cuffs, and cut straight. The kimono type of sleeve was also in use.

The Norman shirt of the higher ranks was embroidered round the neck and at the wrists,[1] but the neckband did not appear until the fourteenth century; this, and the band at the wrist, in the following century, were often embroidered in colours. The neck opening was fastened usually by being tied, though there is evidence that from the middle of the fourteenth century a button was sometimes used, as can be seen in *The Adoration of the Shepherds*, by Hugo van der Goes, 1475. The neck opening was generally in front; a few, however, appear to have been fastened behind.

The shirt of the fifteenth century had a low neck except for the period 1430 to 1450 when, in fashionable circles, it acquired an upright collar high enough to show, in front, above the edge of the outer garment (*figure* 1(*d*)).

The medieval shirt was made of wool, linen ('holland' shirts of linen made in that country are mentioned in the wardrobe of Edward IV), hemp and, for the wealthy, occasionally silk. In the fifteenth century 'cloth shirts' were sometimes worn between the linen shirt and the doublet.

2. DRAWERS

The Saxon name for this garment was 'braies' or 'breches' (breeches). Both words were used synonymously throughout the Middle Ages to denote a masculine garment concealing the sexual region.

[1] Kelly and Schwabe: *History of Costume and Armour.*

Went sent iohan.

FIG. 2. BRAIES CAUGHT AT THE KNEE WITH RUNNING STRING IN GIRDLE, *c.* 1250

> He didde (put on) next his white lere (skin)
> Of cloth of lake (linen) fin and clere
> A breche and eke a shirte
> And next his shirte an haketon (cassock).[1]

Henry Castyde (*temp.* Richard II) mentioned that the rude Irish 'wore no breeches. Wherefore I caused breeches of fine linen cloth to be made for the four kings of Ireland while I was there.'[2] Again, in a poem of that period, a needy gentleman made the excuse, 'I would have gone to church to-day but I have no hose or shoes, and my breeches and my shirt are not clean.' In a later century we learn from *A Boke of Curtasye* (printed in 1513) that it was the page's duty to prepare for his master's uprising 'a clean shirte and breche.'

Pilgrims, as a mark of poverty, might dispense with the garment. 'In poure cotes for pilgrimage to rome—no breche betwene.'[3] This, however, was quite exceptional since breeches as an undergarment were considered more essential than the shirt. The word 'breche' was also used to indicate, not the garment, but the region of the body. A Norman writer (*c.* 1370) condemned men's short gowns because they 'shewed ther breches, the whiche is ther shame.'[4]

The name 'breeches' finally became applied to an outer garment only; and therefore to avoid confusion we propose to use the word 'braies' throughout, for this medieval undergarment.

Saxon braies, often brightly coloured, were in effect an outer

---

[1] Chaucer: *The Rime of Sire Tophas*, 1387.   [2] Froissart.
[3] *Piers Plowman*, 1362–92.   [4] *The Book of the Knight of La Tour Landry.*

garment, only becoming a true undergarment in the middle of the twelfth century, when they were largely concealed by the Norman tunic. Then, too, the colour interest faded, and drawers of white linen, or of drab woollen cloth for the peasant class, became established.

In the twelfth century most breeches, when still a surface garment, had wide baggy legs often slit up behind for a short distance and reaching to mid-calf. Others, chiefly worn by the peasant class, were often drawn in round the ankle very much like pantaloons. Both types were tied round the waist with a string or girdle, and because of the close fit they required a front opening.

During the second half of the twelfth century, when braies became definitely an undergarment, the seat was made very much fuller, and the front opening was discarded. The legs were shortened and the stockings, made long and wide above, were pulled up over them and attached by cords in front to the braie girdle. This was a running string which emerged at intervals from the hem at the waist for this purpose. A man's purse or keys were sometimes slung from the girdle, since in this position they were safely hidden from view.

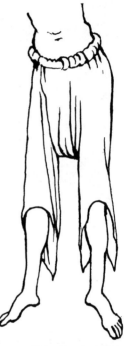

FIG. 3. BRAIES WITH UPWARD CURVE IN FRONT. 13TH CENTURY

This custom continued through the following century.

During the thirteenth century the length of braies varied, reaching to the ankle, to mid-calf or the knee, the tendency being to become progressively shorter. The general pattern had wide legs, a full seat, and no waistband, the top being turned over into a deep tubular hem or (French) 'coulisse,' through which was threaded the girdle or (French) 'braier.' This was pulled in over the hips, puckering the hem and giving it a puffed out appearance. The 'in and out' threading was also used. Two straps or cords, some six inches long, were attached to the girdle on either side, and escaped from the coulisse through eyelet holes. Their function was to hitch up the

FIG. 5. LOOSE BRAIES. EARLY 14TH CENTURY

FIG. 4. SHORT BRAIES. LATE 15TH CENTURY

legs of the longer braies and keep them out of the way. This was done in two different ways. Either the braie leg was turned straight up and attached to the cord direct (*figure* 8); or it was given an outward half-twist before being tied up to the cord (*figure* 7). The latter

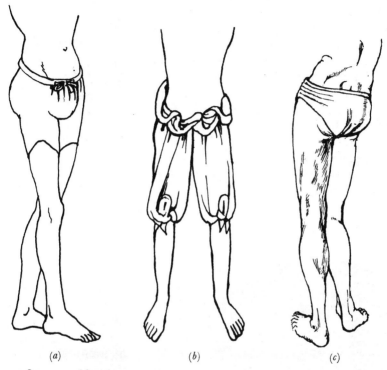

(a)   (b)   (c)

FIG. 6. BRAIES: (<i>a</i>) POUCHED BRAIES TIED WITH A BOW. FIRST HALF 15TH CENTURY.
(<i>b</i>) BRAIES TIED AT THE KNEE. (<i>c</i>) SHORT BRAIES. LATE 15TH CENTURY

method effectively closed the gap when, as was sometimes the case, the leg was slit up behind.

These devices implied that the long braies were in fact cumbersome, and so by a natural development a knee-length garment became general about the middle of the thirteenth century. Some were tied at the knees with strings (*figure* 6b); an example of this style can be seen in the *St. Christopher* of Matthew Paris. Other braies hung loose (*figure* 3), the lower borders of the legs generally unevenly cut, dipping in front or behind, the latter being the more usual. Braies at this period did not reach to the waist, but were pulled in by the girdle just above hip level.

In the fourteenth century braies became shorter and shorter and the shirt could no longer be tucked in but hung outside over the thighs. After 1340 the costume on the surface somewhat resembling modern 'tights,' began to display the shape of the male leg as a form of sex attraction. Under these long tight hose, braies scarcely reached to mid-thigh, while some were shorter still, and the hose, formerly attached to the girdle of the braies, were now fastened to the overgarment called the gipon by ties known as 'points.'

As the braies became shorter they also became tighter, so that some required a slit at the hem of each leg, sometimes made in front, sometimes at the side, to enable the garment to be pulled on.

FIG. 7. COUNTRYMAN IN BRAIES. 14TH CENTURY

FIG. 8. BRAIES TURNED UP STRAIGHT AND HITCHED TO BRAIE GIRDLE, *c.* 1250

Towards the end of the fourteenth century the turned-over hem or coulisse containing the girdle became much narrower, and the girdle, becoming known as the 'brayette,' was often buckled in front. From 1340 onwards it not only ceased to function as an attachment for the hose, but also for purse and keys.

During the first half of the fifteenth century, braies had been so shortened both above and below that they had become little more than a loin-cloth. The buckled girdle was discarded and replaced by a narrow running thread 'en coulisse.' The two ends emerged in front through two eyelet holes placed some six inches apart. These threads, however, running side by side in the intervening space between these holes, crossed each other so that the right-hand end of the cord emerged from the left-hand eyelet hole, and the left-hand end of the cord emerged from the right-hand eyelet hole. When pulled up and tied in a bow outside, this caused a pouching of the material, which can be seen in contemporary illustrations (*figure* 6*a*).

By the close of the Middle Ages, braies had become less like loin-cloths (*figure* 6*c*), and more like modern bathing trunks.

It should be understood that during these centuries the peasant and labourer did not attempt to keep pace with the changes of fashion but, as we see in contemporary illustrations, continued, as a rule, to wear the long braies of their forefathers. We see among the higher ranks how this garment reflected the changes of the outer modes, and close attention to its variations will often help an observer to date contemporary illustrations. For that reason we have described them in some detail.

∽ WOMEN ∽

I. THE SMOCK

This is the Saxon name for the only known undergarment belonging to women.[1] The Normans introduced the name 'chemise.' It was worn next the skin and slipped on over the head, the neck opening probably being wide enough for this purpose, though later, about 1400, there is evidence that some chemises were slit down the front for a short distance. It was flowing, ankle length, and during the eleventh, twelfth and thirteenth centuries had long straight sleeves and a small round neck.[2]

Smocks were often pleated and embroidered, particularly round the neck and hem. In Chaucer's time even a carpenter's wife had a smock

> . . . brouded all before
> And eke behind on her colere about
> Of cole-blak silke, within and eke without.[3]

[1] *Eric and Enid* (c. 1164). '. . . her daughter who was clothed in a full-skirted chemise, white and pleated. Over it she had put on a white robe; she had no other garment.'
[2] E. R. Lunquist.   [3] 'The Milleres Tale' (*The Canterbury Tales*).

The materials used were fine linen, hemp, silk textiles (cendal and samite), and chainsil (a silk mixture).

In the twelfth century there was a fashion for slashing the sides of the outer garment, with corresponding openings in the chemise, so that the bare skin was revealed. Preachers denounced this practice, calling these apertures 'windows of hell.'[1]

FIG. 9. WOMAN'S SMOCK, c. 1400

FIG. 10. LACED-UP BODICE RESEMBLING STAYS. 12TH CENTURY

After 1340, women's surface garments became close fitting so as to display the shape of the figure, and sleeves were long to the wrist, moulding the arm. There is no contemporary evidence of any corresponding change in cut of the chemise, but it is difficult not to presume that this must have been the case. Certainly in Chaucer's day the texture of some of the smocks was thin or even transparent;[2]

[1] Marie de France: *Le Lai de Lanval, c.* 1180. 'She was dressed in such a way, in a white gown and chemise, that both her sides were bare where they were laced from side to side.'
[2] Chaucer: *The Romaunt of the Rose, c.* 1370.
    '. . . through her smocke ywrought with silke
    The fleshe was sene as white as milke.'

and the scantiness of the undergarment may be judged by the comment of the Knight de la Tour Landry (1370), who declared that while the long-trained robes kept their backs and feet warm, the fine ladies '*meurent de froid à leur ventres et à leurs tétines.*'

2. STAYS

It is uncertain whether women wore, at least occasionally, something in the nature of corsets. In an illuminated MSS. of the twelfth century (B.M. Nero C.IV) there is a singular figure of a demon, dressed as a woman, and wearing a laced-up bodice closely resembling a pair of stays (*figure* 10). Some of the gowns worn about 1170 appear to be so tight fitting as to suggest a corset beneath; alternatively some kind of tight bandaging may have been used to contract the waist.[1] In the wedding trousseau of Princess Joan (1347) 'a double cotehardie for riding, and corsets' are mentioned. Again, towards the end of the fifteenth century, certain female effigies have been given waists equally suggestive of tight lacing.

There is, however, no reliable evidence that actual stays were ever a usual accessory garment.

3. THE BUSTLE

That the fashionable ladies of the middle of the fourteenth century sometimes employed a device corresponding to a bustle, is indicated in the reproof uttered by Douglas, monk of Glastonbury, in 1343, who complained that they 'weredde such strete (tight) clothes that they had long fox-tails sewede within ther garments to hold them forthe for to hede ther arses, the whiche disguising and pride afterwards broughte forthe and causedde many mischiefs and mishappes that hapned in the (realm) of Englond.' A primitive but doubtless effective form of bustle; though surely employed not to hide the outlines of Nature, but rather to exaggerate them.

When we observe the fantastical 'fashions' of the fifteenth century, with frequent changes of design, it is very remarkable that the underclothing should have remained undisturbed and unaffected by the novel expressions of class distinction and sex attraction which were so lavishly displayed in the outer garments.

[1] Kelly and Schwabe: *History of Costume and Armour.*

II

1485—1625

THE end of the Wars of the Roses, which in England brought the Middle Ages to a close, saw the end of the medieval conception of dress. The changes associated with the Tudor regime were sufficiently profound to affect the nature and purpose of underclothes. Ceasing to be merely a layer serving to protect the skin, they now began to assist the external costume of both sexes in expressing class distinction. In women's dress they also played a subsidiary, though not unimportant, part in the art of sex attraction.

The new fashion for slashing men's outer clothes exposed the fine quality of what lay beneath, and immediately brought the shirt itself, or a lining simulating it, into prominence. In order to attract still greater attention, the edge of the shirt was ruffled at the neck, a decoration which soon developed into a separate accessory, the ruff. This emergence of the shirt for occasional display is not the sole instance of this tendency in the wearing of underclothes in this period. For instance, the waistcoat, which originally was an under-garment, was shown, when the doublet was taken off, *en deshabille*.

With women, underclothing had the new function of supporting the growing size and shape of the skirt. Petticoats became necessary for that purpose until the expansion reached a degree where a hooped contrivance—the farthingale—had to be employed. The huge skirt has always been woman's most conspicuous method of expressing class distinction, either in the form of a sweeping train or as a circular shape supported on a hooped petticoat.

Thus we see that for both men and women in the sixteenth century the undergarment was no longer an obscure drudge, but was promoted to serve in the general mode of expressing what the whole costume so extravagantly announced; and likewise to share in that extreme degree of finery and physical discomfort which became the acceptable hall-mark of the Social Superior.

The excessively small waist of the Elizabethan lady, familiar in portraits, could only have been produced by a very unmerciful corset. We might be tempted to regard this as a method of sex attraction but the fact remains that the male waist seems to have been similarly constricted. The male silhouette resembled a caricature of the female outline, suggestive of a (perhaps unconscious) homo-sexual trait, and appearing to indicate that the pinched waist of both sexes was not so much 'attractive' as a sign of social superiority, like other devices for restraining physical freedom.

We have to recollect that all female parts on the stage were played by male actors, often famous for their skill in 'female impersonation,' so that the appearance of males in female dress was quite familiar; and that in the literature of the period there is a lack of that erotic interest which men normally take in the concealed garments of women. In his *Anatomie of Abuses* (1583), the Puritan-minded Philip Stubbes, though fulminating against the extravagance of costume in both sexes, ignores the eroticism of feminine underclothing, which he surely would not have done if that aspect had been one of the 'social evils' of his day. His target is the abominable use of clothes for the purpose of class distinction. It remained for a later generation of poets to sing the charms of 'the tempestuous petticoat' and 'the sweet disorder of her dress.'

In the period under consideration, then, from the Tudors to the end of the Jacobeans, the new function of underclothes was much the same for both sexes; to exploit the grandeur of the costume as evidence of rank, and only by that indirect method to add to the wearer's sex attractions.

As such, this century and a half composes a distinct and unusual phase in the history of costume, and an interpretation of its underclothes helps us to comprehend the significance of its fashions.

Moreover, with the sixteenth century we begin to obtain far more reliable information than previously on the subject from contemporary literature (especially the drama), portraits, and indeed a few actual garments.

I. THE SHIRT[1]

Shirts were usually made of cambric or holland. They were very full and, until about 1510, had low necks. Here the material was finely gathered into a narrow band, which was often cut square in

front, but sufficiently open to allow the shirt to be put on over the head. The sleeves also were full and were gathered into narrow bands at the wrists. The bands both at the neck and wrist were generally embroidered with gold thread and coloured silks, black and red predominating. Embroidery went out in the second half of the sixteenth century and was replaced by ornament in drawn or cut-work edged with bobbin lace.

The shirt at this period, and until about 1545, was very largely exposed to view. From 1510 the front was also embroidered and its decoration revealed by leaving the doublet open.[2] When no

FIG. 11. SHIRT AND COLLAR SHOWING HOOKS AND EYES. AFTER PIETER BRUEGEL, c. 1567

stomacher was worn the front was open as far as the waist. When worn with a low-necked doublet, the shirt emerged above it; with a short one, it would bulge out between the lower edge of the doublet and the waist. The wristbands protruded below the doublet sleeves. The decorative slashing of the doublet also showed portions of the shirt; and even when this fashion changed and the slashes

[1] Shirts surviving from these periods are naturally exceedingly rare. We therefore give a note in the Appendix on the best known examples, the Sture shirts. See Appendix (*figure* 117).

[2] 'Shertes brodered and displayed in fourme of Surplys.' Alexander Barclay: *The Ship of Fools*, 1509.

were filled in with coloured silk puffings, the idea was still to simulate the revelation of an undergarment.

Important changes were made in the line of the neck throughout the period. From 1510 a small frill was added to the neckline; but after 1525 the neckline was cut high and finished with a broad band fitted close round the neck, the front opening being fastened with strings or buttons. The band was edged with a small, turned-down collar, which developed into the 'falling band' or 'fall,' or else with a small frill, the origin of the ruff (*figure* 12).

The upright neckband increased in height as the period advanced. At the same time frills or 'ruffles' were added to the wristbands of the shirts with ruffs, while turned-back cuffs were worn with the falling bands, and also occasionally with the ruffs. The 'falling band'[1] or turned-down collar continued with many variations to be worn throughout this period. It was usually attached to the shirt, and was very high when turned over the high collar of the doublet, but low, and spreading wide over the shoulders, when the doublet became collarless in the early years of the seventeenth century. The 'standing band,' or 'whisk,' was an alternative collar at the beginning of James I's reign and lasted until about 1630. It was supported on a wire frame, known as an 'under-propper,' or 'supportasse'; it fitted close round the neck, and had a straight horizontal edge in front, spread out fanwise round the back of the head, and was fastened under the chin by 'band strings.' Both standing and falling bands were edged with broad lace.

The ruff, at first a frill edging the neckband, developed into a goffered collar open in front (*c.* 1560). In 1580 it reached immense proportions and was usually put on separately from the shirt and fastened by band strings. By this time it was closed all round the neck, to form the large, 'cartwheel' ruff. The organ-pipe pleats or 'sets' radiated evenly outwards from the neck; and when the ruff was several layers deep it was popularly known as 'three steps and a half to the gallows.'

Ruffs were made of 'cambric, holland, lawn, and the finest cloth that can be got,' and were often embroidered with silk and edged with lace. They were stiffened by starch, introduced into England in Elizabeth's reign, and coloured, yellow being a popular choice.

Stubbes' scornful, realistic comment—'if it happen that a shower

---

[1] 'Band' was the general term for collar.

FIG. 12. NECKS AND CUFFS, 1523–38. AFTER HOLBEIN

of rain catch them, before they can get harbour, then their great ruffs strike sail and down they fall as dishcloths fluttering in the wind'—indicated an objection which, however, could be avoided by wearing an under-propper, as used for whisks. The high ruff went out after 1620 and was replaced by the falling ruff which spread out over the shoulders in less formal pleats.

The gradual change which marked the shirt during the first half of the sixteenth century has a psychological interest. At first the low-cut horizontal line exposing the top of the chest emphasized the breadth of shoulders and its broad masculinity was no doubt sex attractive. Gradually the neckline rose, the emphasis on the shoulders diminished, and with increasing constriction round the neck a new symbol of gentility developed (which survived in various forms of collar-like devices down to modern days).

Henceforth the gentleman's shirt was concerned chiefly to express his social rank. This change of symbolism in such an important garment, taking place in so short a time, is very remarkable. Its new function, in the eyes of some, seemed more detestable than its old. The Puritan Stubbes, always infuriated by the sight of his betters, declared: 'I have heard of shirts that have cost some ten shillings, some twenty, some forty, some five pounds, and (which is horrible to hear) some ten pounds apiece.' A marked contrast with the countryman's

> Shirt of canvas, hard and tough,
> Of which the band and ruffles were both of one;
> So fine that I might see his skin them through.[1]

In 1533 a Sumptuary Law enacted that no one under the rank of a knight might wear 'plaited shirtes or shirtes garnished with silk, gold, and silver,' evidence of the growing significance of the only undergarment which has obtained the honour of an Act of Parliament.

Silk shirts, as worn by the country gentleman, were mentioned in 1582 (Essex Quarter Sessions Records), and early in the next century cambric, holland, and lawn were the materials which the travelling salesman usually offered his customers for shirts.

> Pure Holland is his shirt, which proudly faire
> Seems to outface his doublet everywhere.[2]

[1] Francis Thynne: *Animadversions*, 1599.   [2] Fitzgeffery: *Poems*, 1617.

FIG. 13. SHIRT WITH LOW COLLAR AND SMALL FRILL, 1531

A curiosity were 'historical shirts,' described by Fairholt as those 'adorned with worked or woven figures.' They seem to have been favoured by lovers. 'Having a mistris, sure you should not be without a neat historical sherte.'[1]

2. WAISTCOAT

This garment was worn under the doublet except when the doublet was taken off *en deshabille*. It was waist-length, with or without sleeves, and usually quilted or bombasted. Early in the seventeenth century, if not before, it was often called a 'vest,' the term still used by tailors. That it had pockets of some size is implied in these stage directions:

> KATHERINE . . . 'Brother, I'll look after yours' (takes up his vest) . . . (FRANK searches first one pocket, then another, finds the knife, and then lies down.)[2]

It was made of cloth, velvet, silk, or linen, and often embroidered. We read of waistcoats 'of cloth of silver quilted with black silk and tuffed out with fine cambric,' or 'of white satin, the sleeves embroidered with Venice silver.' Apparently the waistcoat was slipped on over the head like a vest—'he puts on his armour over his ears, like a waistcoat.'[3]

3. DRAWERS

Drawers corresponded to modern pants, and were known as 'trousers' or 'strossers.' A youth, waiting for his tailor to bring his suit, is described as dressed 'in his gown, waistcoate, and trouses.'[4] They were either knee or ankle length, cut on the cross to give a close fit,[5] and made of linen.

4. NIGHTCLOTHES

Wrought nightshirts are included in the wardrobe accounts of Henry VIII, and are alluded to in the drama (e.g. Thomas Kyd's *Spanish Tragedy*, 1594). We assume them to have been similar to the day-shirts.

[1] Fletcher: *The Custom of the Country*, 1625.
[2] Dekker: *The Witch of Edmonton*, 1621.
[3] Nicholas Breton: *Bower of Delights*, 1591.
[4] Ben Johnson: *The Staple of News*, 1625.
[5] Shakespeare mentions 'your straight (i.e. close-fitting) strossers': *Henry V*.

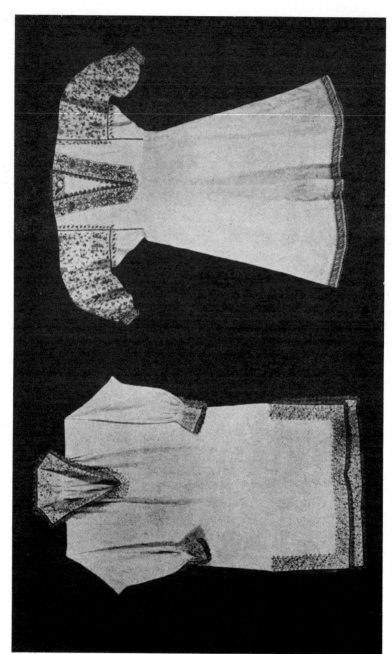

FIG. 14. (*left*) SHIRT, LATE 16TH CENTURY; (*right*) CAMICIA, LATE 16TH CENTURY (ITALIAN)

Night-caps were usual; frequently they were red in colour, perhaps to suggest the idea of warmth. Dr. Andrew Borde, in 1557, advised: 'Let your nyght cap be of scarlet . . . to be made of a good thycke quylte of cotton, or els of pure flockes or of cleane wolle, and let the covering of it be of whyte fustyan.' But William Vaughan's theory was slightly different. 'Let your night cappe have a hole in the top through which the vapour may goe out.' (1602.)

Night-caps were of sufficient value to be mentioned occasionally in wills.[1] A 'night cappe of black velvet embroidered' would be for a fine gentleman, while the social inferior might have to content himself with

> A knit nightcap made of coarsest twine
> With two long labels buttoned to the chin.[2]

5. CORSETS

Though there is no definite evidence that the 'exquisites' of the late Elizabethan and Jacobean periods constricted their waists with corsets, it is more than suggested in Satire VII of Bishop Hall (1598):

> His linnen collar labyrinthian set,
> Whose thousand double turnings never met:
> His sleeves half hid with elbow pineonings,
> As if he meant to fly with linnen wings.
> But when I looke, and cast mine eyes below,
> What monster meets mine eyes in human shew?
> So slender waist with such an abbot's loyne,
> Did never sober nature sure conjoyne.

6. PRICES

1522. '3 ells for a shirt, 6/. 3 ells of linen for two shirts, 1/1. an ell. Two yards of canvas to make the kitchen boy a shirt, /8.'

From the wardrobe accounts of Prince Henry, eldest son of James I:

> Holland for shirts, 13/4 an ell.
> Night clothes 11/.
> Two waistcoats of fine cambric wrought in coloured silks, lined with sarcenet, bound in silver lace, £2.10.0.

(An ell equals 1¼ yards.)

[1] John Corbett in 1557 left to his father 'my beste velvet nighte cappe.' (Saffron Walden Wills. *Walden Muniments*, Vol. 5.)
[2] Joseph Hall: *Satires*, 1598.

FIG. 15. EMBROIDERED LINEN DRAWERS. LATE 16TH CENTURY (ITALIAN)

∽ WOMEN ∽

I. THE CHEMISE

In this country the garment was spoken of as a 'smock,' even in its most elegant forms. The only specimen we know of is the Italian 'camicia' in the Metropolitan Museum of Art, New York. As its lower portion is of later date, we do not know the original shape; but presumably the general outline corresponded to that of the man's shirt, without the side vents.

Following the masculine mode its collar developed and appeared above the top of the gown in a frilled border, becoming often a high collar, splayed open, and loosely tied at the neck with strings (c. 1540). The collar and the borders of the short neck-opening were embroidered in a manner similar to that of the male shirt.

This type of chemise was worn with the high-necked gown. With the square-cut, deep décolletage, which persisted until the middle of the century, was worn a low-necked chemise, the border of which

FIG. 16. CHEMISE. AFTER HOLBEIN, 1541-3

was either not seen or seen only as a narrow edging above the line of the décolletage. Sometimes the space above was covered by a 'chemisette,' or 'fill-in,' which in pictures may be mistaken for a high-necked chemise.

Again in consonance with men's fashions, the smock was no

FIG. 17. CHEMISE. AFTER HOLBEIN, 1543   FIG. 18. CHEMISE. FLEMISH, 1529

longer entirely concealed; and the edging was often left visible at the neck and wrists as well as through the slashed sleeves. Such devices displayed the quality of the material (e.g. *figures* 16, 17).

Chemises were usually made of cambric or holland; silk was only used occasionally. The unfashionable wore lockeram. Embroidery was in common use,[1] and it seems to have been an acceptable compliment for courtiers to present Queen Elizabeth with elaborate specimens of this garment. Thus, 'a cambric smock, wrought with black silk in the collar and sleeves, the square and ruffs wrought

---

[1] E.g.   My maids, gae to my dressing-room
              And dress me to my smock
              The one half is o' the Holland fine,
              The other o' needle-work.
Percy: *Reliques of Ancient Poetry*: The Ballad of Lord Thomas and Fair Annis.

with Venice gold and edged with a small, bone lace of Venice gold,'
was given her in 1577. Spenser also describes:

> . . . a Camis lighte of purple silke
> Woven uppon with silver, subtly wrought,
> And quilted upon satin white as milke,
> Trayled with ribbands diversely destraught,
> Like as the workmen had their courses taught;
> Which was short tucked for light motion
> Up to her ham; but when she list, it raught
> Down to her lowest heele.[1]

The chemise and many other garments of both sexes were often
heavily perfumed. This was not only necessary to counteract the
smell of our ancestors' unwashed bodies. Their laundry methods[2]
are to us just as objectionable. The washing was performed in tubs,
wood-ash being used in place of soap, and the laundress was directed
to procure much 'sweet powder, herbs, and other sweet things
for the sweet keeping' of the linen. This was perhaps more necessary from the practice, common in early times, of extracting the dirt
by smearing the clothes with mud or scouring them with dung,
which, says Harrison, gave them 'such a savour that I cannot abide
to weare them on my bodie.'[3]

One curious custom connected with the smock, which can be
traced back at least to the sixteenth century, deserves notice here.

There was an old vulgar error, which lasted for several centuries, to
the effect that a man was not liable for his bride's debts provided that
he married her in no other apparel than her smock or shift. The strangest
thing about this odious custom is that any priest or minister could be
found to administer the sacred rite with the woman in such a guise. In
1547 at Much Wenlock, August 4, here was married early in the morning
Thomas Munslow, smith, and Alice Nycols, which wedded to him in
her smock and bareheaded.

                    (*The Parish Registers of England*, by L. Charles Cox, 1910.)

[1] *Faery Queene*: from the fight between Redegund and Artegal.
[2] Medieval laundry bills throw light on the condition of underclothes as worn by
our ancestors. Thus in the thirteenth century the washing bill for the entire household
of Bishop Swinfield for one year amounted to 43/2 (household rolls of Bishop Swinfield).
In the reign of Henry VIII, the Duke of Northumberland's establishment of 170 persons
had an annual washing bill of 40/- (Northumberland household book). The charge
for washing one of Henry VIII's shirts was a penny or twopence—roughly a day's wage
for, doubtless, a day's work.
[3] Harrison's 'Description of England,' 1577, quoted in *Our English Home*. J. H. Parker,
1861.

2. THE WAISTCOAT

An undergarment which, like a man's, was slipped on over the head and so resembled a vest. The materials were flannel, velvet, damask, sarcenet, and linen.

During Elizabeth's reign the waistcoat was lavishly enriched with 'wrought work,' and by the beginning of the seventeenth century the shops were 'stored with rich and curiously imbroydered waist-coats of the full value of tenne pounds apiece, twentie, and some forty pound.'[1]

From the nature of the material we must suppose that some were quite concealed while the more ornate were intended to be partly visible. Lady Anne Clifford's description (1616) suggests a negligée attire: 'All this time since my Lord went away I wore my black taffety nightgown and a yellow taffety waistcoat.'

3. THE CORSET

This may have taken the form of an underbodice (made in two parts and so called 'a pair of bodies'), stiffened with busks of wood or whalebone inserted into casings in the 'bodies,' and tied there by 'busk points.' We read of '12 pairs of busks of whalebone.'[2] The *Book of Customs Rates* (1631), speaks of 'Bodies for women and children of whalebone or leather.'[3]

A good deal of masculine scorn was provoked by them. Thus Philip Gosson:

> These privie coats by art made strong,
> With bones and steels and suchlike ware
> Whereby their back and sides grow long,
> And now they harnest gallants are;
> Were they for use against the foe
> Our dames for amazons might go![4]

There are occasional references to 'iron bodies,' and specimens of these, resembling armour, perforated with holes, exist in museums. These, however, are now regarded as orthopaedic instruments, when they are not—as is commonly the case—fanciful 'reproductions.' There is no evidence that they were worn by women as stays.

[1] John Stow: *Annals of Angland*, 1601.   [2] Egerton MS., 1583.
[3] Linthicum, *Costume in Elizabethan Drama*.
[4] *Pleasant Quippes for Upstart New-fangled Gentlewomen*, 1591.

4. THE PETTICOAT

We do not know when the petticoat was first worn in England as a separate garment hung from the waist. Unfortunately the word is used in contemporary references both for the undergarment and also for the skirt when separate from the bodice (e.g. in the case of an open robe). We assume that when the material was specially rich or ornamented it was a visible garment—a skirt; when of a more homely nature, it may have been an under-petticoat, and not seen.

Clearly, however, it was well established in the sixteenth century. Kiecher says, in 1585,[1] that 'the women of England wore three cloth gowns or petticoats, one over another.' Dekker confirms its existence in 1604,[2] and Thomas Middleton mentions that the depth of a woman's petticoat was a yard and a quarter. Some household accounts speak of 'two yards of kersey for a petticoat.'

The under-petticoat was usually tied by 'points,' or laces, to the body, though some appear to have resembled the princess petticoat.

Various materials were used for this garment—red cloth (note the colour again), a kind of serge called 'fryzado,' and something like velveteen, 'mockado.'

As the circumference of the skirt expanded during the second half of the sixteenth century we may safely suppose that the under-petticoats followed suit, in order to support the shape, until, about 1550, the outline was sustained by the artificial hooped petticoat or 'farthingale.'

Though we may suppose that the gentlewoman wore under-petticoats, it seems that the countrywoman often wore none. When William Kempe danced from London to Norwich (1599) he mentions that 'a lusty country lasse' danced a mile with him, and 'tucked up her russet petticoate' (i.e. skirt) and 'garnished her thick short legs' with morris bells:

> Her stump legs with bells were garnish'd,
> Her brown brows with sweating varnish'd,
> Her brown hips, when she was lag
> To win her ground, went swig a swag;
> Which to see all that came after
> Were repleate with mirthful laughter.

[1] Linthicum, loc. cit.   [2] *The Honest Whore.*

Near Norwich Kempe had an accident:

It was the mischaunce of a homely maid that, belyke, was but newly crept into the fashion of long-wasted petticotes tyde with points and had, as it seemed, but one point tyed before—as I was fetching a leape it fell out that I set my foote on her skirts, the point breaking off fell her petticoate from her waste, but as chance was, though her smock was coarse it was cleanly; yet the poor wench was so ashamed, the rather that she could hardly recover her coate again from unruly boys, that looking before like one that had the greene sicknesse, now had her cheekes all coloured with scarlet.

Even less seems to have been worn in Ireland. Fynes Moryson[1] (1617) reported that the Irish 'goe naked in very winter time, onely having their privy parts covered with a rag of linen . . . so as it would turn a man's stomacke to see an olde woman in the morning before breakfast.' He describes 'sixteene women, all naked except their loose mantles, whereof eight or ten were very faire and two seemed very Nimphs; sitting down by the fier with crossed legs like Taylors and so low as could not but offend chaste eyes. . . .'

5. THE FARTHINGALE

About 1545 appeared the Spanish *verdingale* or farthingale, a petticoat reinforced by a series of graduated hoops of cane, whalebone, or wire. Its shape was that of a cone, closely resembling that of the Victorian cage-crinoline. The material used was woollen, silk, satin, or velvet, usually of a brilliant colour (crimson, purple, or peach). Fifty yards of whalebone[2] might be used, in addition to buckram.

Although at first a fashion of the Court circle the farthingale rapidly spread to all classes.[3] That this fashion was inspired by class distinction was noted by Hugh Latimer in a sermon. 'It is nothing but a token of fair pride to wear such farthingales.' To be 'exclusive' a garment has to be not only very inconvenient but also very expensive; the former, by itself, is insufficient. Sometimes a 'double farthingale' was worn (*c.* 1550). The size of the garment may be gathered from Heywood's *Epigrams* (1560):

[1] *Itinerary*, 1605–17.
[2] Whalebone cost 2d. a yard, and red buckram 1/2 a yard, in 1594.
[3] Nicholas Udall: *Ralph Roister Doyster, c.* 1577.

FIG. 19. BUM-ROLLS. FROM AN ENGRAVING, 1600

Alas, poor verdingales must lie in the streete,
To house them no doore in the citee made meete,
Syns at our narrow doores they in can not win,
Send them to Oxforde, at Brodegates to get in.

About 1570 a variation, the French farthingale, began to compete with the Spanish form, without ever completely replacing it. It was shaped like a horizontal cartwheel, the hooped petticoat being tub-shaped with vertical sides, while round the hips, under the skirt, was worn a thick bolster-like 'bustle,' commonly known as a 'bum-roll.' It was tied in front, and often this sufficed to throw out the skirt without the addition of a farthingale. The tub-shape varied much in size but always gave the wearer the appearance of standing within a rampart; and we read of one woman:

> Placing both hands upon her whalebone hips,
> Puft up with a round circling farthingale.[1]

The size of the fashionable French farthingale is indicated by a description of James I's Queen Anne wearing 'so expansive a farthingale that I do not exaggerate when I say it was four feet wide at the hips.'[2] Its decline is implied in Lady Anne Clifford's statement (1617), 'All the time I was at the Court I wore my green damask gown embroidered without a farthingale.'

[1] *Micro-cynicon*, 1599.　　　　　　　　　　[2] Linthicum, p. 181.

Compare also:

> Her fardingale is set above her ears,
> Which, like a broad sail with the wind doth swell
> To drive this fair hulk headlong into hell.
> . . . Then gird herself close to the paps she shall,
> Shap'd breast and buttock, but no waist at all.
>
> (Michael Drayton, *The Mooncalf*, published 1627.)

A homely substitute for the farthingale was, as its name implies, the 'bum-roll,' which was covered with tape or ribbon.[1] That the wearing of them carried a sort of social stigma is suggested by Ben Jonson:[2]

> Nor you nor your house were so much as spoken of before I debased myself from my hood and my farthingale to those bum-rowles and your whalebone bodice.

6. DRAWERS

It does not seem that Englishwomen wore drawers before the very end of the eighteenth century. Fynes Morison, in his *Itinerary* (1605–17), makes it clear that the Italian women of his day wore them: 'The city Virgins, and especially Gentlewomen . . . in many places weare silke or linnen breeches under their gownes'; and Leloir states that the fashion for wearing 'calecons,' or drawers, was introduced into France from Italy by Catharine de Medici; but there is no evidence that the fashion crossed the Channel during this period.

7. NIGHTCLOTHES

Smocks, with varying degrees of embroidery and openwork, were worn by all women of any social pretension. Cambric smocks, often heavily perfumed, are mentioned at the close of the Elizabethan period. It seems to have been a garment very similar to the day chemise and in contemporary descriptions the name is used indifferently for both.

Night-caps were worn; in the 'Linnen List' of Winnifred Barrington[3] are mentioned 'Two night quayfes,' or coifs: also 'night cross-cloths,' apparently worn across the forehead at night.

---

[1] 'One roole (bum-roll) covered with Karnacion ribben'; 'a roole covered with wyght tape.'—Essex Record Office; Winnifred Barrington's Linnen List, 1589.
[2] *The Poetaster*, 1601.   [3] Essex Record Office, 1589.

III

1626—1710

In this romantic period of the Stuarts, underclothes, with both sexes, developed new significance. Ceasing to be merely utilitarian in function, they were being exploited to indicate class distinction and sex attraction to a striking degree. We may regard this as a natural antagonism to Puritanism which persistently disapproved of the display of underclothes for erotic purposes though it had no objection to class distinction in costume.

Up to this period, as we have seen, underclothes had very much the same significance in both sexes, but from now on there is a division; the male garments are designed mainly to express social rank, the female mainly to attract.

Man's shirt, for example, is in the Stuart period an integral part of the visible costume of the fine gentleman while the neck and sleeves of the lady's chemise are equally conspicuous. But it was the change of design of her skirt, from rigid to flowing, which enabled provocative glimpses of under-petticoats to be seen, and so gave her a new weapon of attack. The petticoat became the recognized symbol of feminine charm and poets discovered in it an appropriate theme for erotic verse. Herrick's familiar lines (c. 1650) struck a new note in English poetry—namely a greater interest in feminine clothing than in woman herself.

> A sweet disorder in the dress
> Kindles in clothes a wantonness;
>
> .   .   .   .
>
> A winning wave (deserving note)
> In the tempestuous petticoat . . .
> Do more bewitch me, than when Art,
> Is too precise in every part.

If we examine the fashionable portraits of both sexes, of the period just before, as well as just after, the Restoration of 1660, it will be noted how the shirt and the chemise are glorified. Still more remarkable and significant was the masculine fashion, therein portrayed, of exhibiting the shirt extruding between the bottom of the waistcoat and the top of the breeches (which, indeed, often appear as though about to slip down): while the feminine chemise is shown sliding off the shoulders and the gown itself in as precarious a position as the man's breeches.

The meaning of this impulse affecting the costume of both sexes is obviously erotic, and it can be said that never before, or since, have fashionable folk elected to be painted for the benefit of posterity in such hazardous toilets.

The period is important in that it was the last time that the male attempted to give his underclothing an erotic suggestion. In one of Mrs. Aphra Behn's licentious comedies, *The Rover* (1677), the stage presented an amorous scene with the man dressed only in 'his shirt and drawers.' This was evidently accepted, at the time, as highly attractive to the female part of the audience—a sort of masculine 'strip-tease act.' It is significant that to-day this kind of exhibition is limited to women; male underclothing has become, on the stage, merely comic and we are beginning to view the female display in the same spirit unless it is done with infinite skill and tact to avoid exciting ridicule.

Laughter is a psychological resistance to would-be erotic appeals, and in our attitude towards underclothes *'du sublime au ridicule il n'y a qu'un pas.'* But as we view and criticize the use for erotic purposes which the Stuart fashions made of those garments, we have to allow for the fact that at the time spectators discovered in them a charm just because they 'were not amused.'

Portraits and museum specimens fail to convey to us another aspect of those underclothes but on which, however, we must insist, if we are to appreciate an obstacle to sex appeal which they had to overcome. Men and women, even of high rank, were generally dirty and often verminous.[1] Exquisite lace ruffles did not entirely conceal grimy hands and black finger-nails, and the fashion for heavily perfumed undergarments imperfectly distracted attention from less agreeable odours. It was their experience that silk and linen

---

[1] Thomas Verney asks for 'a lace shirt to keep me from lice.' *Verney Memoirs,* 1639.

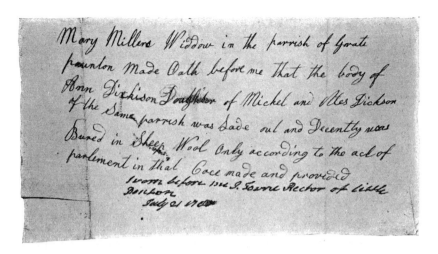

FIG. 20. CERTIFICATE OF BURIAL IN WOOL, 1707

garments next the skin were less liable to harbour lice than the wearing of woollens, which did not become usual for undergarments until the era of physical cleanliness opened a century later.

The nineteenth century accepted cleanliness as a sign of class distinction; to-day it has become so general that it has ceased to be significant of class; instead it has become almost an essential of sex attraction, so that to the modern taste those fine folk of the seventeenth century, in spite of their clothes, would have been physically repellent. Our eyes would have admired the quality of their underclothes and recognized their attraction—at a certain distance.

The apparent dislike of wearing 'wool next the skin' was perhaps accentuated by the Act of 1678, which provided that:

'No corpse of any person (except those who shall die of the plague) shall be buried in any shirt, shift, sheet, or shroud, or anything whatsoever made or mingled with flax, hemp, silk, hair, gold, or silver, or in any stuff, or thing, other than what is made of sheep's wool only.' The Act was not repealed till 1814, and parish registers constantly stated that the deceased had been 'buried in wool' (*figure* 20).

It would have been natural, therefore, that 'wool next the skin' had disagreeable associations. The more fashionable folk[1] ignored the Act and the famous actress, Mrs. Oldfield (Pope's 'Narcissa'),

[1] 'Take care I ain't buried in flannel, 'twould never become me, I'm sure.'—Lady Brampton in Sir Richard Steele's *The Funeral.*

had herself buried in Westminster Abbey arrayed in 'a very fine Brussels lace Head, a Holland shift, with tucker and double ruffles of the same lace and a pair of new kid gloves'; a circumstance inspiring Pope's lines:

> Odious! In woollen! T'would a saint provoke
> (were the last words that poor Narcissa spoke);
> No; let a charming chintz and Brussels lace
> Wrap my cold limbs, and shade my lifeless face:
> One would not, sure, be frightful when one's dead—
> And—Betty—give this cheek a little red.

A rare form of 'undergarment' of the period deserves historical notice as illustrating social customs; this was the 'Sheet of Repentance,' in which a woman had to be clad when confessing in church that she had committed adultery. The Saffron Walden churchwarden's accounts for 1629 has this entry: 'for five yardes of callico for making of a sheete to do Pennance withall, 5/.'

∽ MEN ∽

I. THE DAY-SHIRT

At the beginning of this period the front and back of the doublet were slashed, and until the middle of the century its sleeves gaped down the front seam, were unbuttoned, and turned back at the wrists. The shortened doublet of 1640 exposed still more of the shirt all round above the breeches, the doublet being left unbuttoned. The shirt was thus conspicuously displayed. 'I hope you will consider to buy me some good shirts or else some sort of wastcoat, for it is not fashionable for any gentleman to go buttoned up either winter or summer.'[1] Its neckband was narrow; to it the material was gathered, with a short centre-opening in front, edged with lace or a linen frill. The opening was tied at the neck with strings or buttoned. Sometimes the neckband was extended into a 'stand-up turned down' collar, tied with strings, or fastened by two buttons (*figure* 21).

Throughout the period the sleeves were full and were caught in at the wrist (sometimes at the elbow as well) with ribbon ties, which produced puffing between the ties. These ribbons survived till the

[1] *Verney Memoirs*, 1688.

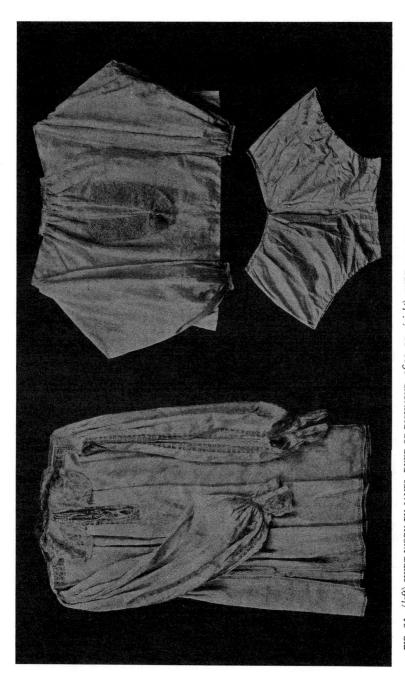

FIG. 21. (*left*) SHIRT WORN BY JAMES, DUKE OF RICHMOND, 1612–55; (*right*) SHIRT AND DRAWERS FROM THE EFFIGY OF CHARLES II, WESTMINSTER ABBEY

end of the period.[1] For instance, the shirt on the funeral effigy of Charles II, in Westminster Abbey, is contemporary in date (1686). Its sleeves are gathered into full puffs at elbow and forearm; the wristbands have four buttonholes to which lace ruffles were attached. Strips of lace edge the front opening. The narrow neckband has two buttonholes on the left (the neck has been cut out and mutilated). The length of the garment is 43 inches.[2]

The materials for the shirt were fine holland, linen, lace, frieze holland, and for inferior qualities a coarse kind of linen called lockeram.[3]

At the beginning of this period the neck region was concealed by the falling bands of fine linen or lace. The band gradually spread until it entirely covered the shoulders. About 1640 it became smaller and was replaced at the middle of the century by the cravat hang-

FIG. 22. SHIRT, *c.* 1635. FROM LODGE'S ENGRAVING OF JAMES, DUKE OF RICHMOND, 1612–55

ing down over the front. This became longer and narrower, often extending down nearly to the waist by the end of the century. A form of the cravat, the 'Steinkirk'—in which the ends were twisted ropewise together (*figure* 33), appeared about 1690, but may be seen in some portraits even before the date of the battle after which it was called. The cravat concealed the front opening of the shirt which was edged with a gathered frill of lawn or lace (the 'jabot'); but it was narrow enough to expose the shirt on either side of it, and

---

[1] 'He took the very ribbons out of his shirt.'—Farquhar: *The Recruiting Officer*, 1706.
[2] Tanner and Nevinson: *Society of Antiquaries*, 1936.
[3] From the accounts of John Masters, 1646: '11 ells of lockeram to make my footboy 4 shirts.' '12 ells of fine holland at 6/. an ell to make me 4 whole shirts.' (An ell was 45 inches).

as the vest was usually left unbuttoned, from the 'nineties onwards, an extensive area of shirt was thus visible.

The termination of the sleeves at the wrist underwent changes. Reversed cuffs of lace or lawn, with vandyked edges, by the middle of the century were worn limp and ruffled; and with the Restoration of 1660 the wrist ruffles of lawn or lace expanded on to the hands —a very characteristic expression of superior rank. A number of portraits, however, show no ruffles but simply a coat-sleeve, shortened to expose a narrow wristband buttoned, with the shirt puffed out above. Sometimes the coat cuff was left unbuttoned to reveal still more of the shirt. In a garment designed to indicate social finery there will always be a considerable range of degree. Portraits, especially towards the close of this period, may show sitters with no ruffles, or with only a slight amount of shirt visible at the wrist; others wear no cravat at the neck. The more magnificent examples are to be found, as we should expect, in those who

FIG. 23. SHIRT AND CRAVAT (CHARLES, DUKE OF SHREWSBURY) c. 1690

ruffled it in Court circles, and the shirt served to indicate these finer shades of gentility.

2. THE HALF SHIRT

This was a short under shirt, about hip length, apparently corresponding to the garment which M. Leloir[1] describes as a 'camisole,' which, he states, was made of flannel in winter and linen in summer. We have not found evidence of flannel used for it in this country.

The first reference to this garment comes from Scotland about

[1] *Histoire du Costume.*

1578—'6 fine whole sheirtes. 1 fine laced halfe sheirte.'[1] An early mention of it in England comes from the steward's accounts to Viscount Scudamore, of Holme Lacy, Hereford, recently discovered in the cathedral archives by Mr. F. C. Morgan: '3 ells and a halfe of holland at 9/ a yarde £1 11. 0. making shirtes and half shirtes 6/.'[2] This is in 1632. Next come the household accounts of the Marquis of Hertford for 1641–42, which record '10½ ells of bone lace for six halfe shirtes for my Lord Henry'—from which it seems that the garment required two and a half yards of material. Pepys has some information to give: 'This day put on a half shirt first this summer, it being very hot; yet so ill-tempered I am grown that I am afeard I shall catch cold' (June 28, 1664); and again, October 31, 1661, 'this day left off half shirts and put on a wastcoat'—presumably for greater warmth. The half-shirt was also a Continental fashion; and two youths, doing the Grand Tour with their tutor in 1670, recorded their purchases in Paris: '4 half-shirts laced, 4 payr of cuffs laced, 4 cravattes, 2 payr of drawers, two payr stockings fr. 90. 10.' '2 payr half shirts for me, a cravatte, 2 payr of cuffs fr. 32.' Half-shirts with point de Paris are also mentioned.[3]

3. DRAWERS

These were of two types. An example of the first are the drawers for the effigy of Charles II, in Westminster Abbey. They are silk trunks, 13 inches long, cut full and square; they are fastened with ribbons in front, have a small slit behind, and are tied at the back.

The second type consists of long drawers with 'stirrups'—a band, which passed under the instep to prevent the garment from slipping up the leg. 'A paire of Longe Linnen Drawers to put under the Breeches' was bought for 7s. for the Duke of Albemarle's effigy (1670). Richard Legh paid £2 for '2 pairs of large worsted drawers with stirrups' in 1675.[4] Worsted was an unusual material for this

---

[1] *Edinburgh Inventories*, ed. 1845. From information kindly given by Mr. J. L. Nevinson.
[2] This information is published by permission of the Dean and Chapter of Hereford Cathedral. The accounts proceed to give interesting details of prices and quantities of the materials required: 'for lineing yor Lordships drawers 1/. 2 cambric fringed Ruffes at £1 13. 0. the peec and 4 payer of Cufes £3. 1 laced ruff and 2 payer of Cufs £2. 8. 0. Holland to make yor Lordhp Cuffes 5/. 2 payer of linnen drawers /8. 7 yards of linnen cloth at /11 the yard for shirtes for the foole (*a curiously late survival*) 6/5. for thrid and making them /11. Laundres for washing: 9 Ruffes at /9 pr. Ruf. 6/9 3 ruffes and cufs 1/6 6 shirts at /4 the peec 2/ 12 half shirts at /3 the peece 3/.'
[3] T. Barrett-Lennard: *Account of the family of Lennard and Barrett*, 1908.
[4] Lady Newton: *Lyme Letters*, 1925.

garment, and suggests that it was intended for winter wear or for riding.

Pepys mentions lying 'in my drawers and stockings and waste coate till five of the clock' in hot weather, and also refers to his 'cool holland drawers.' But in neither entry nor in Mrs. Behn's *The Rover* is there a clue to their cut.

4. NIGHTCLOTHES

That of the fine gentleman was as elaborate as the day-shirt, often with lace insertion at the neck and down the sides of the sleeves, with ruffles at the wrist. The sleeves were very full; the neck opening was somewhat deeper than in the day-shirt and the collar lay flat. It was customary for the bride and bridegroom to give each other their wedding nightclothes; the cost may be gathered from a letter written by one of the prospective mothers-in-law to the other: 'I believe stockings and slippers is usual for lovers to give before the wedding. I think the nightclothes may be spared; they will cost £4 at least. I doubt £4 will not do it if of lace that will be commendable. These things will draw money, do what you can.'[1]

Gentlemen in mourning wore black nightclothes. 'Two black taffety nightclothes with black night capps' are mentioned in the *Verney Memoirs* (1651).

This wife a wondrous racket meanes to keepe,
While th'Husband seemes to sleepe but does not sleepe:
But she might full aswell her Lecture smother,
For ent'ring one Eare, it goes out at t'other.

FIG. 24. NIGHTCLOTHES.
FROM AN ENGRAVING, 1646

Night-caps, usually of wrought linen, might be equally ornate. Thomas Verney has 'six fine night capps laced, marked V in black silks; four plain capps marked in blew silke.' There is also mention of 'thirty fine peaked night capps.'

[1] The Gurney papers, 1661.

↷ WOMEN ↶

1. CHEMISE, OR 'SMOCK'

This was usually made of holland and was heavily perfumed. It was plain except for a frill, sometimes edged with lace, at neck and sleeves. The neck line was cut low, with a short V opening in front where it was tied by means of a threaded draw-string. When in the 1650's the décolletage of the bodice was cut horizontally off the shoulders, the chemise, previously exposed and acting as a 'tucker,' was reduced to a narrow white line or completely hidden. The lace border, however, reappeared in the sixties and was usually much in evidence to the end of the period.

The large balloon sleeves, reaching just below the elbows, and protruding beyond the bodice sleeves, were finished with stiff lace ruffles, which, after 1630, were replaced by funnel-shaped turn-up cuffs. These were frequently scarcely visible below the dress

FIG. 25. CHEMISE, 1678–80. FROM LELY'S PORTRAIT OF ELIZABETH, LADY OXENDEN

sleeves, which were worn long until the sixties, when the shorter style again exposed the sleeves of the chemise. The cuff was then discarded for a soft drooping frill, either plain or edged with lace, and falling from the narrow band to which the sleeve was gathered (*figure* 27). This band was pierced with buttonholes through which ribbon ties were fastened. Occasionally the frill was omitted and the sleeve was puffed by means of a ribbon tied higher up.

2. THE CORSET

The corset itself has to be distinguished from the *boned corsage* of the gown. When the latter was in fashion, with its tight back lacing

FIG. 27. LINEN CHEMISE, *c.* 1700, OR EARLIER

FIG. 26. SHIRT WORN BY CHRISTIAN IV OF DENMARK, *d.* 1648

and long pointed busk in front, the wearing of a corset in addition would have been superfluous, if not impossible.

The corset, heavily boned, had a long busk in front and was laced up behind. The lower edge was tabbed. The extreme décolletage of the bodice would have required the corset to be without shoulder straps, though there may have been, as in the next century, straps across the upper arm. Near the end of the century some stays appear to have been made in two parts and laced up front and back, but the older form persisted. The degree of tight-lacing may be gathered from the comment:

'Another foolish affectation there is in young virgins, though grown big enough to be wiser; but they are led blindfold by a custom to a fashion pernicious beyond imagination, who, thinking a slender waist a great beauty, strive all they possibly can by straight-lacing themselves to attain unto a wand-like smallness of waist, never thinking themselves fine enough till they can span the waist. By which deadly artifice, while they ignorantly affect an august or narrow breast, and to that end by strong compulsion shut up their waists in a whalebone prison, they open the door to consumptions.'[1]

3. PETTICOATS

The farthingale ceased to be fashionable about 1625, and as the skirt of the gown then became trained and flowing it would doubtless have required a number of under-petticoats (not to be confused with 'skirt-petticoats') to support it. There is, however, little direct or detailed evidence about this garment. Mrs. Isham asks:[2] 'I pray you send me word if wee bottone petticoates and waste-cotes whear they must be botoned.' The Hertford Household Accounts enter '17 yards of white flannel to make under-petticoats for the three young ladies, at 1/8 a yard'; and the two playwrights, Etherege and Mrs. Aphra Behn, concur a generation later in references to flannel as a petticoat material. Red seems to have been a popular colour.

4. THE BUSTLE

About 1690, with the overskirt becoming bunched up at the back, it was natural that the bustle should return—at least for a brief spell[3]—only to be replaced early in the eighteenth century by the

---

[1] Bulwer: *Artificial Changeling*, 1653.   [2] *Verney Memoirs*, 1639.
[3] Mrs. Centlivre mentions 'rump furbelows,' meaning this type of bustle, in *The Platonic Lady*, 1707.

hooped petticoat. A precisely similar development occurred in the middle of the nineteenth century when the cage crinoline replaced the bustle.

5. THE WAISTCOAT

That women often wore this as an undergarment—even, apparently, next to the skin—may be gathered from the will of the Countess Rivers (1644), where mention is made of 'Holland wastecotes to wear under my gowne; two yellow wastecotes to wear next me. . . .' Presumably this undergarment corresponded to the gentleman's 'half-shirt.'

6. DRAWERS

M. Leloir[1] describes 'les caleçons' as habitually worn by French ladies from the middle of the sixteenth century, and he gives quotations to support the statement. We, however, have failed to find evidence of drawers being worn by Englishwomen of any rank, except for a solitary reference in Pepys' diary (1663); when he suspected his wife of intended infidelity and watched her dressing. 'I am ashamed to think what a course I did take by lying to see whether my wife did wear drawers today as she did use to, and other things to raise my suspicions of her.' Mrs. Pepys, however, was a Frenchwoman and may have acquired the habit before her marriage.

We should, perhaps, qualify the above statement by mentioning that in the country festivals when such items as 'smock races' were run by young women (the prize being a new smock) the competitors sometimes, at least, ran in 'drawers.' Thus, a seventeenth-century ballad, *The Virgins' Race or Yorkshire's Glory*,[2] describes how:

> In half-shirts and drawers these Maids did run
> But bonny Nan the race hath won.

—each sprinter wearing drawers of a different colour.

We must suppose that, in this case, 'half-shirts' were something in the nature of blouses.

The materials used by country folk may be gathered from a libellous 'poem' which the composer was charged with having

[1] *Histoire du Costume.*
[2] Ashton: *Ballads, etc., of the Seventeenth Century.*

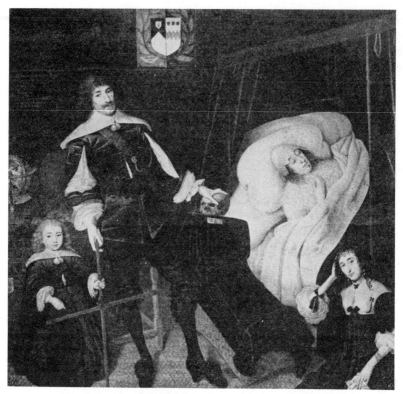

FIG. 28. SIR THOMAS ASTON AT THE DEATH-BED OF HIS WIFE, 1635

uttered, at the Essex Quarter Sessions of 1644: the first verse being:

> I prithee little Martin amend thy life,
> And ly no more with Dick Graygoose wife;
> Though he sell nothing but canvas for frocks,[1]
> Yet thou hast holland to make fine lasses' smocks;
> If any one would know how thou art bent
> They may know more of thy lechery in Kent . . .

7. NIGHTCLOTHES

We have no precise description of the nightdress, though pictures give us some idea of its nature and show that, for the higher ranks, it was lavishly trimmed with lace. Mrs. Aphra Behn refers to 'point night clothes.'[2] A coif covered the head.

---

[1] 'Frock' probably meant the countryman's smock-frock.　　　　[2] *The Rover*, 1677.

It seems to have been a fashion, when a wife died, to have her 'portrait' together with that of her (living) husband and children, painted as the body lay in its nightclothes. Such pictures supply us with most of the information we have as to this garment. But there are a few later references. For instance, Mrs. Centlivre mentions 'modish French night-clothes' in her play *The Platonic Lady* (1707); and that they were sometimes made of silk is indicated in Colley Cibber's *She Would and She Would Not*—'steal out of her bed . . . with nothing but a thin silk night-gown about her' (1703).

8. POCKETS

These were detachable, in the shape of a narrow bag with a centre slit, and were fastened round the waist under the petticoats.

Sometimes the pocket was a single one:

> Therefore all the money I have, which,
> God knows, is a very small stock,
> I keep in my pocket, ty'ed about my middle,
> Next to my smock.[1]

Sometimes there were two of these bag-pockets attached together by a band and carried one on each hip.

The underclothing of the period was sufficiently uncomfortable to tempt ladies to discard some of it when circumstances permitted. We learn from Vanbrugh's *The Provok'd Wife* (1697) that 'One may go to church without stays on'; and we hear of one 'with nothing on but her stays and her quilted petticoat.' Another admits 'If there were no men, adieu fine petticoats, we should be weary of wearing 'em.' That there were other mysteries of the wardrobe is suggested by Vanbrugh in his comedy *The Confederacy*, in which 'Mrs. Amlet, a seller of all sorts of private affairs to the ladies,' supplies, among other things, 'false hips.' We regret she is not more explicit.

[1] Swift: *Mrs. Harris's Petition*, 1699.

IV

1711—1790

Almost the whole of costume in this period was dominated by the hoop, which gave woman's skirt a special importance and underclothes a peculiar significance.

We naturally associate this fashion with its predecessor, the farthingale of the sixteenth–seventeenth centuries, and with the Victorian crinoline which followed it a century later. But although the three types had the same primary function of expressing class distinction, their erotic associations differed. As Englishwomen did not wear drawers until the nineteenth century, the thighs were bare beneath the petticoats, so that, with the farthingale and the hoop, accidental exposures must have been embarrassing. It is noticeable, however, that the Elizabethan–Jacobean literature seldom dwells on the erotic possibilities of such accidents; the farthingale was sufficiently substantial and the material of the skirt generally weighty enough to make exposure unlikely.

But the eighteenth-century hoop was otherwise, and the skirt material flimsier. Not only was the hoop liable to be blown about or even turned inside-out, but it was the fashion, in walking, to give it a side tilt exposing the under-petticoats. The attitude is described by Mrs. Haywood in *The Female Spectator* (1744–6): 'What manner some ladies come into public assemblies—they do not walk but straddle and sometimes run with a kind of frisk and jump—throw their enormous hoops almost in the face of those who pass them. . . .' The men of these times are strangely happy; in my time a fine woman was not to be gained without a long application, but now a game of romps reduces the vanquished fair to accept of what conditions the conqueror is pleased to give.' The same author adds: 'If the ladies would retrench a yard or two of their extended hoops they now wear they would be much less liable to the many embarrassments one frequently sees them in when walking in the streets. How often do the angular corners of such immense machines as we sometimes see, tho' held up almost to the armpits, catch hold of obstacles. . . .' Thus: 'A large flock of sheep were driving to the slaughterhouse and an old ram ran full butt into the footway where his horns were immediately entangled in the hoop of a fine lady as she was holding it up on one side, as the genteel fashion is. In her fright she let it fall down (on the ram). She attempted to run—he to disengage himself; she shriek'd, he baa'd, and the dog barked. Down fell the lady and a crowd of mob shouted. . . . Her gown and petticoat which before were yellow, the colour so much the mode at present, were now most barbarously painted with a filthy brown.'

While the woman writer viewed the hoop fashion with indignation and disgust, the male observer might complain of its inconvenience while recognizing its erotic possibilities.

> What fancy can the petticoat surround
> With the capacious hoop of whalebone bound,

exclaimed the poet Gay (1714); Soame Jenyns is more explicit:

> Dare I in such momentous points advise,
> I should condemn the hoop's enormous size;
> Of ills I speak by long experience found,
> Oft have I trod the immeasurable round,
> And mourn'd my shins bruis'd black with many a wound.
> Nor should the tighten'd stays, too straightly lac'd,
> In whalebone bondage gall the slender waist.
> Nor waving lappets should the dancing fair,
> Nor ruffles edg'd with dangling fringes wear.
> Let each fair maid, who fears to be disgrac'd
> Ever be sure to tie her garters fast;
> Lest the loos'd string, amidst the public ball,
> A wish'd for prize to some proud fop should fall,
> Who the rich treasure shall triumphant show,
> And with warm blushes cause her cheeks to glow.[1]

We gather, from *The Spectator* of 1712, that a popular amusement was to send young ladies sky-high on swings. 'In this diversion there

[1] *The Art of Dancing*, 1730.

are very many pretty shrieks, not so much for fear of falling off as that their petticoats should untie. The lover who swings his lady is to tie her clothes very close together with his hat band before she admits him to throw up her heels.' By such means she would claim that 'he cannot tell the colour of her garters.' A somewhat similar 'exposition' is a popular amusement at fun fairs to-day.

Evidently the hoop had dynamic functions as well as the merely static such as we see in the stately portraits in picture galleries. There one gets an impression of a vast expanse of skirt forming a solid foundation immobilized on the ground. We do not appreciate that the hoop, in action, had the liveliest propensities; that it enabled the wearer to reveal the outline of the legs through the slender under-petticoat. Unlike the farthingale, the hoop of the eighteenth century and the crinoline of the nineteenth, being flexible, possessed a peculiar erotic attraction in movement; as indicated in a song by Soame Jenyns:

> Oh, torture me not, for love's sake,
> With the smirk of those delicate lips,
> With that head's dear significant shake,
> And the toss of the hoop and the hips!

The centre of erotic attraction had, in fact, changed. During the seventeenth century it had been the breasts, either completely exposed or very nearly so. One notes, for instance, that all through the Restoration drama the breasts are specially admired and freely spoken of, and that the women characters accept such compliments with approval. The last occasion that a male character pays such a direct compliment to a woman is in one of Farquhar's comedies (1707). From about 1710, when the hoop became fashionable and the interest shifted to the legs, what might be called the 'breast taboo' began, at first in direct conversation between the sexes, later in the novel, and ultimately in poetry. A striking illustration of this taboo may be seen in a number of portraits of young women painted during the early part of the seventeenth century; in these originally the breasts were completely or nearly completely exposed, but at some date in the eighteenth century that region has been painted out, and we now see a vague slab of unnatural flesh as an improvement on Nature, and a tribute to the 'new look.'

It has become almost an established custom that the male interest

—and consequently the female fashion—has oscillated in this manner between those two physical regions; and that whichever happens to be temporarily in the ascendant is the more freely spoken of, while its rival is veiled in prudish euphemism, legs becoming 'limbs' and breasts the 'figure.'

The career of the eighteenth-century hoop, as in the case of the Victorian crinoline, was preceded and followed by the bustle, an erotic device to emphasize the appropriate region. By the addition of 'false hips' (which have subsequently been called panniers) the hoop was developed laterally and so produced a curious feature, unique in feminine fashions. Henry Fielding observed how many fashions were but forms of class distinction, or, as he put it: 'Numberless are the devices made use of by the people of fashion of both sexes, to avoid the pursuit of the vulgar. . . . Of all the articles of distinction the hoop hath stood the longest, and with the most obstinate resistance. Instead of giving way, this, the more it hath been pushed, hath increased the more; till the enemy hath been compelled to give over the pursuit from mere necessity; it being found impossible to convey seven yards of hoop into a hackney-coach, or to slide with it behind a counter.'[1]

This extraordinary exaggeration of the lateral dimensions of the skirt seemed an attempt to deny any suggestion of sex attraction, as though seeking to insist that the huge skirt was essentially to indicate social rank; one notes that it provoked hilarious comment from the men.

> Make your petticoats short that a Hoop eight yards wide
> May decently shew how your garters are tied. (1773.)

A discussion between two gentlemen on the stage expressed the masculine attitude towards this momentous subject:

'I would have her begin with lengthening her petticoats, covering her shoulders and wearing a cap upon her head.'

'Don't you think a tapering leg, falling shoulders and fine hair delightful objects, Sir John?'

'And therefore ought to be concealed. 'Tis their interest to conceal them; when you take from the men the pleasure of imagination there will be a scarcity of husbands.'[2]

[1] *The Covent Garden Journal*, 1752.
[2] Garrick: *Bon Ton*, 1775.

There in plain prose is the principle of sex attraction in costume;
here it is more gracefully expressed by the poet:

> At times to veil is to reveal,
> And to display is to conceal;
> Mysterious are your laws!
> The vision's finer than the view;
> Her landscape Nature never drew
> So fair as fancy draws.[1]

We may well suppose that both sexes found their fashions almost
intolerable in very hot weather. In Italy, for example, at informal
evening gatherings in summer, there was a measure of relaxation
'the gentlemen being all in light night-caps and nightgowns (under
which, I am informed, they wear no breeches) and slippers, and the
ladies in their stays and smock-sleeves, tied with ribands, and a
single lute-string petticoat; there is not a hat or a hoop to be seen.
It is true this dress is called *vestimenti di confidenza*, and they do not
appear in it in town but in their own chambers and that only during
the summer months.'[2]

Male underclothing during this period preserved in the shirt its
former qualities, though somewhat diminished. The habit of leaving
much of the waistcoat unbuttoned to display the fine quality of the
shirt was more than evidence of social rank; it appears to have had
its attractions to the other sex. We are told 'A sincere heart has not
made half so many conquests as an open waistcoat.'[3] But in other
respects man's underclothing was sinking into obscurity. This was
due, in a great measure, to the closer fit of his suit, designed to
exhibit the shape of his legs in breeches and stockings, leaving little
opportunity for the display of garments beneath.

Towards the close of this period we find reference to the wearing
of stays by 'smart' officers in the army.[4] The term 'smart' was
coming into vogue to indicate the well-dressed man, and for at
least a century after the word implied tight-fitting garments which,
of necessity, reduced underclothing to a very subordinate function,
so that only the shirt front survived for display purposes. In women's

---

[1] John Logan: *Ode to Women*, 1770.
[2] Lady Mary Wortley-Montague: *Letters*, 1753.
[3] *The Tatler*, 1710.
[4] One is described with 'his stays laced' in General Burgoyne's comedy, *The Lord of the Manor*, 1781.

costume 'smart' came to mean 'well cut' but not necessarily tight-fitting.

With the latter part of the eighteenth century, man's under-clothing ceased to serve for sex attraction, a function it has never regained, while continuing—in the shirt front and cuffs—to indicate class distinction, until, in modern times, that too has disappeared.

ᗡ MEN ᗡ

I. THE SHIRT

Its essential shape remained unchanged. The bottom was cut square, with the usual side vents, and the back flap slightly longer than the front; the body and sleeves were ample and the material was gathered into the neckband. The beginning of the period, however, introduced some important changes.

Hitherto the front opening, edged with a narrow 'jabot,' had been concealed by the hanging cravat which was either flat or twisted into a 'Steinkirk' and reached nearly to the waist, the upper part of the waistcoat being left unbuttoned. From about 1710 the hanging cravat was commonly dispensed with so that the jabot—or frilled border of the central opening—becoming more elaborate, often embroidered, was exposed to view, and allowed to project between the gap of the unbuttoned waistcoat. With this mode the cravat became a horizontal neckcloth, folded round the neck, at first narrow and later developing into a stock. By the end of this period the stock became deep enough to be a true 'choker,' buckled or tied at the back.

The neckband of the shirt, formerly quite narrow, became higher and developed into a collar attached to the shirt, though concealed by the neckcloth, if such was worn. Leloir[1] describes it as high enough to be turned down over the border of the neckcloth but this does not seem to have been a common English mode until the end of this period. The narrow neckband was closed by a single button; with an attached collar this might require two or even three, set one above another, or, in the absence of a neckcloth, buttoning might be replaced by a ribbon threaded through two holes in the neckband and loosely tied across. The buttons appear to have been

[1] *Histoire du Costume.*

FIG. 29. SHIRTS. 'CRICKET ON THE ARTILLERY GROUND, WOOLWICH,' BY FRANCIS HAYMAN, R.A.

the Dorset thread type.[1] The jabot varied much in its width and depth. *The Spectator* of July 1711 describes 'his new silk waistcoat which was unbuttoned in several places to let us see that he had a clean shirt on which was ruffled down to his middle.' When, after about 1760, the waistcoat was usually buttoned higher the amount of jabot exposed was necessarily much reduced.

The jabot was popularly known as 'chitterlons' or 'chitterlings.'[2] Parson Woodforde (1782) mentions: 'I bought a piece of Holland for shirts at 3/ a yard; for half a yard of cambric for chitterlons 5/.' It was essentially the display feature of the shirt and its quality— and perhaps its extent—was an outward and visible sign of the wearer's social position, being inconvenient, uncomfortable and readily soiled.

The sleeves were voluminous, with carefully pressed pleats along the outer side, and closed by a narrow wristband, buttoned. To this was usually, but by no means always, attached a ruffle. Roderick Random, 1748, possessed 'half a dozen ruffled shirts, as many plain.' (But whether the distinction referred to the wrists or to the jabot we cannot tell.) The ruffle, of lace or cambric, often embroidered, was variable in size, tending to become smaller towards the close of the period, when those imbued with democratic principles, such as Fox and his friends, discarded this symbol of class distinction (*figure* 30).

During the first half of the century the large open coat cuff allowed the lower part of the shirt-sleeve to protrude; later as the coat-sleeve became a closer fit only the ruffle was visible. Occasionally, during the first half of the century, the coat cuff was slit up at the side and the ruffle of the shirt was carried up the gap for a few inches.

The function of the ruffle was to indicate that the wearer was not a 'worker,' at least with his hands. Although Adam Smith in 1776 declared that 'a creditable day-labourer would be ashamed to appear in public without a linen shirt' it was certainly not ornamented with jabot and ruffles.

Although the ruffle was often made detachable for washing purposes the jabot was not; consequently a man of fashion would need

[1] An advertisement for some stolen garments (*Daily Advertiser*, January 29, 1755) mentions '7 full-trimmed shirts, 5 of which have one buttonhole at the wrist and a thread button; 2 shifts with 3 flat thread buttons on each.'

[2] This popular name for a goffered material is of even greater antiquity: 'I learned to make ruffs like calves's chitterlings.'—Ulpian Fulwell: *Like will to Like*, 1568.

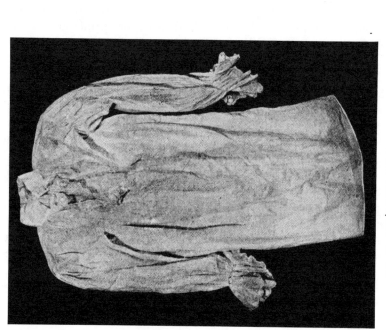

FIG. 31. CHEMISE, AFTER 1740

FIG. 30. MAN'S SHIRT. FRENCH, c. 1750

a large number of shirts. *The Tatler* (1710) mentions a fop who 'wears twenty shirts a week.'

In attempting to date specimens of shirts of this period—and equally in attempting to date portraits by the shirt displayed—we have to allow for the considerable variations due to personal taste and to the occasion when they were worn. Much can be learnt from the statuary and monumental effigies of the time. There was, for instance, the negligée costume, so often modelled by Roubiliac, in which the neck of the shirt is left gaping, the collar loosely turned down, sometimes with a ribbon band fastening, sometimes with buttons visible; the shirt itself may or may not show the top of a

FIG. 32. SHIRT. FROM THE BUST OF L. F. ROUBILIAC
BY HIMSELF

jabot. With such a costume the wig is seldom worn, its place being generally taken by the informal indoor cap. But in 'full dress' with wig the shirt is closed and a neckcloth worn concealing the upright collar.

We have also to remember that the earlier modes of the flat hanging cravat and the twisted 'Steinkirk' did not entirely disappear until about 1780. In Garrick's play *Bon Ton* we read of 'one of the knots of his tie hanging down his left shoulder and his fringed cravat nice twisted down his breast and thrust through his gold button-hole.'

Thus, for half a century, hanging cravat and jabot were rival fashions; and sometimes the shirt-front would be enriched with jewelry. The waistcoat, unbuttoned above, might 'display a brooch set with garnets, that glittered in the breast of his shirt, which was of the finest cambric, edged with right Mechlin.' (*Roderick Random*, 1748.)

2. THE DRAWERS

These were usually short, tied in at the knees, and closed by a string fastening round the waist. From Somerville[1] we hear of: 'his drawers beneath his hanging paunch close ty'ed.' And: 'In his best trousers he appears and clean white drawers.'

Breeches are often mentioned as having 'linings' of washable material, presumably detachable for that purpose. Indeed the term 'linings' to denote washable drawers was still employed by the artisan till the end of the nineteenth century. *Roderick Random* describes 'our money sewed between the lining and waistband of our breeches.' When the breeches became closer-fitting, Jeremy Bentham, about 1770, mentions taking a long country walk 'in a pair of breeches woefully tight'—the drawers presumably became shorter and tighter too.

Although the garment was generally short it was not invariably so. Benjamin Franklin describes how 'during a hot Sunday in June 1750 I sat in my chamber with no other clothes on than a shirt and a pair of long linen drawers.'[2]

The drawers, in the eighteenth century, had entirely lost whatever power of sex attraction they may once have possessed; *The Spectator* of 1711 wrote with disapproval of Mrs. Aphra Behn's comedy in which, as already mentioned, the garment had been exhibited on the stage in an amorous setting. Sex attraction devices of one generation are so often disapproved by the next, either because of their indelicacy or their inefficiency.

A curious glimpse of a bit of the garment may sometimes be obtained in the marble effigies of semi-recumbent figures, between 1720 and 1740, where the knee-buttons of the breeches have been left gaping above the line of the rolled up stockings on the outer side of the leg; the space could only be occupied by the undergarment—a device reminiscent of the former fashion of 'slashing'; we have not seen it in paintings, where the white pigment would be too conspicuous (*figure* 33).

[1] *The Officious Messenger*, 1730.
[2] *Autobiography*.

FIG. 34. SHIRT. BUST OF SIR EDWARD WALPOLE
BY L. F. ROUBILIAC, 1735

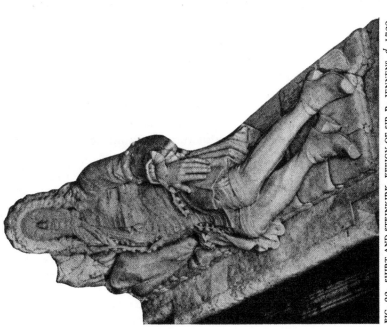

FIG. 33. SHIRT AND STEINKIRK. EFFIGY OF SIR R. JENNENS, *d.* 1722,
ACTON CHURCH, SUFFOLK

3. NIGHTCLOTHES

The linen nightshirt (always to be distinguished in this, as in former centuries, from the 'nightgown' or negligée) resembled the day-shirt except that it was slightly longer and fuller in cut.

It had, however, a wide, flat, turned-down collar, the neck being closed with two buttons.

The neck opening descended somewhat lower than in the day-shirt, and often there were no cuffs at the wrists but merely a short frill and side openings.

Night-caps of linen or dimity embroidered in colours were the usual mode, and were always worn in bed. They were baggy and had no tassel. Fielding and Smollett provide us with some evidence. A lady describes as a spectacle far from attractive the appearance of her elderly bridegroom 'in his three-fold nightcap, his flannel shirt . . .'[1]; we read of a quilted night-cap fastened under the chin in *Humphrey Clinker* (1771), and in *Roderick Random* of a worsted night-cap buttoned under the chin. Worsted, however, was worn only for extra warmth; otherwise it was an unfashionable material.

4. ARTIFICIAL CALVES

This accessory was introduced by the Macaronis—from about 1770 onwards. Its purpose was to accentuate the shapeliness of the male calf of the leg, which below the tight breeches of the period was regarded as so captivating. The importance of this device lies in its proving—if proof indeed were needed (*figure 35*)—that the male leg was then in the ascendant as a feature of sex attraction. It is sufficiently described in Sheridan's version, brought up to date, of Vanbrugh's comedy *The Relapse*, and renamed *A Trip to Scarborough* (1777).

LORD FOPPINGTON. . . . The calves of these stockings are thickened a little too much; they make my legs look like a porter's. . . .

MR. MENDLEGS. My lord, methinks they look mighty well.

LORD FOPPINGTON. Ay, but you are not so good a judge of these things as I am. I have studied them all my life. Pray therefore let the next be the thickness of a crown-piece less.

MR. MENDLEGS. Indeed, my lord, they are the same kind I had the honour to furnish your lordship with in town.

[1] Henry Fielding: *The Miser*, 1733.

FIG. 35. MAN'S TOILET, SHOWING CALF-PADS. ETCHING BY LEWIS MARKS, *c.* 1796–1800

LORD FOPPINGTON. Very possibly, Mr. Mendlegs; but that was in the beginning of the winter; and you should always remember, Mr. Hosier, that if you make a nobleman's Spring legs as robust as his autumn calves, you commit a monstrous impropriety, and make no allowance for the fatigues of the winter.

Similarly in *The Lord of the Manor*[1] we are told that 'the military leg, with six yards of flannel roller to sweat the small and prop the calf . . . will be all the go.'

The same play also introduces us to an undergarment which the fop had recently revived; we read of one with 'his stays laced.' Henceforth for the next hundred years or so the elegantly dressed gentleman, proud of his close-fitting 'smart' clothes and shapely waist, not uncommonly wore stays.

WOMEN

I. THE CHEMISE

This reached to just below the knees. The top of the garment, edged with lace and threaded with a draw-string, was scarcely on the shoulders, and followed the line of the low décolletage of the bodice, above which the lace edging showed. The full sleeves, gathered in at the top, were elbow length with a lace frill which was revealed below the sleeve of the gown. But when, about 1740, the bell-shaped sleeves came into fashion, the chemise sleeves ceased to be visible.

A chemise, dated 1775, is at the National Museum, Copenhagen. Its length is 44 in., the hem 79 in., the width at base of sleeve gore $26\frac{1}{2}$ in., and sleeve length $14\frac{1}{2}$ in. It is gathered into a narrow band

FIG. 36. CORSET, CHEMISE AND UNDERSKIRT. FRENCH, *c.* 1780

[1] A comedy by General Burgoyne, 1781.

with two buttonhole fastenings. During this century the chemise or shift varied greatly in quality; and in the less fashionable classes was often quite plain. The usual material was linen, but Richardson's Pamela (1741) is described as making her shifts of Scots cloth, though she speaks of 'two yards of black ribband for my shift sleeves,' and the rest of her underclothing comprised a linsey-wolsey petticoat, two flannel 'undercoats' (i.e. 'waistcoats') and a 'pair of pockets.' She was a domestic servant aged fifteen.

2. HABIT-SHIRTS

This relatively short-lived garment appears for the first time in the eighteenth century. Since it has not been described elsewhere, we propose to quote some accepted examples of the type.

In the eighteenth century woman's riding costume resembled in many respects a man's and included a 'habit-shirt' worn under a waistcoat. Parson Woodforde bought '4 yards of long Lawn at 3/6 per yard for Nancy to make her riding Habit Shirts and ½ yard of corded Muslin for Ruffles at 9/ per yard.'[1] The City Museum, Hereford, has recently been given three specimens of this rare garment, hitherto not described in the books on costume. They are identical in design and made of fine cambric; the construction resembles that of a modern 'coat-shirt,' the front being 15 in. deep and the back 11 in. To the back hem is attached a long tape for tying round the waist (*figure 37*).

A frilled jabot, 12 in. deep and 2 in. wide, surrounds the upper part of the front opening which is without fastenings.

The neckband, 14 in. round, has an attached collar 2 in. deep with two Dorset thread buttons, one above the other, by which it is closed. The sleeves, 21 in. long, and 8½ in. wide at the elbow, are attached at the shoulder, with a gusset in the armpit and a narrow gusset above pointing to the neck and reinforced by lateral bands.

The wristband, with a 3-in. side slit, is square cut and has a frill 1 in. deep, which also surrounds the side slit. It is closed by a single button.

On the three shirts all the buttons are of the Dorset thread ring type except one which is of the 'high top' pattern.

[1] *Diary of a Country Parson*, April 24, 1782.

FIG. 37. (*above*) WOMAN'S HABIT-SHIRT, SHOWING LINK-HOLES. EARLY 18TH CENTURY: (*below*) WOMAN'S HABIT-SHIRT, *c.* 1780

The garment has in many respects a masculine appearance but the tape attached to the back for tying round the waist is surely a feminine device.

We have provisionally assigned a date of about 1780 to these interesting garments, and in this we have been supported by Dr. Boucher of L'Union Française des Arts du Costume, who has examined them with us.

They differ from the 'habit-shirts' of the nineteenth century, which were sleeveless and scarcely more than 'fill-ins' above the top of the habits. As such those may be regarded as 'dress accessories'; but these of the eighteenth century, worn like a man's shirt under a waistcoat, may reasonably be included as undergarments.

So too, perhaps, may be the habit-shirts worn about the turn of the century. In 1801, Susan Sibbald thus describes her sister and herself: 'how smart I thought we looked in our hats and feathers, habits with lapels, which when opened displayed waistcoats, frilled habit shirts, stand-up collars and black silk handkerchiefs round our necks, so that to look at us through the windows of the carriage if it were not for the feathers and curls, we might have been taken for two youths.'[1]

The City Art Gallery, Leeds (Sanderson collection) has a specimen of habit-shirt which we assign to the early part of the eighteenth century when *The Spectator* (1712) commented on the masculine appearance of the woman rider's costume (*figure* 37).

It is of fine homespun linen, the front panel 15 in. deep, the back 12 in., the two joined at the sides and gathered into the neckband. The opening extends $8\frac{1}{2}$ in. down the front and is surrounded by a frilled jabot 1 in. wide. The attached stand-up collar, 13 in. round, is $1\frac{1}{2}$ in. deep and fastened by two 'high top' buttons.

The front and back hems have each a narrow band, 7 in. long, in the centre, to which the material is gathered; tapes are attached to the sides of the back for tying round the waist.

The sleeves, 18 in. long and 12 in. wide at the middle, have a small gusset below the collar attachment and a large one in the armpit; a narrow reinforcing band runs from the neck across to the shoulder. The narrow wristband is closed by *link holes*, with a 1-in. frill attached which also surrounds the 3-in. side slit. The 'link holes' were probably for a ribbon fastening. The sleeves are gathered into

[1] Francis Paget Hett: *Memoirs of Susan Sibbald*, 1926.

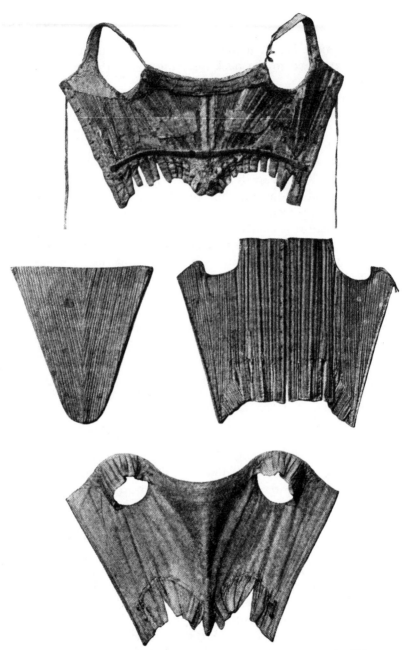

FIG. 38. (*above*) INTERIOR OF CORSET, SHOWING THE REINFORCEMENT, *c.* 1777 : (*middle*) CORSET
AND SEPARATE STOMACHER, 1730–40 : (*below*) CORSET OF WHITE FLOWERED SILK, *c.* 1770

the shoulders and wrists. Unlike the Hereford specimens, this had to
be put on over the head.

3. THE CORSET

This was singularly rigid and compressing throughout the period,
and was worn from childhood. The coarse material of which it was
made was closely stitched in rows
from top to bottom, enclosing
stiffenings of cane or whalebone.
Its lower margin was cut into tabs
so that the garment could be
adapted to the shape of the hips.
The front, supported by bones,
ended in a point below the waist.
The back, also boned and usually
made higher than the front, had
attached shoulder straps which
were brought forward and fastened
to the top edge in front, while the
sides were hollowed out under the
armpits. For the low décolletage of
Court dress these shoulder straps
were passed round the tops of the
arms (*figure* 38).

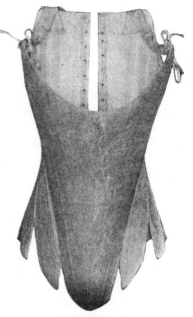

Back lacing with a single thread
was usual; the eyelet holes over-
sewn with silk since metal eyelets
had not yet been invented. (This

FIG. 39. CORSET SHOWING BACK-LACING,
c. 1770

point is important in dating specimens) (*figure* 38). The 'open
corset' was laced in front and behind, and for stout people extra side
lacings might be added. The discomfort of the fashionable corset in
1779 may be gathered from *The Sylph*, a novel by Georgiana, Duchess
of Devonshire: 'Poor Winifred broke two laces in endeavouring to
draw my new French stays close. You know I am naturally small at
bottom, but now you might literally span me. You never saw such a
doll. Then they are so intolerably wide across the breast that my
arms are absolutely sore with them; and my sides so pinched! But
it is the ton, and pride feels no pain.' Occasionally corsets were
covered with dress material, and formed the bodice of the gown,

with eyelet holes round the armholes by which detachable sleeves could be secured.

Specimens of corsets of the eighteenth century are often difficult to date with precision. A type may be found with an iron stiffener curved round the upper border in front and embedded in the material. A letter of Horace Walpole's (March 28, 1777) clearly refers to this as a new fashion:

'There has been a young gentlewoman overturned and terribly bruised by her *Vulcanian stays*. They now wear a steel busk down their middle, and a rail of the same metal across their breasts. If a hero attempts to storm such strong lines, and comes to a close engagement, he must lie as ill at ease as St. Lawrence on his gridiron.'

The projection of this iron 'rail' would support the bouffante or 'pouter pigeon' corsage which was fashionable for the next ten years or so (*figure* 39).

A comfortable substitute for such a corset as was usually worn was the negligée known as 'jumps,' a loose kind of unboned bodice. 'Bought my wife a new pair jumps instead of stays. She paid 36/6 for them.'[1]

4. THE HOOPED PETTICOAT

This was made of a strong material stiffened with whalebone hoops increasing in circumference from the waist downwards. Until about 1720 the shape was pyramidal. The *Weekly Journal* of 1718 remarked: 'Nothing can be imagined more unnatural, and consequently less agreeable. When a slender virgin stands upon a base so exorbitantly wide, she resembles a funnel (inverted)—a figure of no great elegancy; and I have seen many fine ladies of a low stature who, when they sail in their hoops about an apartment, look like children in go-carts' (*figure* 40).

At first its function, to the male eye, seemed clear. *The Spectator* of 1711 stated: 'The hooped petticoat[2] is made use of to keep us at a distance.' The unsophisticated country folk were astounded when the fashion first reached them. The shape, steadily expanding, became in the 1720's dome-shaped, and in the next decade the front and back were flattened, with extra width at the sides. In 1739 a

[1] *Marchant Diary*, 1716.
[2] A hooped petticoat cost 17/- in 1731 and another 10/6 in 1732. A cane French hoop cost 18/-.—Essex Records, Chelmsford.

FIG. 40. (*above*) BLUE LINEN PANNIERS, *c.* 1740; (*below*) HOOPED PETTICOAT OPENING AT
THE BACK, *c.* 1740–50

lady writes that hoops are 'two and three-quarter yards wide.'
By the 1740's the width was so vast that to pass through a doorway
the wearer had either to go sideways or else to flatten the hoop by
pressure on the flexible rings. But the headlong career of a fashion
is not to be baulked by such obstacles; by the half-century two
devices were employed. Either a pair of hooped bustles (then called
'false hips,' to which the Victorians preferred the nicer name of
'panniers') were worn, one on each hip (*figure* 40); in each of these
was an opening for a pocket suspended within. Or, to obtain still
greater breadth, the substructure was crowned on each side with

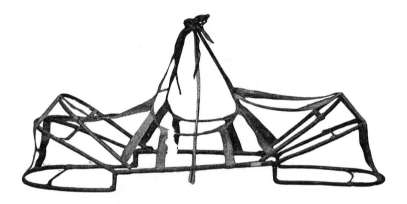

FIG. 41. HOOPED PETTICOAT SUPPORT IN BENT WOOD, *c.* 1750

three metal hoops which, being hinged, could be folded up under
the arms when occasion required (*figure* 41).

A lady, aged 68, whose waist was only 20¼ inches, writes in 1741:
'I desire you will send mee a very good whale bone hoop Peticoat
of the newest fashion. It must be three yards and a quarter round at
the bottom and it must draw in a Top for a wast half a yard and a
nail round, and the length from the hip to the bottom a yard and
a quarter.'[1]

The breadth continued unabated till the end of the 1760's when
the dome-shape returned and, except for Court dress, by 1775 the
hoop had given place to the bustle.

[1] G. Eland: *Purefoy Letters*, 1931.

From the household accounts of a County family (obtained from a private source) we extract some prices:

1745. A hoop 8/6.
1756. Miss ——'s stays bound round the top and cut lower before, 2/.
Her loose slip altered and made to fit the new stays 5/.
Mrs. ——'s stays let out a lap on each side and bound 5/.
Mrs. ——'s stays let out three bones on each side /3.

5. THE BUSTLE

This was a large roll pad, tapering at the ends and tied round the waist. It was stuffed with cork or any light cushion stuffing (*see figure* 42). The revival of this ancient device seems to have appeared, in the fashionable world, early in the 1770's. *The Universal Magazine* of 1776 describes the structure of 'the modern girl':

> Let her gown be tucked up to the hip on each side,
> Shoes too high for to walk or to jump,
> And to deck the sweet creature complete for a bride,
> Let the cork-cutter make her a rump.

> Thus finished in taste while on Chloe you gaze,
> You may take the dear charmer for life.
> But never undress her, for out of her stays,
> You'll find you have lost half your wife.

In more elegant language, Horace Walpole, writing to the Countess of Ossory (January 7, 1783) comments:

'*On prétend* that certain invisible machines, of which one heard much a year or two ago, and which were said to be constructed of cork, and to be worn somewhere or other behind, are now to be transplanted somewhere or other before, in imitation of the Duchess of Devonshire's pregnancy. . . .'

That the purpose of this appliance was something more than a mere *arrière pensée* seems to be implied in a letter from a disconsolate damsel of nineteen, complaining that she has so far failed to capture an admirer:

'. . . I begin, indeed, to think there is nothing at all in beauty; what a deal of pains have I taken to improve my face and my shape! But if you cannot put me in the way to make something of myself after all, I will actually unfrizzle my hair, throw my rouge in the

FIG. 42. BUSTLES. FROM AN ETCHING, 1787

fire, stuff a cushion with my bustle, press down my handkerchief to my bosom—and in short appear exactly as Nature made me. . . .'[1] A desperate remedy indeed.

From the same source we gather a description by an admiring husband of his wife's charms, as displayed at Ranelagh: '. . . She was without any stays and being quite free from such an encumbrance the fine play of her easy shape was exhibited in a very advantageous light. She had nothing on but a white muslin chemise, tied carelessly with celestial blue bows; white silk slippers and slight silk stockings, to the view of every impertinent coxcomb peeping under her petticoat. Her hair hung in ringlets down to the bottom of her back, and even rested upon the unnatural protuberance which every fashionable female at present chuses to affix to that part of her person.'

6. THE UNDER-PETTICOAT

Contemporary illustrations reveal that the under-petticoat was generally quite narrow and tubular, and that it did not reach below

[1] *Lady's Magazine*, 1786.

FIG. 43. (*above*) WOMAN'S UNDERSKIRT, *c.* 1770: (*below*) WOMAN'S UNDERSKIRT, *c.* 1780

the small of the leg. A hoop raised in walking would have freely exposed a flimsy petticoat which could have revealed the shape of the legs. The petticoat was made of cambric, dimity, flannel or calico, frequently with coloured bands bordering it (*figure* 43). For warmth some preferred a quilted under-petticoat.[1] 'You must send a neat white quilted Callico petticoat for my Mother, which must be a yard and four inches long.' 'The Marseilles Quilt petticoat is so heavy my Mother cannot wear it.'[2] For evening the garment would be more elaborate and carry embroidery.

We do not know whether more than a single under-petticoat was usually worn, but illustrations suggest not. 'Send my Mother for under petticoats 16 yards of tufted Dimmothy to wear under an Hoop, and three or four yards of very fine cambric,'[3] suggests materials for day and evening respectively.

The under-petticoat was known as a 'dicky.' 'Of all her splendid apparel not a wreck remained . . . save her flannel dicky' (1787).[4]

7. NIGHTCLOTHES

According to Leloir the night-shift resembled the day-chemise except for being somewhat longer; and he states that (in France) over it was worn a 'camisole' or sleeping jacket tied with ribbons.

On the head was worn a night-cap.

[1] 'A scarlet quilted petticoat, 14/5. 2 dimothy and 2 flannel petticoats, 12/–.'—Essex Records, Chelmsford.
'7 yards of dimothy for her petticoats, 10/6.'—Ibid.
[2] *Purefoy Letters*, 1739.
[3] *Purefoy Letters*.
[4] Compare 'the hips ashamed forsooth to wear a dicky.' (P. Pindar, 1800).

FIG. 44. NIGHTCLOTHES. FROM AN ENGRAVING BY CHOFFARD AFTER BAUDOUIN, 1782

V

1791—1820

HITHERTO information on underclothes has had to be obtained, here and there, from chance references, from accidental revelations in contemporary illustrations and pictures, and from satirical and therefore biased comments. As he pieces together the fragmentary finds of knowledge, the historian always remains conscious of the gaps in his story as well as of the conflicting accounts from which it is composed.

But from the close of the eighteenth century, apart from the increasing abundance of actual garments available in museums, a new source of information becomes available—the fashion magazine. *The Lady's Magazine or Entertaining Companion for the Fair Sex*, from about 1786 onwards supplied a monthly 'fashion article'; and with the dawn of the nineteenth century a number of others appeared. At first they ignored underclothes entirely, but gradually information even on that branch of fashions was allowed to intrude.

While the fashion magazine is, for the historian, a fairly reliable source, we must not overlook the influence it exerted on contemporary taste. It gave readers all over the country descriptions of standard fashions, and was therefore instrumental in persuading a much more general adoption of current modes. It helped to establish uniformity at least throughout those classes who habitually accepted it as a guide, and enabled the middle class to imitate very closely the styles favoured by 'the leaders of fashion.' Incidentally it thus became increasingly difficult for those select few to preserve such modes as their exclusive property. Unfortunately for the historian, journals dealing primarily with masculine fashions did not appear till well into the Victorian era.

The last quarter of the eighteenth century saw the introduction of two important changes of social habit, both destined to affect costume, and in particular the whole range of underclothes, to a notable extent. The first was the development, spreading from the middle class and eventually reaching far beyond it, of that peculiar attitude of mind associated with the term 'prudery.'

Previously the conventional attitude towards underclothing, for example, had been essentially frivolous; it was a legitimate topic for jests and practical jokes. It was part of the artificial comedy of sex. But prudery, which is an unconsciously exaggerated fear of sex, began to regard the subject more gravely. The fear extended to any kind of object or expression which seemed to be associated, however indirectly, with that dreadful, though commonplace, instinct. Underclothing, especially woman's, came to be shrouded in a moral fog of reticence, at times very baffling to the enquiring historian.

The development of prudery, destined later to become a national characteristic, was temporarily arrested by the Napoleonic wars from 1793 to 1814. During that epoch, as is so usual in war-time, the moral attitude swung, for the time being, in the opposite direction in the world of fashion. There, indeed, was not only prudery apparently suspended, but with it was banished much of the material forming our subject. Feminine underclothing was reduced to a point where it almost ceased to express either class distinction or sex attraction. For the latter purpose the physical features of the body were allowed full play; youth was in the ascendant and exercised its sway untrammelled. It was in this respect that the Regency period certainly struck an original note in feminine fashions. While the dress itself, aping the classical modes of ancient Greece, was but an indifferent attempt, though the first in our history, to revive a former style, what was really original was the discarding of superfluous undergarments. The Englishwoman of the fashionable world succeeded in reducing the total weight of her clothing to a couple of pounds. Such a thing had never previously been attempted in this country. The materials worn were sufficiently flimsy to reveal the real shape of the body. That this was a war-time method of sex attraction, rather than an expression of physical emancipation, differentiates the Regency modes from similar experiments in modern times.

There was nothing corresponding to it in male attire. The masculine shirt-front continued to play its former role of announcing the gentleman, but the introduction of voluminous trousers tended, rather, to conceal the shape of the legs, formerly so conspicuous in tight breeches.

The second important change of habit, which affected both sexes and their undergarments, was the singularly novel idea of personal cleanliness. This was introduced by the Macaronis of the 1770's, and it was largely due to their influence that physical cleanliness became fashionable, an extraordinary revival of a habit which had lapsed since the days of the Romans.

It was in this period that the figure of Beau Brummell—in his youth himself something of a Macaroni—stands out as the creator of this new 'fashion.' It would be more correct to say that he saw its possibilities as a symbol of social superiority, and established it as a permanent mark of the gentleman. 'Cleanliness was the touchstone upon which his acquaintances were invariably tried, to detect in them any deviation from that virtue was a sufficient reason for his declining any further intercourse with them.'[1] He made this a test, enunciating as the principle which denoted the gentleman, 'no perfumes, but very fine linen, plenty of it, and country washing.' He re-established, in fact, cleanliness as *the* social virtue, which had been in danger of lapsing.

This new social virtue inevitably affected the condition of the garments worn next the skin and necessitated a larger supply of them. Insensibly the money spent on underclothes increased. Moreover this new standard of physical cleanliness created a new form of class distinction, limited for the time being to the fashionable world, and extending beyond it only slowly. The habit of frequently changing the underclothes—and the ability through wealth and leisure to make these changes—became, in fact, distinctive of gentlefolk.

A philosopher of clothes, in 1800, contemplating the future of these social changes, might well have supposed that presently the human body, resplendent with soap and water, would emerge from its trappings into the light of day, and that underclothes were destined to shrivel into trivial accessories. But no philosopher who overlooked the possibilities of prudery could have foreseen the irony of embedding the Victorian body in layer upon layer of undergarments, all scrupulously clean, and all scrupulously hidden.

[1] Jesse: *Life of Brummell*, 1844.

Could he have foretold that those shrewd Victorians would be aware that the human body, freely exposed, is apt—after all—to be a sorry sight?

ᴥ MEN ᴥ

The turbulent years of this epoch produced a divergency in masculine fashions. The opening phase of the French Revolution excited a wave of sympathy in this country among those who held, in theory at least, democratic views on 'equality.' Charles Fox and his friends, for example, who had previously cultivated elegance in dress, now affected to despise the symbols of social refinement, and sported a style that was almost slovenly. 'Dress never fell till the era of Jacobinism and Equality, in 1793 and 4. It was then that .... the total abolition of buckles and ruffles . . . characterised the men.'[1]

I. THE SHIRT

This garment suffered, for a time, a singular eclipse. In most cases the shirt-front became completely concealed under the immense wrapping of the voluminous neckcloth; and the frill was omitted. The collar, even though five or six inches high (*figure* 45), was no longer visible; the less advanced school, however, allowed its edge to peep over the circumvallum that swathed the throat. Others, still more conservative, clung to the old insignia of rank with 'frilled shirt and lace ends to neckerchief'[2] (1802). This was usually reserved for evening dress; the ruffles at the wrist disappeared finally by the turn of the century. During the latter part of the 1790's not even a glimpse of shirt-cuff was shown, the coat-sleeve reaching down on to the wrist. That thin white line which cut the community in two, separating the gentleman of leisure from the manual worker, was thought to be 'undemocratic,' a brief phase of pseudo-equality that did not last.

It was soon after 1800 that George Brummell 'was the first who revived and improved the taste for dress, and his great innovation was effected upon neckcloths; they were then worn without stiffening of any kind. He used to have his slightly starched. . . . The collar, which was always fixed to his shirt, was so large that before being folded down it completely hid his head and face, and the white

[1] Wraxall's *Memoirs*.   [2] Francis Paget Hett: *Memoirs of Susan Sibbald*, 1927.

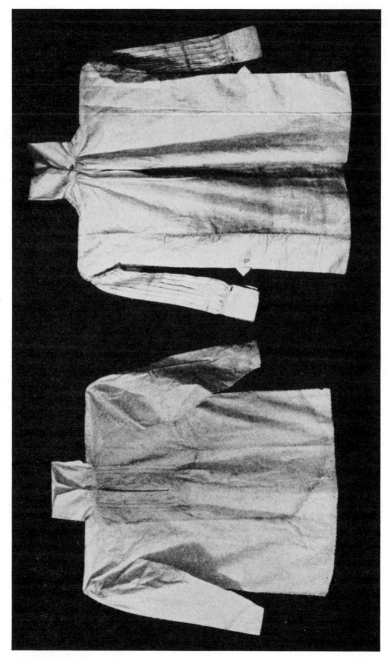

FIG. 45. (*left*) WEDDING SHIRT, *c.* 1795–1800: (*right*) MAN'S SHIRT, DATED (18)13

neckcloth was at least a foot in height. The first *coup d'archet* was made with the shirt collar which he folded down to its proper size; and then—with his chin poked up to the ceiling—by the gentle and gradual declension of the lower jaw, he creased the cravat to reasonable dimensions.'[1] 'When he first appeared in this stiffened cravat the sensation was prodigious; dandies were struck dumb with envy and washerwomen miscarried.'[2]

A letter of Maria Josepha, Lady Stanley, comments on this mode:[3]

1800. Pray, is it the fashion for the shirt collar to stand as high as the corners of the eyes? It is of consequence I should be informed before the new set I am making is finished. . . . Pray inform me if there is anything like a shirt annexed to the hideous ears you have described, because I think that part would be very comfortable to keep one snug from flies and sun. . . . There is nothing I have felt a stronger aversion to in men than that same fashion which I have seen in a few puppies.

(The points of those high collars were known as 'ears.')

By 1806 the ruffled shirt-front had become, once more, the general mode,[4] both for day and evening wear, though as yet no shirt-cuff was visible. A variation, however, for day use then began to appear. 'The bosom of the shirt now presents an air of peculiar neatness; the shirt itself is plaited and is without a frill, the opening being united with three or four linen buttons.'[5] And by the next year 'the day plaited shirt, buttoned, without frill, the waistcoat being buttoned only the lower two or three buttons,'[6] was capturing the fancy of the 'fashionables,' the shirt collar at the back just beginning to show above the coat collar.

The ruffled shirt persisted for evening. The delicate ruffle must

---

[1] Jesse: *Life of Brummell*, 1844.
[2] *The English Spy*, 1826.
[3] Jane Adeane: *The Early Married Life of Maria Josepha, Lady Stanley*, 1899.
[4] The effigy of Lord Nelson in Westminster Abbey is dressed in the clothes belonging to him at the time of his death in 1805. They were described by L. E. Tanner and J. L. Nevinson in 1934 and their account (see *Archeologia*, Vol. 85, 1936) states:
    'Shirt. Linen. Collar 5 in. Neck 15 in. Front slit 10¾ in. Left sleeve 22 in. Right stump 6 in.
    'High standing collar with three buttons (linen thread over a metal ring). The slit in front is edged with a linen frill; the body is full, tail slits at sides, marked with "HN. 24" in blue cross-stitch. There is a gusset on each shoulder towards the neck, and again under the arms. The left sleeve is long and full, gathered at shoulder and wrist, the centre part ironed into pleats; at the wrist there is a band, with slits for links. The right arm is only a stump, the fullness caught in with a draw-string.'
[5] *Beau Monde*, 1806.
[6] Ibid., 1807.

easily have become soiled; hence, no doubt, the disproportionate number of shirts to drawers found in wardrobe inventories of the time. For instance, the naval officer, Captain Fremantle, had in 1810:—'56 shirts' in his wardrobe, of which 14 are described as 'coarse,'[1] and were perhaps nightshirts. But there are only nine pairs of drawers. He required thirty-two neckcloths, an article which was readily spoiled in the tying, so that plenty of spares were necessary. A well-dressed gentleman would require at least two clean shirts daily.

With the return of the ruffled shirt most gentlemen, thanks to Brummell, wore a collar whose points commonly projected upwards in front with a wide gap between. The dandy would wear these collar-points projecting well up on to his cheeks.[2] With the reaction from democratic principles the white cuff of the shirt began to peep forth from the coat-sleeve; the shirt cuff being unstarched and its side opening unfastened. Cuff links were seldom used. Towards the end of this period the shirt-cuff became rather more noticeable, and the cuff of the coat-sleeve was often left unbuttoned at the side.

A specimen of this date, at the City Art Gallery, Leeds (Sanderson collection, *figure* 45) is of linen, the front $33\frac{1}{2}$ in. long, back 34 in., width 30 in., square cut with 12 in. side vents. Collar $5\frac{1}{2}$ in. deep, with one buttonhole at the base. Sleeves 19 in. long, 12 in. wide at the middle. Cuffs starched, 4 in. deep, square cut, buttoned at the base.

A narrow reinforcing band $1\frac{3}{4}$ in. wide passes from the neck to the top of the sleeve, and a vertical band 2 in. wide descends 10 in. in front and behind the shoulder.

A small gusset at the neck and a large one in the armpit.

The front opening has no jabot edging.

The stitching of the edge of the collar indicates that it was worn upright as a 'winker' and not turned over (which would have shown the less neat side of the stitches). Probably worn with a deep stock and full cravat.

This shirt is marked with initials and '13.' This is probably the date 1813.

---

[1] A. Fremantle: *The Wynne Diaries, III.*

[2] Cf. 'I must have a cambric *chemise* with the collar highly starched for dressing time —one of those that look like winkers.'—*The Hermit in London,* 1819.

'Winkers' was the popular name for the collars whose points projected almost into the eyes.

In spite of these changes of fashion there was a considerable number of men, especially the elders and professional men, who continued to wear the older style of day-shirt with frill. Portraits of the time are therefore somewhat contradictory, especially when they are of the seniors of that generation. As the war progressed, any original sympathy towards 'equality' faded, and a return to class distinctions was in a subtle manner indicated even in the shirt.

The shirts of the first half of the nineteenth century are often difficult to date, being still 'home made,' and sometimes having had their fronts or cuffs renewed at a later date. A notable specimen in the Castle Museum, Norwich, is a 'wedding shirt' of fine cambric enriched with needle-point lace and drawn thread work showing initials and two entwined hearts at the base of the front opening, which is nine inches deep and without a frill (*figure* 45). There is a gusset in the armpit, and the sleeves, wide at the top (9 in. at the widest point) slope to a narrow wrist where they are embroidered to simulate a cuff. The length of the shirt is 29 in., width 27 in., side slits 9½ in. deep, and the side slits and bottom are edged with embroidery. It was evidently to be worn with the tight buckskin breeches of the 1795–1800 period.

A 'dickey' (or false shirt-front), originally known as a 'Tommy' (*figure* 46) is mentioned[1] as a thing permissible in the country when fine dressing was impossible.

For the purpose of dating shirts of the nineteenth century the following points are helpful, though not wholly reliable. The construction at the shoulder presents a small triangular gusset at the base of the neck with the point towards the collar, and a large gusset in the armpit. These features, seen first in the eighteenth century, continued in use until near the middle of the nineteenth, the armpit gusset surviving longer than the neck gusset.

Until about 1840 a horizontal band, about 1½ in. wide, was added along the top of the shoulder to reinforce the material. In the Leeds shirt (*figure* 45) of 1813 there is in addition a vertical band surrounding the shoulder seam and descending some 10 in. in front and behind. This band was at first narrow, about 2 in. wide. It gradually became wider until by about 1840 it was often 5 in. wide, when the horizontal band above was no longer required. This broad vertical band survived, in evening shirts, till the end of the century.

[1] *The Hermit in London*, 1819.

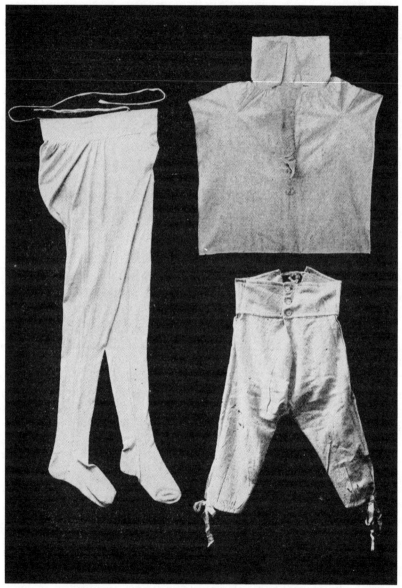

FIG. 46. (*left*) FOOTED LONG DRAWERS, 1795: (*above right*) MAN'S DICKEY, *c.* 1820: (*below right*) FLANNEL DRAWERS, *c.* 1805, WORN BY THOMAS COUTTS

The bottom of the shirt was cut square until about 1850 when it became curved, sometimes markedly so, a shape which continued up to the first World War.

Evidence of machine stitching indicates a date after 1850—in practice after 1860; but a great many continued to be sewn by hand after that date.

The presence of a frilled jabot can be misleading as that type of shirt was worn by the upper servant and by old-fashioned professional gentlemen at least into the 1860's.

The stud-hole at the back of the neckband is rare before 1860.

2. DRAWERS

These appear to have been of two lengths, short when worn under breeches (*figure* 46) and 'smallclothes' (i.e. breeches with a short extension on to the calf); long when worn under pantaloons and trousers.[1] In the Victoria and Albert Museum is a pair of man's long drawers, of stockingette with feet (*figure* 46). The legs, separately woven, are attached to a three-inch waistband of homespun, and fastened together only for some four inches behind. At the back of the band are two internal strings for tightening. Its probable date is about 1795. In the same collection is the pair of short flannel drawers, which belonged to Thomas Coutts. They are cut in the eighteenth-century style with spreading legs and are tightened at the back by tapes. The knees are tied with sarcenet ribbon. The waistband is three inches deep and is fastened down the front with three buttons.

3. BRACES

Man's undergarments received this useful addition shortly before 1800. It doubtless met a long-felt want. We read of a plump gentleman, in the tightest of buckskin breeches, attempting, at a ball, to bow to his partner, whereupon the breeches, stretched to capacity, suddenly shut up like a concertina round his ankles, so that he was immobilized. It may have been a war-time product that had let him down.

The material used was leather, e.g. 'a pair of morocco-leather braces, 5/–.'[2]

---

[1] From domestic bills (at the Hollytree Museum, Colchester) :—
'1811. Flannel drawers 6/6.' (Presumably the long variety).
'1813. Pair of drawers 4/6.' (Presumably the short variety).
[2] 1811. Accounts at the Hollytree Museum, Colchester.

The word used by the man of fashion for this appliance was, in his case, very appropriate. A 'brace' tightens a grip and his braces served not merely to suspend but also to tighten the buckskin breeches as much as possible. The name has survived long after a tight fit to breeches and trousers has ceased to be the mode.

The labourer, on the other hand, who naturally could not work in tight garments on his legs, retained the old-fashioned word 'gallows,' which had been formerly applied to any kind of suspensory device for holding up a garment, and henceforth spoke of his braces as his 'gallows.'

4. CORSETS

The dandy frequently wore this aid to beauty. Satirical caricatures show us the Prince Regent and others (e.g. *figure* 47) being laced in with difficulty, and Creevey also informs us that 'Prinny has left off his stays and his belly now hangs over his knees.' We also have a description of the fashion: 'A man is to be pinched in and laced up until he resemble an earwig.'[1] Contemporary illustrations show that after Waterloo the male waist became a conspicuous post-war attraction, and remained as a symbol of the exquisite for at least a generation. We are assured that 'all people of fashion wore them in town,' and that the exquisite would discuss the relative merits of 'the Cumberland corset and the Brummell bodice.'

That they were not always reliable is clear from the entry in *The Diary of a Dandy* of 1818.

FIG. 47. MALE CORSETS. 'TIGHT LACING.'
ENGRAVING, *c.* 1815

[1] 'He was dressed in the ultra pitch of fashion, collared like the leader of a four-horse team, and pinched in the middle like an hourglass, with a neck as long as a goose, and a cravat as ample as a tablecloth.' *The Hermit in London,* 1819.

'Sent for the tailor and stay-maker—ordered a pair of Cumberland corsets with a whalebone back. A caution to the unwary! The last pair gave way in stooping to pick up Lady B.'s glove. The Duke of C. vulgar enough to laugh and asked me in the sea slang if *I had not missed stays in tacking.*'

Ten years later a London tailor advertised that he had a stay-maker on his staff 'who designs and fashions the most approved stays for Gentlemen, from the Glasgow Stiffener to the Bath Corset.'[1]

5. NIGHTCLOTHES

These appear to have undergone no important change. Examples originally belonging to Thomas Coutts, the banker, may be seen at the Victoria and Albert Museum—a linen nightshirt, thirty-five inches wide, with a high folding collar and one button; and two knitted night-caps of jellybag shape, one single and the other double.

6. UNDER-WAISTCOAT

An example, which belonged to Thomas Coutts, is made of stockingette with a woollen lining, and is fastened down the front by thirteen Dorset thread buttons. The sleeves have a gap under the armpits and a narrow wristband with one button. It is twenty-eight inches long.

✑ WOMEN ✑

A revolutionary change in the structure of costume took place at the beginning of this epoch. The English invention of the high waist crossed the Channel and was shortly returned in the guise of the 'classical' style of dress, accompanied by an extensive shedding of superfluous undergarments. The English spirit of moderation, however, checked the 'near-nudity' movement in this country except for a few daring exponents of the ultra-French modes. For a few years stays were discarded by the 'fashionables,' but returned early in the new century.

All through this period there was a continual outcry at the scanty garb of 'the New Woman,' but, by modern standards, the amount of underclothes worn was not alarmingly small. Indeed, its total weight was not less than was often worn, in summer, some twenty

[1] We are indebted for this to Messrs. Drew & Son, of Bath, from whose brochure on corsets it is taken.

years ago.[1] What was so shocking to the sense of prudery in Regency times was the novelty of a dress of such transparent material as to allow of a liberal revelation of the human shape, such as had not been seen in this country before.

'Mrs. John Villiers was lately walking about Brighton in a muslin gown over a pair of grey pantaloons tied at the ankle with black twist, like those you may have seen William have,' Lady Stanley wrote in disgust[2] in 1801.

We may regard it as a kind of veiled exhibitionism. The centre of attraction, throughout the period, was the breasts, emphasized by the high waistline. 'One cannot see so many Ladies of high ton with the straps over the bosom, without thinking how much better they might have been employed over the shoulders.'[3] Three years later the same paper comments: 'The fashion of *false bosoms* has at least this utility, that it compels our fashionable fair to wear *something*'[4] (*figure* 48). The voice of prudery is heard in the comment: 'When I see a young lady displaying to every licentious eye her snow white bosom and panting breasts, with stays cut down before, the better to expose them to view—or when to shew a fine ankle the petticoat is shortened until half the leg is exposed—I blush for her indelicacy.'[5]

The spirit of class distinction was temporarily suspended, and with it went the hoop and wide skirt, which survived only in Court dress until George IV abolished it when he came to the throne in 1820. Those Court hoops had become an anachronism. 'You can form no idea what torments they were; it was like carrying a house

---

[1] That the urge to discard superfluous clothing extended far beyond the world of fashion is evidenced in the lament of a Yorkshire farmer, whose daughter, he declared, had died as a result. The poem also shows how rapidly new fashions were able to spread at that date, about 1800:

> And when she fust cam yam tae me
> She had nae petticoats ye see,
> At fust Ah fund she'd but a smock
> An' ower that her tawdry frock.
> Her shoon had soles so verra thin
> They'd naught keep out but let wet in.
> Besides, thou sees, she had nae stays,
> An' scarce enuf by heaf o' claies!
> Her naked arms, she liked to show
> E'en when t'cawd bitter wind did blow,
> An' noo i'toon as each yan passes
> You can't tell ladies fra bad lassies!

(Quoted by permission of the authorities of the Castle Museum, York.)

[2] *Letters of Maria Josepha, Lady Stanley*, 1899.
[3] *The Times*, 1796.   [4] Ibid., 1799.   [5] *The Mirror of the Graces*, 1811.

FIG. 48. PATENT BOLSTERS. ETCHING DATED 1791

on one's back; so frightful, and so ridiculous too,' exclaimed a lady subsequently.[1]

The important innovation in this period was the introduction of drawers, which had hitherto been a purely masculine garment. The adoption of it by women was the first of that long series of larcenies from the male wardrobe by which woman has marked each stage of her emancipation, until now 'the cupboard is bare and so the poor dog has none' that he can call his own (*figure* 50).

For us there is a certain irony in the fact that at first the wearing of drawers by women was considered extremely immodest. No doubt everyone was aware that it was a male garment; obviously only women of easy virtue would so demean themselves. So exceptional was it before 1800 that an instance obtained notice in *The Times*: 'At the late Fandango ball in Dublin a certain Lady of Fashion appeared in the following very whimsical dress:—flesh coloured pantaloons, over which was a gauze petticoat, tucked up at each side in drapery, so that both thighs could be seen. . . .'[2]

Early in the new century, however, the invidious garment was being adopted by 'the dashers of the haut ton,' and when Royalty, in the person of Princess Charlotte, not merely wore them but freely revealed the fact, its future career was assured. She was herself extremely 'modern,' being 'forward, buckish about horses and full of exclamations very like swearing. She was sitting with her legs stretched out after dinner and shewed her drawers, which it seems she and most young women now wear. Lady de Clifford said, "My dear Princess Charlotte, you shew your drawers." "I never do but where I can put myself at ease." "Yes, my dear, when you get in or out of a carriage." "I don't care if I do." "Your drawers are much too long." "I do not think so; the Duchess of Bedford's are much longer, and they are bordered with Brussels lace." "Oh," said Lady de Clifford in conclusion, "if she is to wear them, she does right to make them handsome".'[3]

The desire to exhibit a trophy so recently looted from man was natural enough; Regency prudery had not yet converted the garment into that Cimmerian mystery which so intrigued the Victorian male.

The early years of this period was marked by a singular taste for

---

[1] Mrs. Hudson : *Almacks*, 1825.
[2] 1796.   [3] *Glenbervie Journals*, 1811. Ed. F. Bickley, 1928.

wearing a bustle *in front* as well as behind. Noted by Horace Walpole in 1783 (*see* p. 91), we find it still being commented on ten years later. 'The pretty prominent pads which now grace the first circles of female fashion, if they have no sanction in decency, can certainly find one in precedent.'[1] Evidence of pregnancy, real or pretended, has always rather shocked the chaste male mind. 'When our grandmothers were pregnant they wore jumps to conceal it. Our modern young ladies, who are not pregnant, wear pads to carry the semblance of it. From thence it may be inferred, our grandmothers had some shame, while their descendants had none.'[2]

FIG. 49. AN OPERATIC SINGER, SHOWING THE CHEMISE. FROM AN ENGRAVING, 1798

1.   THE CHEMISE

(The old term 'shift' had by now become quite unfashionable, even 'vulgar.') The garment, made of cotton or linen, was straight and ungathered, the shape being almost oblong. It was knee length. The neck opening was square and edged with a gathered muslin frill. The short sleeves were set in with a gusset in the armpit. Being wide, the chemise was sometimes omitted when the dress itself was narrow (*figure* 49). 'Some of our fair dames appear, in summer and winter, with no other shelter from sun or frost than one single garment of muslin or silk over their chemise—*if they wear one!*—but that is often dubious.' 'The chemise, now too frequently banished.' 'The indelicacy of this mode need not be pointed out; and yet, O shame! it is most generally followed.'[3]

2.   THE PETTICOAT

This was made of cotton, cambric, linen, or, for winter, sometimes fine flannel. The attached bodice was of coarser material, and the upper third

[1] *Chester Chronicle*, 1793.   [2] Ibid., 1794, quoted in 'Browns and Chester.'
[3] *The Mirror of the Graces*, 1811.

of its skirt was opened down the sides to form a flap in front (to enable the garment to be put on), which was then fastened by tapes round the waist. The bodice was tied or buttoned in front and the back was cut high except when a low-necked dress was worn. This form of construction was known as 'a low stomacher front.' That even this garment was discarded by the more daring is expressly stated: 'The only sign of modesty in the present dress of the Ladies is the pink dye in their stockings, which makes their legs appear to blush for the total absence of petticoats.'[1]

'A lady with a well turned ankle should never wear her petticoats too short; cheap exhibitions soon sink into contempt; a thousand little natural opportunities occur to disclose this attraction without ostentatious display'[2] (1806).

In 1807, when dresses were narrow and tubular, there were advertised: 'patent elastic Spanish lamb's wool invisible petticoats, drawers, waistcoats, all in one.' 'The "invisible petticoats" were woven in the stocking-loom and drawn over the legs so that when walking you were obliged to take short and mincing steps.'[3] Elastic petticoats were advertised at 3/6 in 1811, and cotton petticoats, 3/6. Elastic at this period meant stretchable material such as stockinette.

From about 1815 onwards the petticoat had a pocket-hole on the right side through which a hanging pocket could be reached. By that date also the lower border was usually scalloped and trimmed with small flounces or a deep border of 'Moravian work' (later called 'broderie anglaise'), while circular rows of piping, known as 'rollios,' extended upwards, often nearly to the waist. In these later years the petticoat was gored.

By 1818, 'women have learnt to wear full petticoats but not to lengthen them.'

3. DRAWERS

These began to come into fashion about 1806, and were at first made on the lines of the masculine article, the waistband drawn together by back lacing. The leg was either tubular or gathered into a band below the knee. A specimen, said to have been from the wardrobe of the Duchess of Kent, *circa* 1820, and now in the Gallery of English Costume, Platt Hall, Manchester (Cunnington collection) is illustrated. The legs are attached to a wide waist-

---

[1] *Chester Chronicle*, 1803.   [2] *The Beau Monde*.   [3] *Memoirs of Susan Sibbald*.

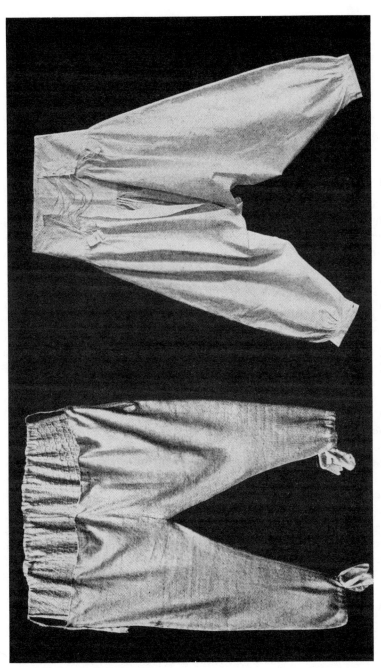

FIG. 50. (*left*) WOMAN'S DRAWERS IN KNITTED SILK, 1810–20 : (*right*) WOMAN'S DRAWERS OF LAWN, *c.* 1820. WORN BY THE DUCHESS OF KENT

band, and each is buttoned just below the knee (*figure* 50). 'Cotton drawers at 3/9, worth 5/–' are advertised in 1806. In 1811 'Ladies' Hunting and Opera drawers in elastic India cotton,' and in 1813, 'drawers with attached feet' were being advertised. These were made of knitted cotton.

We have to distinguish between drawers, which reached to just below the knee, and

4. PANTALOONS

This garment was distinct from drawers, which only reached just below the knee. Its name was quickly given a more feminine sound, and changed to 'pantalettes.' It differed in being extended down the leg to just below the calf, where it was bordered with lace and trimmed with four or five rows of tucks. In fact, the lower part was intended to be seen. This display was so opposed to the spirit of prudery that, at least in this country, the fashion for pantalettes did not survive beyond the 1830's, except as a style for small girls.

A fine example of the prudish comment comes from Lady Stanley's letter of 1817—'We were insulted by the presence of (Lady) Charlotte (Lindsay) in a green silk Spencer, green silk boots, and trowsers to the ankle much below the petticoat' (i.e. pantalettes).[1]

In some cases the two legs were constructed as separate items, very inadequately held in place, to judge from a lady's complaint in 1820: 'They are the ugliest things I ever saw: I will never put them on again. I dragged my dress in the dirt for fear someone would spy them. My finest dimity pair with real Swiss lace is quite useless to me for I lost one leg and did not deem it proper to pick it up, and so walked off leaving it in the street behind me, and the lace had cost six shillings a yard. I saw that mean Mrs. Spring wearing it last week as a tucker. . . . I hope there will be a short wearing of these horrid pantalets, they are too trying. Of course I must wear them for I cannot hold up my dress and show my stockings, no one does.'[2]

It may be noted that French writers attributed the introduction of drawers for women to the English custom of schoolgirls wearing such things when doing physical exercises; this, observed by the French *emigrées*, inspired the Parisian women of the Empire to

[1] *Letters of Maria Josepha, Lady Stanley.*
[2] Mrs. Earle: *Two Centuries of Costume in America.*

adopt the garment. That the generality of English women did not, as yet, wear this garment, is frequently proved by the caricaturist of the time, who did not hesitate to indicate the bare fact of its absence.

5. CORSETS

From 1794 to 1800 corsets were short, and were not worn universally. 'Corsettes about six inches long, and a slight buffon tucker of two inches high, are now the only defensive paraphernalia of our fashionable belles, between the necklace and the apron strings.'[1] From 1800 to about 1811 corsets were long, and from then to the end of the period they were, once again, short. It will be seen, therefore, that the phase of 'no corsets,' was, in this country, very brief and by no means general.

The Long Corset was made of jean or buckram, well stiffened with whalebone. It extended downwards to cover the hips, and upwards to push up the breasts. The lower edge was often straight and not cut into tabs as before, though tabbing persisted as an unfashionable device almost till 1820 (*figure* 51). Sometimes the edge was vandyked; but as an alternative method padded, cup-shaped supports for the breasts were also used to ease the rigidity of the bosom. The corset was laced up behind, its back being made with a rigid bone or steel busk. As formerly the eyelet holes were over-sewn and had no metal protectors.

The Short Corset was equally rigid, and had back lacing. As the mode was to have small hips and a full bosom, there were sometimes bitter complaints.

'By the newly invented corsets we see, in eight women out of ten, the hips squeezed into a circumference little more than the waist; and the bosom shoved up to the chin, making a sort of fleshy shelf disgusting to the beholders and certainly most incommodious to the wearer.'

The fashion magazines of the period abound in advertisements of stays. In 1807, 'The long elastic cotton stay obviates every objection complained of in Patent stays, not being subject to the disagreeable necessity of lacing under the arm, or having knitted gores . . . adapted to give the wearer the true Grecian form.' Another maker assures us that her product (at three to four guineas, ready money) has

[1] The Times, 1795.

FIG. 51. WOMAN'S TOILET, SHOWING CORSET WITH BUST SUPPORT. ETCHING BY LEWIS MARKS,
c. 1796–1800

succeeded in five thousand cases in removing with perfect ease the
fullness of the stomach and bowels. We learn that 'the present mode
of bracing the digestive portion of the body in what is called Long
Stays . . . compass into form the chaos of flesh.' And we accept,

FIG. 52.   WOMAN'S CORSET. 'A LITTLE TIGHTER'. FROM A CARICATURE BY ROWLANDSON, 1791

without surprise, the news, in 1810, that 'long stays are wholly
exploded.'

To apply effectively the new short stay a mother is advised that
her daughter should lie face down on the ground so that, by having
a foot in the small of the back, the mother can secure a firm purchase
on the laces.

The Divorce Corset appeared in 1816. The name is misleading;

at least it has misled a modern author into supposing that it reflected the current laxity of marital morals; whereas it was merely a device —not to separate husband and wife—but to separate one breast from the other. It consisted of a triangular piece of iron or steel, padded and with curved sides, the point projecting upwards between the breasts, thrusting them apart to produce a Grecian shape. It had almost the effect of a modern brassière.

The 'Pregnant Stay' was described, in 1811, as completely enveloping the body from the shoulders to below the hips, and elaborately boned 'so as to compress and reduce to the shape desired the natural prominence of the female figure in a state of fruitfulness.' There was also the 'Lucina belt for every lady expecting to be hailed by the endearing title of Mother.'

6. THE BUSTLE

For a few years before and after 1800 the bustle was discarded. By about 1810 it returned in the form of small rolls sewn into the back of the skirt; by 1815 it had become detached in the shape of a long sausage with tapes at each end by which it was tied round the waist. (Both types may be seen in the Gallery of English Costume, Manchester.) It seems that English ladies called the article a 'Nelson,' perhaps in compliment to the hero of the battle of the Nile when he was Rear-Admiral.

Towards the end of this period the French fashion of wearing an *outside bustle*, known in this country as a 'frisk,' was a momentary mode. For a few years after Waterloo, the fashionable stance, known as the 'Grecian bend,' was effected by a forward stoop assisted by a large bustle, placed high up the back.

7. POCKETS

The former device of a detached pocket hung round the waist under the skirt became impracticable with the scanty dresses of the period, and so they became replaced by the handbag or 'reticule,' commonly called a 'ridicule.' An observer in 1805 remarked that it was out of the question for ladies to wear pockets. When in a novel of 1817 a countrified lady admits to having a pocket, it provoked the comment: 'Your pocket, Madam! Do you wear a pocket?'

'Absolutely,' tittered a lady behind her chair, 'she confesses to wearing pockets.'[1]

8. NIGHTCLOTHES

That these remain more or less unchanged is suggested by a letter from Susan Ferrier, 1814: 'I must have been tying my nightcap or buttoning the collar of my nightgown' (*figure* 53).

[1] E. S. Barrett: *Six Weeks at Longs*, 1817.

FIG. 53. 'DAMP SHEETS,' SHOWING NIGHTCLOTHES AND CORSET. AFTER ROWLANDSON, 1791

VI

1821—1840

THE twenty years of war had seen some bizarre experiments in the clothing of both sexes. There had been violent efforts at novelty signalized, in the main, by a conspicuous distortion—even abandonment—of class distinction, and in consequence a notable crudity in sex appeal. By 1820 or so order was restored to chaos, and costume settled down steadily to emphasizing and developing the expression of class. The age of the genteel had begun in grim earnest.

This entailed a careful regulation of the forms of sex attraction permissible, especially in the apparel of the lady. Thanks to the increasing social importance of the middle class the spirit of prudery recovered from its war-time set-back, and became the dominating influence over the costume of both men and women. The 'high priestess' of this moral cult was the mythical figure known as 'Mrs. Grundy.' The name of that eminent Victorian is now almost forgotten, yet she reigned as a totalitarian dictator for nearly a century. This is curious and yet curiously English. She had never had a corporeal existence; being merely a character mentioned, though never seen, in an obscure comedy (Thomas Morton: *Speed the Plough*, 1800). Yet from about 1830 onwards her name became the convenient censor of social morals and dress, the personification of the spirit of prudery; this soon began to regulate polite speech. In 1818, Lady Susan O'Brien had noted that the language of society was becoming 'more refined. No one can now say "breeding," or "with child," or "lying in," without being thought indelicate. "Colic" and "bowels" are exploded words. "Stomach" signifies everything.'

This psychological 'black-out' began to affect various parts of the body; 'legs' became 'limbs,' 'breasts' became 'bosom,' and as a substitute for a more precise term, 'the lower back' served to indicate a region that has baffled the descriptive fashion writer ever since. When a gentleman's trousers masqueraded as his 'inexpressibles' (a term appearing first in 1805) and, later, as his 'nether integuments,' his underclothes could only be described as his 'linen.' With the ladies the rule was more discriminating; in polite society one might mention only such feminine undergarments as were in part exposed to view. It was permissible, therefore, to use the word 'petticoats,' and, with circumspection, 'stockings'; the rest was silence. Happily the abundance of fashion journals, designed for the female eye only, are available for the social historian who does not shrink from playing Peeping Tom.

We cannot properly appreciate the growing importance of feminine underclothes in this and subsequent periods unless we realize the atmosphere of secrecy which gave them at the time an attraction which has not survived in the museum cases where they may hang to-day. Yet they were endowed with the charm of mystery, not hitherto possessed by such inanimate objects. It was not surprising that so convenient a means of appeal should have multiplied. If a glimpse of one petticoat could produce agitation, what effect might not be obtained by half a dozen?

From the beginning of this period for nearly a century petticoats and prudery combined as a gigantic force; the steadily expanding skirt—concealing Heaven knows what—dominated the social scene and marked the growing importance of the lady; her underclothing had become, as it were, an integral part of her personality. It expressed, even more truly than the outward dress, a statement of the higher morality. Instilled with the principle that ugliness is next to Godliness, she was careful to avoid any suggestion of aesthetic beauty in such garments as were wholly invisible. A concession was allowed in those of which an occasional glimpse was permitted; the border of a petticoat might be exquisitely embroidered, but this concession was corrected by austerity elsewhere, with the body itself in the bleak embrace of plain white longcloth. The notion of wearing coloured undergarments would have caused her a moral shudder. The policy was to obliterate all recollections of those indecorous habits which had disfigured the past.

The eighteenth century had regarded woman as a creature of the chase, and the garments which concealed her person as a frivolous affectation of false modesty. The advance of prudery altered all that. Feminine underclothing became a serious, even a solemn subject, expressive of a conscious rectitude of outlook. Yet human nature and the basic instincts could not be smothered even by longcloth, and so a new and more subtle method of attraction developed out of the very materials intended to obliterate the old. Prudery was found to have, in itself, an erotic appeal. Effective underclothing developed into an art, serving sometimes as an accessory to nature's gifts and sometimes as a substitute for their lack. It is true that this art did not arrive at its sublime apotheosis till Edwardian days, but we see the process in its initial stages during the period now under consideration. The lesson which those pioneers surely teach is how profound and irresistible is the attraction which prudery exerts when skilfully practised by one sex on the other. The old saying that 'what the eye doesn't see the heart doesn't grieve over' applies specially to the defects of the human form, which it becomes the function of underclothes to conceal.

They also serve not merely to accentuate the real differences of physique between the sexes, but even to create illusory ones. For to the masculine mind, a creature so exquisitely delicate that she needs to swathe herself in such a multitude of wrappings must be of a peculiar fragility remotely unlike his own substance. How could natural curiosity resist such an enigma? We must not give all the credit to the dressmaker; her handiwork, admirable though it might be, was sustained and given its alluring outlines by the invisible but essential foundations. These too, then, were instrumental in creating the great illusion.

Nor are the underclothes of this period to be ignored as a method of displaying social rank. The vast circumference of the crinoline skirt, or the trailing train of its successors, were not—in spite of the common saying—garments which 'stood by themselves.' They owed their impressive form to their substructure. In fact, to build up the framework of the fine lady, and to add to her importance, a host of ingenious implements were required. We are to witness, in this epoch, the initial stages of that ingenious structure, and in the spirit of the archaeologist we have to explore the depths of its foundations.

By comparison, man's underclothes in this period present an

infinitely less ambitious aim. Only the visible portions of his shirt seem to be purposive; *there* is still stamped the insignia of the gentleman.[1]

∽ MEN ∽

1. THE SHIRT

The differences between day and evening styles came to be accentuated. Although the frilled front persisted for many as day wear (*figure* 54) all through this period, the man of fashion tended more and more to reserve that ornament for his evening shirt, wearing by day the tucked front; but inasmuch as the immense day cravat often concealed almost the whole of the shirt-front, it is impossible, in such cases, to judge of its nature. 'Some of our dashers wear cravats of red Merino, the ends of which entirely cover the bosom.'[2] The same source informed its readers of a dandy, staying at a country house, who came down to breakfast 'in a redingote vest of plain velvet, waistcoat of flowered marcella, shirt of embroidered muslin, cravat of foulard, and—satin pantaloons.' A sceptic in a rival magazine declared that he would give fifty pounds to see a man in such a dress, and fifty more to shoot the beast. When contemporary authorities differ, how shall we, at this distance decide? But we must always remember that a fashion journal is not a scientific work but a branch of romantic fiction tinged with truth.

As formerly, the collar was usually attached, and sufficiently high to be folded down over the cravat. The stock, previously intended

[1] Inventory of a gentleman's linen. August 1829:
    Day-shirts, 23.
    Nightshirts, 5.
    Night-caps, 9.
    Flannel drawers, 2 pairs.
    Calico drawers, 4 pairs.
Inventory of the same in 1837:

Day-shirts	19
Nightshirts	3
Double night-caps	3
Single ditto	2
Thin drawers	2 pairs
Thick drawers	2 pairs

Both inventories show a disproportionate number of day-shirts (which probably included evening shirts). The amount of laundry work entailed by ruffled shirts would have been immense; an exclusive luxury of the well-to-do. Incidentally the inventories include a vast wardrobe of suits and outer garments, indicating a gentleman of wealth. (The total absence of (detached) collars and of under-vests is to be noted.)

[2] *The Gentleman's Magazine of Fashion*, 1830.

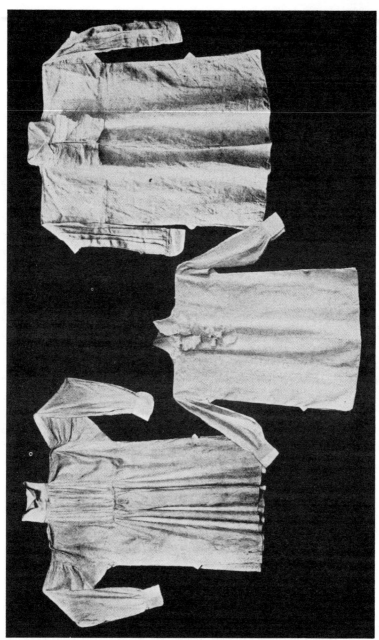

FIG. 54. (*left to right*) MAN'S SHIRT, MARKED AND DATED 1827, WORN BY GEORGE IV; MAN'S SHIRT, DATED 1823; MAN'S DAY-SHIRT, *c.* 1815–25

to be worn only by the military, came into civilian use in 1822. There is some evidence, however, that the detached collar was not unknown. It was tied round the neck, and not fastened with a back stud. 'When travelling take three dozen cravats and at least three dozen shirt collars.'[1]

For the evening 'the bosoms of dress-fronts are invariably composed of lawn or worked cambric which is puckered and furbelowed with a variety of ruffled shapes.' 'Nothing can be more handsome, manly, and unassuming than a plain cambric muslin frill.' 'The wristbands, which should only be turned down the last thing on going to a party or ball, should be made of a considerable depth, collars the reverse.' 'The wristbands, collar and front are the only parts displayed'; so that 'the body and sleeves may be made of fine India longcloth instead of linen.' (*The Whole Art of Dress*, 1830.)

Illustrations in contemporary novels, however, show a considerable variation from these rules; elderly gentlemen and professional men, and those of the middle class, commonly wear frilled shirts by day; by the end of this period the frilled shirt is often worn by butlers and upper men-servants by day, as part of their uniform, much as they subsequently wore 'dress suits.'

An important novelty was introduced, a primitive form of 'sports shirt,' known as an 'aquatic shirt,' intended for the river but soon adopted by the unfashionable young man, in the 1830's.[2] The correct form had narrow blue and white, or red and white, stripes or checks of cotton, and the collar and wristbands were not visible.

Notes on Museum Specimens.

Men's Shirts in the City Museum, Hereford.

    1. Day. Of homespun linen, buttoning at the neck. Attached 5-in. collar to fold over neckcloth, with two buttons. Cambric frill 11 in. deep down the centre of front. Sleeves $7\frac{1}{2}$ in. wide at the middle, with gussets at shoulder and armpit. Unstarched cuff with link holes at the base. Dated 1824.

    2. Day. Of linen, length 37 in., width 30 in. Attached collar 6 in. deep, with two buttons (linen covered on brass rings). Cambric frill 11 in. deep. Sleeves 11 in. wide at the middle, with

---

[1] *The Art of Tying the Cravat*, 1828.
  Cf. 'Having tied on a clean shirt collar'—Theodore Hook: *Sayings and Doings*, 1828.
[2] Jack Hopkins, the medical student in *The Pickwick Papers* (1836–7), wore a 'blue striped shirt and false collar.'

gussets at the shoulders. Unstarched cuff with one button at the base. Probable date about 1830.

3. Day. Of linen, length 25 in. front, 35 in. back; width 35 in. Square cut. Collar 5 in. deep, with two pearl buttons. Cambric frill 12 in. deep. Sleeves 8 in. wide at the middle, with gussets at shoulder and armpit. Cuff 2 in. wide, buttoned at base. The garment back-stitched throughout. Worn by a banker, 1830–40. The centre front opening of the frilled shirt is unfastened except for the single button at the neck; the aperture is prevented from gaping by having the frill turned to one side and kept in that position by the waistcoat.

The link holes in the shirt dated 1824 are unusual; in all other specimens there is a button at the base of the cuff, the border being left open, links not being usual until the 1840's. Cuff links appear to have been in occasional use in the seventeenth century—they may be seen in the portrait by Lely of Admiral Jeremy Smith at Greenwich Hospital—but during the period of wrist ruffles in the eighteenth century they would have been invisible. The early nineteenth-century cuff, shorn of its ruffle, remained gaping at the border until the cuff was stiffened with starch when it could more easily be closed by links than by a button.

The shirt of George IV (Castle Museum, York) dated 1827 (*figure* 54), has the front opening closed by three small pearl buttons, the earliest example we know of the use of mother-of-pearl buttons on underclothing.

It seems that the protruding jabot of that period excited some derision. Washington Irving (in *Whim-Whams of Lancelot Langstaff*, 1823) comments: 'They had exuberant chitterlings; which puffed out at the neck and bosom like unto the beard of an ancient he-turkey,' and he is equally scornful of 'his silver-sprigged dickey which he assures me is all the rage.'

A dress shirt of the period 1830–40 (Sanderson collection, City Art Gallery, Leeds) is of linen, the front 41 in., the back 42 in. Width below armpits 27 in. Attached collar 2½ in. high; 16 in. round, with two buttonholes in front, one above the other. The front opening, 10½ in. deep, has a jabot of frilled starched muslin 4 in. wide. The square-cut starched cuffs, buttoned at the base, are 1¾ in. deep.

The shoulder has both types of reinforcing bands described in the previous chapter (horizontal along the top and vertical down the front and back). This transition from the older method of construction to the newer seems to suggest the date we have given to it. The extreme width of the jabot frill, at such a date, almost certainly indicates that it was an *evening* dress-shirt, not a day, though we might be misled by such a specimen as

'A fine, false, four-frilled front to his shirt, embroidered, pleated, and puckered like a lady's habit-shirt. Down the front were three or four different sorts of studs, and a butterfly brooch, made of various coloured glasses, sat in the centre'—and worn by James Green on a boat excursion to Margate. (Surtees: *Jorrocks's Jaunts and Jollities,* 1838–9.) And when he turns back the wrists of his coat he exhibits 'his beautiful sparkling paste shirt buttons' (i.e. links). From such descriptions we learn to appreciate the difficulty in dating Victorian specimens of shirts, unless we know for certain whether they had been worn by a gentleman or by a—gent.

2. DRAWERS

These appear to have been both long and short, the long variety often being called 'trouser drawers.' This distinction is apparent in a bill of John Disney, tailor and draper, 1831:[1]

'Pair of troues Dr. /6. Pair of Dr. of Drill 1/6. Two pairs of Dr. & buttons 1/3. Pair of Dr. & buttons /9.' ('Troues' = 'trouser'; 'Dr.' = 'drawers.')

From various sources we have collected references to men's drawers in this period made of the following materials:

Calico; cotton; worsted (thick and 'extra-thick'), and 'thick China drawers' (i.e. of China silk). Some short drawers were made of white drill, but we have been unable to find a specimen and we do not know their construction.

3. CORSETS

That the man of fashion wore corsets is sufficiently apparent from portraits, such as that of Count D'Orsay by Maclise. The 'pinched-in waist' is described in *Pelham* by Bulwer-Lytton (1828) who was himself labelled by Tennyson as 'the padded man who wears the stays.' According to Fraser, Disraeli's stays were visible through the

[1.] Essex County Records.

back of his coat. It was, in fact, the correct mode of the beau whom, by this date, it was no longer correct to call a 'dandy.'[1]

> Each lordly man his taper waist displays,
> Combs his sweet locks and laces on his stays,
> Ties on his starch'd cravat with nicest care,
> And then steps forth to petrify the fair.[2]

4.   NIGHTCLOTHES

The nightshirt had a plain turned-down collar, buttoned at the neck, the centre opening extending a considerable way down the front. The garment appears to have been otherwise plain. A night-cap with coloured tassel was usual. We have Mr. Pickwick's authority for stating that the night-cap was tied beneath the chin with strings.

ဢ WOMEN ဢ

I.   THE CHEMISE

Usually of homespun linen, this was an unshaped garment with a low square neck edged with a narrow cambric frill. A specimen dated 1825 (Gallery of English Costume, Platt Hall, Manchester) is a yard wide, with short sleeves gathered over the shoulders and set in with large gussets under the arms (*figure* 55).

2.   PETTICOAT

This was often made with an attached bodice, in the form of a stomacher-front. Others were buttoned behind and had low necks edged with lace or insertion, the neck line being pulled in by a draw-string. The border of the evening petticoat would be orna-mented, a specimen at Platt Hall having a deep edging of scalloped and embroidered cambric above which are sixteen rows of heavy piping to the knee (*figure* 55).

The short petticoat (i.e. without a bodice) hung from the waist. Materials: cotton for day and cambric or muslin for evening.

With the steadily expanding skirts we may safely assume that towards the end of this period the petticoats had increased in

---

[1] 'Dandy has been voted vulgar, and Beau is now the word.'—Disraeli: *The Young Duke*, 1829.
[2] *The English Spy*, 1825.

FIG. 55. (*left to right*) CHEMISE, DATED 1825: PRINCESS PETTICOAT, c. 1820: NIGHTDRESS, DATED 1825

number, and that, in winter at least, they were often of thicker materials than formerly.

In 1827, in Paris, 'petticoats are stuck out with whalebone,' a mode which did not affect this country till twenty years later.

3. DRAWERS

The use of this garment was steadily spreading, so that by the end of the 1830's it had become generally accepted by women of any social pretensions. It had, in fact, become a garment of class distinction, not, of course, to be worn by the lower orders. 'Many ladies when riding wear silk drawers similar to what is worn when bathing' (1828). For riding on horseback the French fashion for wearing pantaloons under the habit was appearing in this country by the 1830s.

Pantalettes were sometimes worn (*figure 57*). A French journal of 1824 remarked that 'Drawers of percale are extremely fashionable at present, for children, young girls, and even ladies. In the country they are absolutely essential.' In England, however, the ankle-length garments, though usual with children, were seldom worn by adults in society, though they are not uncommon in pseudo-Victorian stage 'revivals' to-day.

4. CORSETS

Tight-lacing became progressively more severe, partly to accentuate the much-admired 'small waist,'[1] and partly as a moral restraint correcting the looser habits of the Regency. Some lamented the change. 'The general character of youth should be meek dignity, chastened by sportiveness and gentle seriousness. Ladies are implored to maintain something of the ease and grace attached to the once dominant Grecian costume, against all the newly-sprung up Goths and Vandals in the shape of stay-makers who have just armed themselves with whalebone, steel and buckram to the utter destruction of all native-born fine forms' (1824). 'At Paris they recommend the corsets of Delacroix, fitted with paddings to fill up any deficiency. Young ladies may be seen with their breasts displaced by being pushed up too high and frightful wrinkles established

---

[1] 'French corsets producing a graceful and sylph-like tournure' were advertised at 25/– in 1834.

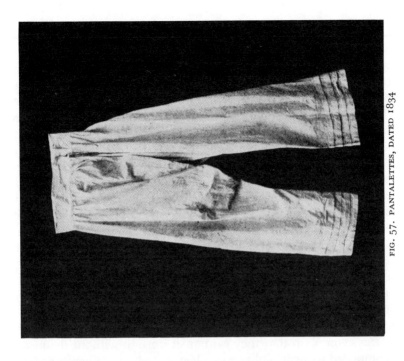

FIG. 57. PANTALETTES, DATED 1834

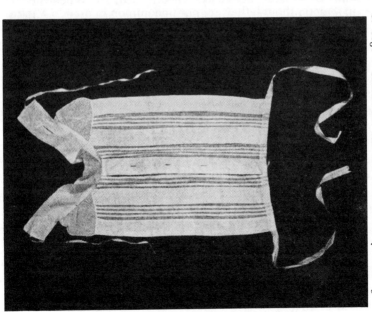

FIG. 56. WOMAN'S HABIT-SHIRT, PLEATED AND TUCKED, c. 1830–40

between the bosom and the shoulders . . . a ridiculous fashion by means of which the body resembles an ant with a slender tube uniting the bust to the haunches which are stuffed out beyond all proportion' (1826).

That the habit was spreading to the middle class may be gathered from a letter from a tradesman (1828): 'My daughters are living instances of the baleful consequences of the dreadful fashion of squeezing the waist until the body resembles that of an ant. Their stays are bound with iron in the holes through which the laces are drawn so as to bear the tremendous tugging which is intended to reduce so important a part of the human frame to a third of its natural proportion. They are unable to stand, sit or walk, as women used to do. To expect one of them to stoop would be absurd. My daughter, Margaret, made the experiment the other day; her stays gave way with a tremendous explosion and down she fell upon the ground, and I thought she had snapped in two.' He adds, 'my daughters are always complaining of pains in the stomach.'

A book of the toilet (1837) informs us: 'Women who wear very tight stays complain that they cannot sit upright without them, nay are compelled to wear night stays when in bed. . . . When the young lady spends a quarter of an hour in lacing her stays as tight as possible, and is sometimes seen by her female friends pulling hard for some minutes, next pausing to breathe, then resuming the task with might and main, till after perhaps a third effort she at last succeeds and sits down covered with perspiration, then it is that the effect of stays is not only injurious to the shape but is calculated to produce the most serious consequences.' (*Female Beauty*, 1837.)

Demi-corsets, some eight or ten inches high, with light whalebones, were worn when performing domestic work by day; when arrayed in her best pair she bent at her peril.

It should be noted that the eyelet-holes began to be strengthened with metal rings in 1828; and that in 1830 'an elastic stiffening of a vegetable substance has been invented, instead of that spiral brass wire now used for shoulder straps, glove tops, corsets, etc. . . . it is said to be made of India rubber.' 'Patent caoutchouc instantaneous closing corsets; this novel application of India-rubber is by far the most extraordinary improvement that has ever been effected' were advertised in 1836.

5. THE BUSTLE

This was becoming larger, either as a crescentic pad stuffed with down, often double or treble, and tied round the waist (*figure* 58); or made of gathered rows of stiffened material, or of whalebone.[1]

A down-stuffed bustle, dated 1833, is in the Cunnington collection, Platt Hall, Manchester.

'The diameter of the fashionable ladies at present is about three yards; their bustles (false bottoms) are the size of an ordinary sheep's fleece. The very servant girls wear bustles! Eliza Miles told me a maid of theirs went out one Sunday with three kitchen dusters pinned on as a substitute.'[2] Another writer declares, 'nothing can be in worse taste than the monstrous and ill-shaped bustles we commonly see sometimes placed altogether on one side; and sometimes so irregular that they look as if some domestic utensil

FIG. 58. BUSTLES: (*top pair*) EARLY 19TH CENTURY; (*below*) DATED 1833

FIG. 59. WOMAN'S-NIGHT-CAP, *c.* 1819–33

were fastened under the dress.'[3] We are also informed that the bustle 'has the drawback of being liable to slip out of place, being situated in a region on which the fair wearer is unable to keep an observant eye.' That this was not uncommon may be gathered from the loud comment of the schoolgirls on their form-mistress: 'Miss Trimmer's bustle's on crooked!'[4]

---

[1] Advertisement: 'Worked hair sleeves and bustles, black and white, prepared whalebone covered' (1838).
[2] Mrs. Carlyle: *Letters*, 1834.
[3] Mrs. Walker: *Female Beauty*, 1837.
[4] Surtees: *Jorrocks's Jaunts and Jollities*, 1839.

6. NIGHTCLOTHES

So far as is known these do not show any material change. A linen nightdress, dated 1825, in the Gallery of English Costume at Platt Hall (*figure* 55), is plain and unshaped, and has a falling collar with a frill which is continued down the front opening as a border. The sleeves are gathered into a cuff, which is fastened by a hand-made button.

A Bustling Woman_1829 — after Cruikshank

FIG. 60

VII

1841—1856

THE art of costume seldom develops at a uniform rate of progress; it exhibits phases of activity interspersed with periods of apparent quiescence. Such quiet interludes are, of course, illusory, for changes, especially below the surface, may be going on preparatory to an upheaval of the visible landscape. Of this nature was the period of the 1840's and early 1850's.

Outwardly fashions seemed to pause, as though content to have established on a solid foundation a style of costume indicative of middle-class prosperous gentility. In this it appeared to be more important to express class distinction than sex attraction; or rather the evidence of social rank and wealth was in itself a sufficient form of attraction.

The gentleman's interest in his shirt as a garment of display steadily declined, indicated partly by its stabilized form, and even more by the diminishing exposure of its surface. In estimating this we must not be misled by fashion plates emanating from French sources, even though having English captions, and appearing in English magazines as illustrations of 'the latest London fashions.' If, however, we compare them with actual photographs and portraits of Englishmen (photographs becoming available in the 1850's), we find that there was a considerable difference in taste, and that the English gentleman usually avoided the lavish display of picturesque shirt-front by day, such as decorated the subjects of Louis Phillippe and Napoleon III. This country was then too busy with commerce for its prosperous menfolk to cultivate romantic attitudes in dress. 'The age of ruins is past; look at Manchester' was Disraeli's comment. An Englishman's income made a stronger impression than his shirt-front.

Moreover in the early 1850's an innovation, presaging profound social changes, appeared gradually in the gentleman's garb; thanks, in part at least, to the development of railway travelling it was becoming necessary to have for informal occasions a less exacting type of costume, namely, the 'Tweedside,' or forerunner of the 'lounge suit,' and with it a shirt and collar designed for ease and movement.[1]

Modern progress of this sort scarcely as yet affected the other sex. The lady remained a static creature, more concerned, for the time being, in demonstrating her social importance than her physical charms. That she was not entirely unconcerned with the art of sex attraction in its more primitive forms may be gathered from contemporary advertisements[2] recommending artificial 'bust improvers' and 'lemon bosoms'; so too the wedding dress of the period was specially padded over the 'figure' for that important moment in a young lady's career.

But progress was mainly marked in the skirt, whose substructure was steadily expanding. A complex system of fortifications in depth, and immense circumvallations of petticoats kept the wearer at arm's length from contact with the outer world. It was as though she had become petrified into a monument which, however impossible it might seem, continued to expand. By 1851 the lady was indeed a Great Exhibition. Well might she have supposed that further progress was impossible; the gigantic structure had reached a size which seemed to defy the skill of the dress-architect to increase; mere petticoats could no longer support the burden of Atlas. But necessity is the mother of invention, and by the end of this period nothing could have prevented the introduction of some kind of mechanical support—to wit, the artificial 'cage crinoline.'

Although the 1840's were not conspicuous for striking fashion changes, they nevertheless introduced a number of ingenious items employed in underclothing. For example, the domestic pin, which previously had its head attached round the end of the shank by a separate process, was made with head and shank all in one, from 1840 onwards. The 'three-fold' linen button, introduced in 1841, had the advantage over the pearl button of being able to withstand

---

[1] 'Saxony flannel shirts, suitable for gentlemen travelling, 9/6 each.'—Advertisement of 1855.

[2] E.g. *The Lady's Newspaper*, 1847.

the mangle. The hand-made Dorset thread button, in which cotton thread was sewn across a wire ring, radiating from its centre, had disappeared by 1830.

The 1840's also saw the introduction of a new undergarment for both sexes, namely the woollen vest, or 'under-vest,' worn next the skin, and for women, the camisole. It appears, however, that young ladies strongly disliked the maternal recommendation of wearing 'wool next the skin.' Their existence was notably sedentary; they took little outdoor exercise, and in the home gentility forbade active domestic work. Leading the life of a caged canary they were generally in delicate health, necessitating much 'wrapping up'; additional undergarments seemed the obvious remedy, and the making of them (in private) a very suitable occupation. The sewing machine had not yet been invented, so they had to become experts at the needle.

A less formal generation might suppose that to carry on her person about a stone's weight of clothing, mostly undergarments, would have been sufficient protection for the most fragile of her sex, yet, curiously enough, there were frequent complaints, in the 1840's, that young ladies were insufficiently clad, both for propriety in evening dress and for health in the day. *The Handbook of the Toilet* (1841) ascribed the English habit of 'catching colds' to draughts and imperfect closure of windows, especially in the bedroom. It was sufficient if, in warm weather, the ventilator of the grate was left open. 'Our fair countrywomen fear water; this, with insufficient clothing (a practice arising from the silly vanity of appearing small-waisted) are the true causes.' The undergarments worn 'at least over her vital organs, are totally inadequate, and bare shoulders in evening dress is largely instrumental in starting consumptions. The chest should be carefully guarded but the garments should be porous, and for that reason leather waistcoats and rabbit skins should be avoided. Flannel should be worn next the skin all the year over the whole body and arms and as low as the middle of the thighs, but alas! very few young ladies will do so. Ladies should not be sparing of flannel petticoats, and drawers are of incalculable advantage to women, preventing many of the disorders and indispositions to which British females are subject.'

These admonitions were coupled with stern condemnation of the practice of tight-lacing, especially with stays lacing downwards, 'producing injurious pressure upon those forms which Nature has given women as fountains of nourishment for their offspring; the downward pressure may even produce protrusion of the intestine, which has spoiled the prospects and fortune of many a girl who has brought it upon herself.' While the medical profession declared 'tight lacing and sedentary languishing are the greatest enemies to female health,' the Church was even more explicit. 'Tight lacing, from a moral point of view, is opposed to all the laws of religion.' A more powerful reason, however, for abandoning the habit came presently from fashion itself; by the early 1850's the skirt had become so vast in dimensions that by comparison any waist looked small, and many fashionable young women no longer bothered to wear stays at all. That particular feature of attraction seemed unimportant in contrast to the imperative need for expanding yet further the social symbol of the huge skirt.

☙ MEN ☙

I. THE SHIRT

The stereotyped pattern for day use gradually developed into one with fine lines of vertical tucks on each side of a narrow central panel. The amount of shirt-front exposed depended chiefly on the design of waistcoat, which was sometimes cut to expose a considerable depth, revealing two or three shirt-buttons (*figure* 61); studs often replaced buttons by the end of this period, and might be linked together by a slender gold chain (known as 'tethered studs'). In other cases the front was plain; often the waistcoat was cut high, and where a large cravat was worn practically the whole of the shirt-front was hidden. The morning dress of the Marquis in *Hillingdon Hall*[1] is thus described:—'An immense pearl pin fastened the folding ends of a lilac satin scarf with white flowers, almost concealing the elaborate workmanship of his shirt front.' For informal occasions he wears 'a pink-striped shirt.'

The collar was attached to the back of the neckband by a button, and stood up stiffly above the cravat with a wide gap between the square-cut points. A narrow edge of unstarched cuff was visible, and cuff links appeared after 1840 as a usual fashion.

A specimen in the City Museum, Hereford, of about 1850, is of

[1] R. T. Surtees, 1844.

FIG. 61. MEN'S COLLARS, CRAVATS, AND SHIRTS: C. 1850 (a) LORD CARLISLE,
(b) MR. FRITH, (c) MR. PHELPS, (d) LORD BROUGHAM, (e) MR. SHEE : 1890 (f) MR. GLADSTONE

fine linen; length 37 in., width 28 in. (*figure* 62). The neckband, 1 in. deep., is starched and has a pearl button attached at the back. The starched front has two panels of fine tucks running transversely, and three stud holes down the centre. The cuffs, also starched, are turned back, with a button at the base and link holes at the border.[1] The garment is hand-sewn throughout.

The dress shirts of this period might present fine lines of tucks or be enriched with lines of embroidery. Frequently there was no stud or button in the front. With these a white cravat, wound twice round the neck and tied in a large bow, crossed the front of the neck between the collar points. The cravat was deep enough to conceal all but the rim of the collar. When the shirt-front had studs these were usually gold, two or three, connected by chains. Gold cuff links were usual, though they were still generally described as buttons.

It will be observed, therefore, that the masculine shirt by day was losing its importance. Its former splendour was now being transferred to the neighbouring waistcoat which invariably caught the eye. Only in evening dress did the shirt retain its old class distinction.[2]

About 1850 the bottom of the shirt, front and back, which had hitherto been cut square, was beginning to be cut in a deep curve, as illustrated in an advertisement of 1853 (*figure* 64). This curve persisted well into the twentieth century.

For evening dress the 'Patent Elliptic Collar'—cut higher in front than behind—was introduced. 'How gloriously he is attired. . . . His elliptic collar, how faultlessly it stands; his cravat, how correct; his shirt how wonderfully fine; and oh! how happy he must be with such splendid sparkling diamond studs—such beautiful amethyst buttons at his wrists—and such a love of a chain disporting itself over his richly embroidered bloodstone-buttoned vest. . . . Altogether such a first-class swell is rarely seen. . . .'[3] (*figure* 64).

The term 'swell' had by now lost its earlier significance. At this time the various social grades descended from the gentleman to the gent, and thence by stages to 'downy ones' and 'knowing coves,'

---

[1] The device of a button at the base and links at the border was known as the 'French cuff'.

[2] Advertisement: 'Shirts of longcloth with linen fronts, collars and wrists at 6/6; all linen 10/6. Stocks, fine everlasting cloth, with bows, 3/6; long ends, 4/6; of satin, 4/6—long ends 6/6' (1844).

[3] R. T. Surtees: *Ask Mamma*, 1858.

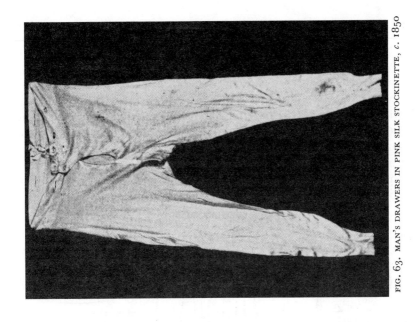

FIG. 63. MAN'S DRAWERS IN PINK SILK STOCKINETTE, *c.* 1850

FIG. 62. MAN'S SHIRT, 1850–60

and each were distinguishable by their attire and their taste in shirts.[1]

If some of those picturesque garments were now to come to light museum curators might find them difficult to date, or even mistake them for modern. How baffling, for instance, would be such a one as worn by Mr. Ledbury in his office—with the figure of a famous prima donna forming 'the pattern of his shirt, on which she was reproduced many times in a chocolate tint.'[2]

Equally puzzling would be the sportive attire of the 'snob' on shipboard, wearing 'a shirt embroidered with pink boa-constrictors.'[3]

THE ELLIPTIC COLLAR.
TO FASTEN AT THE BACK.

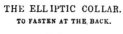

WITH PATENT ELASTIC FASTENING.

A MOST PERFECT AND EASY FITTING SHIRT, and by a simple invention of the Patentee adjusts itself to all movements of the body, both back and front, either walking, sitting, or riding. Price, including the REGISERED ELLIPTIC WRISTBAND, 42s. the half-ozen.

The ELLIPTIC 3 fold COLLAR, quite unique, in all shapes, with PATENT ELASTIC FASTENING, 12s. the dozen. The Patent Elastic Collar Fastening can be attached to any Collar, opening back or front. Six sent by post on receipt of 13 postage stamps.

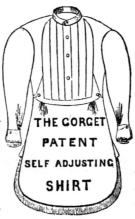

THE GORGET
PATENT
SELF ADJUSTING
SHIRT

THE ELLIPTIC COLLAR.
TO FASTEN IN FRONT.

WITH PATENT ELASTIC FASTENING

Directions for Measurement
1. Round the Chest, over the Shirt.
2. Round the Waist, over the Shirt.
3. Round the Neck, middle Throat.
4. Round the wrist.
5. Length of Coat Sleeve, from centre of Back, down seam of Sleeve, to bottom of Cuff.
6. Length of Shirt at the back.

The first four measures must be taken Tight.
Say if the Shirts are to open back or front.
If with collars attached (3s. the half-dozen extra)
If Buttons or Studs in Front.
If Buttons or Studs at Wrist.

FIG. 64. THE GORGET PATENT ADJUSTING SHIRT, 1853

That these literary fancies were based on fact is proved by an advertisement of 1855: 'Rodger's Improved Shirts for ease, elegance and durability have no rival, 31/6 and 42/– the half doz. Patterns of coloured shirtings, such as horses, dogs and other sporting designs, post free.'

Unfortunately the spivvy adornments of Victorian downy ones have yet to be discovered.

[1] See Albert Smith: *The Natural History of the Gent*, 1847.
[2] Albert Smith: *The Adventures of Mr. Ledbury*, 1847.
[3] Thackeray: *Book of Snobs*, 1855.

2. THE DICKEY

This had, by now, declined in the social scale.[1]

3. DRAWERS

A pair in the City Museum, Hereford, *c.* mid-nineteenth century, of pink silk stockinette is ankle length (*figure* 63). The front opening, 9 in. deep, is closed by an overlap of the 2-in. waistband, fastened by four pearl buttons. A 4-in. opening down the centre of the back is closed by two silk tapes in the waistband. Holes bound with tape, through which the tongues of the braces were passed, are six in number in the waistband, two on each side of the front and one on each side of the centre of the back.

4. UNDER-VEST

'Merino vests for ladies and gentlemen' were advertised in the 1840's but we have no description of them. We have seen how, previously, men used flannel under-waistcoats for extra warmth; now the additional garment began to be worn under the shirt next the skin, while preserving the name originally applied, and still applied by tailors to the waistcoat.

5. BRACES

An advertisement of this accessory (1846) explains its necessity in a polite piece of period copy-writing: 'Henry Powell respectfully invites inspection of his little invention of a Brace to sustain Drawers and Trousers, at the same time. Knowing, from his own trade, the variety of plans tried by Gentlemen to keep their drawers in the right place, such as loops placed horizontally or perpendicularly on the bands, button holes made, or cut in the bands, tapes, strings, pins, etc. etc., all of which answer but very imperfectly (often breaking or tearing out, turning over the tops of the trousers, or producing an unequal draught, besides taking extra time and trouble) H. P. was induced to turn his attention to the subject, and has succeeded by a very simple contrivance in finding a remedy for these defects in the Comprino Brace. . . . 2/ to 6/6 for useful, and 6/6 to 10/6 for more ornamental ones. . . .'

[1] 'Mr. Sponge, being more of a two-shirts-and-a-dicky sort of man.'—R. T. Surtees: *Mr. Sponge's Sporting Tour*, 1853.

Superior articles were often embroidered—'The Marquis throwing back his pea-green cashmere coat lined with silk, and displaying his embroidered braces, pink rowing shirt[1] and amber-coloured waistcoat.'[2] Mr. Pacey, a 'country swell,' favoured 'white satin forget-me-not embroidered braces';[3] but Mr. Verdant Green went up to Oxford 'with a pair of braces from Mary worked in an ecclesiastical pattern of a severe character,' as befitted a student.[4] The labouring class retained the ancient name of 'gallows' for this kind of appliance—'Galusses—things to had your breeks up by,' as James Pigg explains.

6. NIGHTCLOTHES

Contemporary illustrations indicate that sometimes a nightshirt with a small turned-down collar was worn, and sometimes a nightgown reaching to the ankle. The night-cap was usual, of the jellybag shape, often coloured and generally tasselled. White cotton nightcaps, knitted or crocheted, were the less fashionable mode.[5]

ᔐ WOMEN ᔐ

I. THE CHEMISE

Usually of longcloth, advertised at 16/6 a dozen in 1849.

A specimen, for day-wear, dated 1849 (Platt Hall, Cunnington collection) has the front square with a falling flap (*figure* 65), and the sleeves short and full and gathered into a band; there is a gusset in the armpit. A few had long sleeves with worked wristbands with an edging of net or lace. The garment reached the knee and was about four feet round the hem.

An evening chemise, dated 1847, in the same collection is of cambric, the front square with a narrow frill of lace, and a drawstring round the neck; short full sleeves gathered into a band edged with lace. The front has small gussets for the figure, and the skirt is slightly shaped.

The severe plainness of the day garment is characteristic of an article entirely concealed from view.

---

[1] 'Fancy Regatta Shirts, well made, 29/6 a doz.'
[2] R. T. Surtees: *Hillingdon Hall*, 1844.
[3] R. T. Surtees: *Mr. Sponge's Sporting Tour*, 1853.
[4] Cuthbert Bede: *The Adventures of Verdant Green*, 1853.
[5] 'The Templar nightcap for railroad, 6/6 to 18/6'—advertisement of 1844.

2. THE PETTICOAT

A number, ranging from four to six, were worn according to the season. Only the outermost, of which glimpses might be displayed with discretion, was in any sense decorative. It was generally of cambric, elaborately embroidered or trimmed with embroidery, crochet or lace to a depth of six or eight inches above the hem. Some were flounced. Beneath this was worn a plain white longcloth petticoat, both being gathered on to waistbands fastened by strings. A variation of the latter was the petticoat with attached bodice which was then called a 'slip' but later became known as a 'Princess petticoat.' A specimen (Cunnington collection) of longcloth, has the bodice buttoning down the front into a point, the skirt close-gathered and attached to the bodice with a line of piping. Beneath these were worn one or more flannel petticoats, cream-coloured, and plain or scalloped round the hem.

The width of all these petticoats steadily expanded during the period, corresponding to the growing dimensions of the skirt, to some six or eight feet or more round the hem.

Beneath these was worn a knee-length petticoat of some stiff material, of which the most notable was 'crinoline,' composed of horsehair warp and wool weft. The name is derived from the Greek word for hair, and this garment is to be distinguished from the 'artificial crinoline' or 'cage' which later displaced it. 'Horsehair petticoats' are frequently mentioned in *Hillingdon Hall*, together with 'large bustles.' A petticoat (in the Cunnington collection) made of this material pleated on to a waistband, has a hem six feet in diameter. Extra stiffening round the lower half is obtained by five lines of piping. Another specimen is of stiffened wool, heavily pleated at the back, and open down the front, with tapes for tying round the waist (*figure* 65).

Occasionally a longcloth petticoat, heavily trimmed with cording up to the knees, was worn in place of the crinoline one, to sustain the dome-shaped skirt. Towards the end of this period 'the stiff jupon is still worn but very much diminished in all its dimensions' (1852). The burden of underclothing was becoming insupportable, and the shape of the skirt was often maintained by lining the lower part of the dress skirt itself with crinoline, or by having a few rolls of it along the border. For the evening the under-petticoats could be

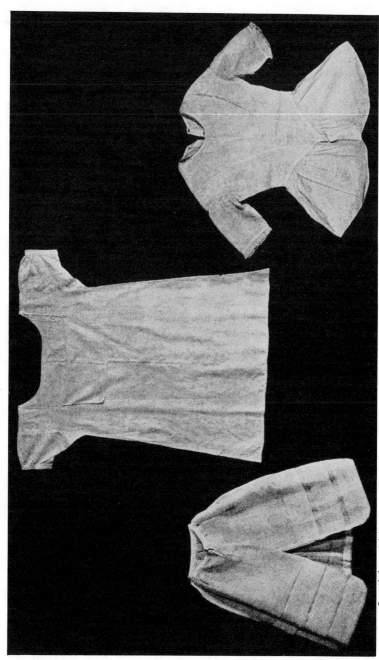

FIG. 65. (*left to right*) CRINOLINE PETTICOAT, *c.* 1840–50: CHEMISE, DATED 1849; WOMAN'S CAMISOLE WITH BACK-FASTENING

reduced in number if they were heavily starched, and a stiff petticoat of book-muslin might suffice with a single cambric one over it.

Early in the 1850's the quilted petticoat,[1] for cold weather, came into use, and about the same time the novelty of petticoats in brilliant colours, especially scarlet.

That the lady of fashion was not infrequently even ahead of the current mode is suggested by the comment, April 1842:—'Lady Aylesbury wears forty-eight yards of material in each of her gowns, and instead of a crinoline (or horsehair petticoat) she wears a petticoat made of down or feathers, which swells out this enormous expanse and floats like a vast cloud when she sits down or rises up.'[2]

3. THE CAMISOLE

This new garment appeared early in the 1840's, and was frequently spoken of as a 'waistcoat.' Made of white longcloth and shaped to the waist by goring, it covered the corset, and thus took the place of the flap front of the old type of chemise, which used to hang down over the top of the corset to conceal it from accidental view (*figure* 65). Double-breasted 'Angola waistcoats' might be worn, instead, in cold weather.

4. THE VEST

'Ladies merino vests, 3/6 and 4/6' were advertised in 1847; but it seems that young ladies were reluctant to wear them as they would increase the waist measurement.

5. BUST IMPROVERS

Advertisements of the 1840's give information about this device: 'The registered bust improver, of an air-proof material; an improvement on the pads of wool and cotton hitherto used'; 'To ladies: The zone of beauty for 18/6, that much improved article of ladies' toilet which imparts a sylph-like roundness to the waist without restraint or pressure.' On the other hand *The Handbook of the Toilet* laments the use of 'lemon bosoms and many other means of creating fictitious charms and improving the work of Nature.'

---

[1] Advertisement 1855: 'Quilted eiderdown slips for their warmth and lightness, giving that graceful fall and fullness to the dress.'
[2] *The Diary, etc., of Mrs. Archer Clive*, 1849.

6. DRAWERS

The purpose of wearing drawers is described in *The Handbook of the Toilet*: 'Drawers are of incalculable advantage to women who expose themselves to a variety of diseases from the usual form of their garments. In France, drawers form a necessary part of female attire, and many indispositions, to which British females are continually subject, are prevented by their use. According to our fastidious notions of propriety it is considered indelicate to allude in any way to the limbs of ladies yet I am obliged to break the ice of this foolish etiquette which is more revolting to modesty than favourable to it, by associating indelicate notions with what is in itself as pure and delicate as the lovely countenance of Eve before her fall. The drawers of ladies may be made of flannel, angola, calico, or even cotton stocking-web; they should reach down the leg as far as it is possible to make them without their being seen.'

'Longcloth drawers, 1/3; drawers, full maids', 8/5 doz' (*Lady's Newspaper*, 1847). 'Ladies' riding trousers, of chamois leather and black feet' (1854).

Although in the 1840's the garment was extremely and severely plain, reaching some way below the knees, in the next decade it was becoming more ornamental. Thus in 1851, 'Longcloth drawers, plain, 2/–; richly trimmed, 3/6.'

Merino and lamb's wool vests and drawers, for winter, were worn during the latter part of the period.

7. CORSETS

'The modern stay extends not only over the bosom but also all over the abdomen and back down to the hips; besides being garnished with whalebone to say nothing of an immense wooden, metal, or whalebone busk passing in front from the top of the stays to the bottom; they have been growing in length by degrees; the gait of an Englishwoman is generally stiff and awkward there being no bend or elasticity of the body on account of the form of her stays.'[1] Such stays were laced up at the back (*figure* 66).

In 1847 we find advertised 'Front fastening stays with patent clips,' and 'Paris woven corsets, 18 to 19½ in., 17/6.' And the next year stays were made with elastic thread woven into the material. But with the

[1] *Handbook of the Toilet*, 1841.

expanding skirt the compressed waist was no longer admirable, and we read that 'the age of stiff stays has departed, and the modern elegante wears stays with very little whalebone in them, if they wear any at all' (1850). Instead there was 'the Corset Amazone which by the aid of elastic lacings yields to every respiration, and by pulling a concealed cord can be shortened three inches.' 'The elastic bodice with front fastening, 10/6' (1854) was a substitute. Nevertheless there were being advertised '100 patterns of stays for Ladies and 50 for children, 7/– for 18 in., waist rising 6d. an inch.'

Stays with front fastenings were displayed at the Great Exhibition of 1851, and gradually became the accepted model.

Day-corsets of the 1840's had shoulder straps and were shaped to the breasts; in the next decade the shaping diminished and straps were dispensed with.

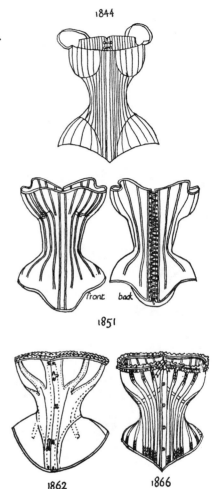

FIG. 66. CORSETS, 1844–66

8. THE BUSTLE

This was no longer confined to the back, but spread round to the sides to help in throwing out the skirt into a domed shape (*figure* 67).

'An immense assortment of dress-improvers' (1849) was the more elegant name for the bustle,[1] which was still being advertised in

[1] 'Bustles of silver hair, from 1/–,' advertised in 1847.

FIG. 67. THE BUSTLE, 1844. AFTER DAUMIER

1854, being only displaced when the 'cage crinoline' arrived. Thus, in that year, we read: 'Not satisfied with the Bustle some ladies of the present day have revived the practice of wearing hoops.'

9. NIGHTCLOTHES

The nightdress, usually of longcloth—costing 29/6 a dozen in 1849—was frilled round the neck and down the front opening, and also at the cuffs. A night cap was worn. This fitted the head like a baby's bonnet and was tied under the chin. The crown was some-times trimmed with insertion and the front edge frilled to frame the face. 'In lieu of the common drawn and frilled nightcap she appeared in a fine embroidered muslin one, trimmed with Valenciennes lace and tied with a blue ribbon.'[1]

Hitherto all these undergarments had usually been home-made, but in 1851 we find ready-made garments much more advertised. 'Longcloth nightdress, 2/6; nightcaps, 6/- to 10/- a doz.; longcloth frilled nightdresses, plain, 3/6; richly trimmed, 7/6.'

The notion that a nightdress should be made 'attractive' by trimmings of lace seemed, at least to the elders, a sign of depravity, and opposed to the highest principles of the English lady.

It will be seen that the underclothing of this period was essentially inspired by the developing force of prudery which arrived at its height by the closing years. The shape of the human body, so suc-cessfully obliterated by the costume, was not merely out of sight but even out of mind. Those layers of wrappings protected the thoughts of the nicely brought up young lady from dwelling upon 'physical facts,' which her training taught her to shun scarcely less than she shunned all knowledge of her internal organs.

In fact, the psychological purpose of all these undergarments was not so much to protect the body as to protect the mind from dwelling upon it. Yet the instincts were not frustrated thereby; masculine imagination must have been tantalized by the contrast of the delicate charm of the dress with the virginal primness of what lay beneath; the connoisseur discovered in prudery itself a subtle erotic appeal. That was the secret of the 1840's—the art of making prudery 'attractive.'

[1] R. T. Surtees, *Hillingdon Hall*, 1844.

VIII

1857—1866

IN the history of English costume this decade is perhaps more important than any other. A wholly new idea, English in origin, began to make itself felt. The notion that ease and comfort must be sacrificed in order to express social rank, had previously governed the design of fashionable clothing. Now, at last, it seemed too great a price to pay.

To adapt fashions to physical needs was an innovation indeed. By a strange irony at the very time when the iron grip of 'fashion' seemed to have secured an extraordinary hold, its victims of both sexes began to revolt. The well-groomed gentleman, corseted and gasping in the tightest of surtouts and pegtop inexpressibles, and the lady, staggering under the burden of multitudinous petticoats, were the prisoners of etiquette. Outside the confines of society there were the workers in clothes allowing freedom of movement. How simple to borrow from the people the principle that clothes should be the servants of their wearers and not the masters!

The decade marks a sartorial revolution, and the yielding of Fashion's Bastille to the encroachments of democracy seemed like the end of an *ancien régime*. What! Were ladies and gentlemen to wear clothes indistinguishable from those of ordinary folk and to have the free use of their limbs?

A superficial view of the changes between the beginning and the close of this period observes only the gentleman becoming comfortable at last in a 'Tweedside' (the prototype of the 'lounge suit'), and the lady in 'walking dress' gladly displaying a good deal of ankles on the croquet field. It is our business, however, to direct attention to the changes which lay beneath the surface, changes without which those novel costumes would have been impossible.

Fundamental changes appear first in man's costume, as a rule, to be followed presently by a corresponding change in woman's. We find him discarding his corsets some years before she escaped from her 'cage.' Characteristically these relaxations from bondage were at first only to be enjoyed on informal occasions. The Tweedside and the walking dress could only be worn in the country, a practice leading to the curious distinction between 'town' and 'country' costume for both sexes.

'Ease is now looked upon as the desideratum in all articles of dress, especially when required to be worn in the country; there it reigns paramount. These two qualities (ease and elegance) strongly mark the peculiar character of the fashions of the period.'[1] To appreciate this comment on the new modes for men we have to note that not merely was the neck freer but also that the waist ceased to be constricted and the trousers were no longer shaped to the leg. Peg-top trousers disappeared in 1861, and the bottom of the trouser leg expanded to $17\frac{1}{2}$ in., presenting a pair of substantial tubes totally devoid of sex appeal. Inexpressible but no longer irresistible, these pillars of society served but to sustain the gentleman's rank; the pageant of colour centred on the waistcoat blazing like a setting sun.

Another observer remarked: 'A garment that fitted a man would be pointed at in the present day as simply ridiculous. Our youths are clothed to please themselves, and so, I presume, are the ladies.'[2] These informal styles soon developed into 'sports costumes,' with gentlemen in knickerbockers, and ladies in spectacular stockings and shortened skirts.

Among the alarming phenomena of that exciting epoch was the novelty of coloured undergarments for ladies, shocking the principles of prudery by their liberal exposure. Chemical dyes were introduced in 1860, the first being solferino and magenta, the latter hailed as 'the queen of colours.' At the same time the sewing-machine had arrived, which made possible an abundance of ready-made underclothes in exuberant hues. Prudery shuddered; it seemed incompatible with a milk-white mind to wear coloured underclothing. It might lead—in fact it did lead—to wilful exposure of them. And the habit might lead to—who knows what indescribable excesses? Thus, in 1866, we read, 'the amount of embroidery put upon under-

[1] *Gazette of Fashions,* 1861.   [2] Whyte Melville: *Good for Nothing,* 1861.

clothing nowadays is sinful; a young lady spent a month in hem-stitching and embroidering a garment which it was scarcely possible that any other human being, except her laundress, would ever see.'ᵗ Such disturbances beneath the social surface were, of course, not effected without strong opposition from authority. It was one of those epochs, not very uncommon, when the younger generation shocks its elders, who foretell the end of civilization.

Popular attention was concentrated upon the crinoline, that ingenious mechanism which in shape—and almost in size—resembled at first the Albert Hall and later the Great Pyramid. The pages of contemporaries echo with the inconvenience caused by this social obstruction; comic papers rejoiced in such a target while sermons dwelt on its moral dangers. Its physical dangers were certainly real, for many wearers of crinolines were burnt to death by inadvertently approaching a fire.

The male sex to a man roared in disgust; with three or four of these giantesses in a room a diminished man could not creep in beyond the door, powerless under the domination of this new Colossus. The hoop of the eighteenth century had been just tolerated in a limited society, but in the bustling Victorian world it was intolerable; and the fashion rapidly spread to all classes. 'Your lady's maid must now have her crinoline, and it has even become essential to factory girls.' In 1863 one of the Staffordshire potteries lost in a single year £200 worth of articles swept down by the crinolines of their workwomen. It was said (in 1859) that Sheffield was producing wire for half a million crinolines each week.

What caused the universal demand for this extraordinary under-garment? For a generation skirts and petticoats had been expanding and the 'cage' was the logical result. Mr. Laver, in his *Taste and Fashion*, has pointed out that the crinoline, as it swung in walking or was lifted when mounting stairs, could be extremely 'seductive.' A garment which frequently revealed extensive glimpses of legs and drawers had erotic functions. Hence, no doubt, the moral disapproval it provoked; for English prudery requires that feminine sex attraction should be static and not dynamic.

We think, however, that the *initial* form of the 'cage,' as it appeared in 1857, was intended to express class distinction. As a contemporary said: 'Perhaps it is the spirit of exclusiveness which

Englishwoman's Domestic Magazine.

has induced the leaders of fashion to surround themselves with barriers of barège and other similar outworks, to keep the common herd at arm's length—or rather, at petticoats' breadth.' But this 'exclusive' device had the fatal defect that it would, in a commercial community, be easily and cheaply copied by the 'common herd,' and so it rapidly lost its original significance and became a device of sex attraction. For it is almost a rule of feminine fashions that when a mode, intended to indicate social rank, becomes universally worn, it is then erotic in function. The Colonel's lady and Judy O'Grady were sisters—under their crinolines.

As this deterioration of purpose became more apparent the wave of moral disapproval rose, and Victorian prudery discovered that this abominable fashion was of French origin; so we established the curious myth that the crinoline had been introduced by—the Empress Eugénie! As a method of attracting the attention of the other sex the crinoline, at its maximum, afforded its wearer innumerable opportunities; she was practising on the susceptibilities of a generation to whom the momentary glimpse of a pair of ankles had been, for years, a precious privilege; on such the vision of scarlet drawers must have acted like a red rag on a bull. It is difficult for us to-day to assess the rich possibilities of such garments bursting beyond the bounds of prudish restraint.

These easy methods of catching the eye have, however, the disadvantage of sometimes attracting *unwanted* attention. Thus a youthful enquirer (one 'Peachblossom') is advised by a magazine editor, in 1858, 'not to attempt the climbing of stiles in a crinoline for the task is impossible. And if she suffers much from the comments of vulgar little boys it would be better, in a high wind, to remain indoors.'

It is startling to learn, from the diary of Lady Eleanor Stanley (1859) that at country house parties the latest 'fast' fashion was for *both* sexes to indulge in paper chases. 'The Duchess of Manchester, in getting too hastily over a stile, caught a hoop of her cage in it and went regularly head over heels lighting on her feet with her cage and whole petticoats remaining above her head. They say there was never such a thing seen—and the other ladies hardly knew whether to be thankful or not that a part of her underclothing consisted in a pair of scarlet tartan knickerbockers (the things Charlie shoots in) —which were revealed to the view of all the world in general and

the Duc de Malakoff in particular.' His subsequent description—
'*c'etait diabolique!*' leaves much to the imagination. Yet, in spite
of such contretemps, the crinoline fashion persisted. Its advantages,
to the wearer, far outweighed its disadvantages. Never before or
since has a feminine undergarment exercised such social power,
enlarging in every sense woman's place in the world and the sphere
of her physical attractions.

The crinoline overshadowed the functions of the corset. We have
seen how the fashion for tight-lacing subsided in the early 1850's,
so that nothing might detract from the importance of the cage. When
this began to shrink, however, in the 1860's, the small waist once
more became a desirable feature and the spotlight of sex attraction
concentrated upon it. The corset resumed its former grasp with
redoubled force. From that very respectable source *The Englishwoman's Domestic Magazine* of 1866 we learn of a girls' boarding school
(the inmates called it 'Whalebone House Establishment') where
stays were compulsory and were sealed up by the mistress on Monday
morning, to be removed on Saturday for one hour 'for the purposes
of ablution.' By such means a waist of twenty-three inches at the
age of fifteen, could be reduced in two years to thirteen inches.

From the same source we learn of a mother urging that daughters
should be made to sleep in their stays, which 'carries no hardship
beyond an occasional fainting fit.' And an enthusiast declares:
"Everyone must admit that a slender waist is a great acquisition;
the so-called evil of tight-lacing is so much cant. To me the sensation
is superb, and I am never prouder than when I survey the fascinating
undulations that Art affords to Nature.' From which it seems the
corset had Narcissus charms. And when other correspondents admit,
a little naïvely, that 'tight-lacing produces delicious sensations, half
pleasure, half pain,' it was obviously an instrument of auto-eroticism.

In the short space of these ten years we see an extraordinary
variation in the functions of feminine undergarments; the cage, at
first a symbol of class distinction, rapidly became a general method
of sex attraction. In the hitched-up skirt and petticoats of the
'walking dress,' an apparent impulse towards freedom was followed
by a reversion to excessive tight-lacing and restriction. Not, of course,
that all these diverse inclinations would have been displayed by
the same individual; they are evidence, rather, of two widely
differing dispositions opposed to each other; and the battle, swinging

to and fro with the ultimate victory as yet uncertain, was being fought beneath the surface.

In the 'hitch-up' walking dress over the crinoline (introduced in 1857) freedom and restriction were curiously combined. 'Next morning they all appeared in looped-up dresses, showing the parti-coloured petticoats of the prevailing fashion which looked extremely pretty, and were all very well—a great improvement on the draggle-tails—until they came to get into the coach, when it was found that, large as the vehicle was, it was utterly inadequate for their accommodation. Indeed, the door seemed ludicrously insufficient for the ingress, and Miss Clara turned round and round like a peacock contending with the wind, undecided which way to make the attempt. At last she chose a bold sideways dash, and entered with a squeeze of the petticoat, which suddenly expanded into its original size, but when the sisters had followed her example there was no room for the Major. . . .'[1]

One thing is evident. The fashions of this period, as shown in pictures of the costumes, are incomprehensible without due appreciation of the underclothing, for they were the weapons that sustained the heat and burden of the fray.

∽ MEN ∽

I.   THE SHIRT

(a) Day. For formal wear enough shirt-front was exposed to reveal the uppermost button or stud, but frequently a large folded cravat occupied the space above the waistcoat, or that garment was cut very high, or the coat might be buttoned high, so that very little shirt-front was visible. Though sometimes a good deal more of it was exposed, the tucked panels were disappearing, the front being plain but not stiff.

The usual type of collar for formal day-wear was upright with a gap between the points; these no longer projected on to the cheek but just touched the jaw. Thus movement of the head and neck was freer. With this collar might be worn the necktie, tied in a flat broad bow, the ends projecting across the top of the waistcoat; or the expansive cravat secured with a pin. (It is convenient from now on

[1] R. T. Surtees: *Ask Mamma*, 1858.

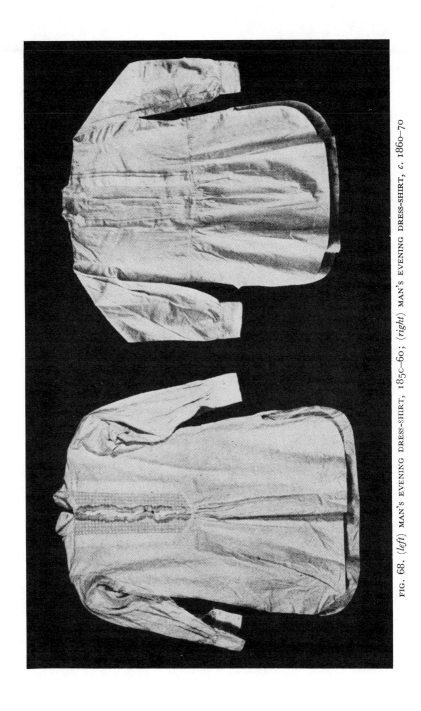

FIG. 68. (*left*) MAN'S EVENING DRESS-SHIRT, 185c–60; (*right*) MAN'S EVENING DRESS-SHIRT, *c.* 1860–70

to speak of the 'necktie' as a band passed round the neck and tied in front either in a bow or a knot with hanging ends. Though in the 1820's and '30's this was called a 'cravat' we now shall reserve that name for the massive wide material folded flat and filling the space above the waistcoat and secured by a pin. The true 'stock' survived only as a hunting 'neckcloth' but the 'Napoleon' preserved its traditional form.)

For informal wear either a shallow single collar with sloping points meeting in the centre and forming a small inverted V opening, or a shallow double collar similar to that of modern times, was worn. With the Tweedside suit, for example, the coat was buttoned so high that scarcely any of the double collar was visible, and the necktie concealed the small space of the shirt-front above the coat.

The cuffs were slightly starched and were closed by links, often jewelled.

A specimen in the City Museum, Hereford, is of fine linen; length $31\frac{1}{2}$ in. front, 37 in. back; width 37 in. The neckband, $1\frac{1}{2}$ in., is without button or stud-hole at the back. The front, slightly starched, has a double-breasted centre panel closed by three pearl buttons, the neck buttoning across with two buttons. The sleeves, set in without gussets, are of the 'bishop' shape, $13\frac{1}{2}$ in. wide, with a narrow cuff buttoned at the base and at the border. It is machine lock-stitched throughout. Date about 1860.

(b) The evening dress-shirt continued to show an expansive front tucked on either side of a centre panel, or the centre panel might be slightly embroidered, the sides being plain (figure 68). There were three, or occasionally only two, studs down the front. A stiff upright collar with the points nearly meeting in front was worn with a white bow.

(c) While the above types were the standard modes, there was also, for country and sporting occasions, a great variety of coloured shirts. Contemporary descriptions remind us that the mid-Victorian male was far from having become the colourless individual sometimes supposed, though the rich polychromatics of the young man's fancy may not be to our taste to-day. Thus 'a dashing looking gent in a red flannel Emperor shirt, a blue satin cravat, a buff vest, and a bright green cutaway coat with fancy buttons,' or an elderly gentleman's morning costume which included 'an elaborately worked ruby-studded shirtfront with stiff wristbands well turned up shewing the magnificence of his imitation India garnet buttons, over a pink flannel vest' (i.e. under-waistcoat), together with 'six rings equally distributed between the dirty-nailed fingers of each hand.'[1] Not perhaps specimens of the best style. The same author speaks of 'magnificently embroidered dress shirts, so fine that the fronts almost looked as if you might blow them out,' worn with diamond studs. He also informs us that a gentleman requires two clean shirts a day.

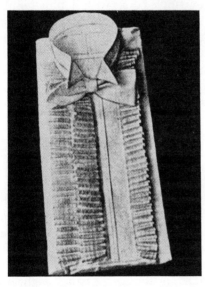

FIG. 69. EVENING DRESS-SHIRT, COLLAR AND TIE, BY WELCH, MARGETSON AND CO., c. 1860

The 'sporting gent' of 1860 in 'a gay butterfly costume with a heartsease embroidered blue cravat, a pink striped shirt with carbuncle studs.'[2] was common enough, but the coloured shirt was not favoured by the Best People, who clung to the symbol of the white shirt and collar as outward and visible signs that they did not earn their living by the sweat of their necks.

Examining a very large number of contemporary photographs, we note that among 'gentlemen' there was a considerable diversity in the style of day-shirt and collar. Mr. Disraeli, like most Members of Parliament and the learned professions, retains the upright collar with a gap between the points, which do not reach up above the jaw, and a necktie in a flat bow (often called a 'once-round' tie); the elders have collars with points on to the cheeks, worn with a swathing neckband, or 'Napoleon,' and these commonly leave the upper two or three buttons of the waistcoat gaping. Artists and writers lean towards the low double collar, which Mr. Dickens wears with a vast satin cravat and a pin, and Mr. Millais wears a hanging necktie knotted through a ring. By such idiosyncrasies a gentleman was able to indicate his personal attitude to life while marking his precise

[1] R. T. Surtees: *Ask Mamma*, 1858.
[2] R. T. Surtees: *Plain or Ringlets*, 1860.

position in the social community. He wore, so to speak, a label round his neck.

An extract from the 1866 trade catalogue of Messrs. J. & R. Morley Ltd. reminds us that our mid-Victorian ancestors had a very wide choice, if not of design, at least of material; and that evidently they believed in being warmly clad:

Men's Shirts, long or half sleeves, in brown cotton, lisle thread, gauze cotton, blue, pink and fancy stripe Imperial Cotton, merino (single or double breasted) in natural, red drab or fancy colours. Summer shirts in gauze merino and India gauze. Winter lambs' wool shirts, Saxony or Cashmere. Scarlet lambs' wool shirts. Worsted and Segovia shirts. Long-cloth shirts with linen fronts, bands and wrists, to button in front or behind. Pure linen shirts, dress shirts with French wrists, printed Regattas and striped Jeans.

Men's Drawers and Pants of merino, lambs' wool, brown and white cotton, and chamois. Calico nightshirts, 45 and 50 inches long.

Women's vests and drawers in merino, lambs' wool, white cotton, and chamois.

2. DRAWERS, AND UNDER-VEST

Of these we have been unable to find any reliable account. In 1857 the Rev. James Round paid 7/6 for linen drawers, 2/6 for cotton drawers and 4/6 for a merino vest.[1]

3. BRACES

At about this period braces[1] embroidered in Berlin woolwork of many colours came into notice (*figure* 70). What is remarkable about them, apart from their colours, is the fact that they were so often worked by young ladies and given as presents to the sterner sex; this at a time when prudery forbade the mention of the garments to which they were destined to be fastened. Perhaps we should regard them as symbols of a secret attachment.

Fashion plates (of French origin) show occasionally gentlemen attired for '*le sport*' in trousers pleated on to a tight waistband and without braces. We have not found an English photograph showing this style.

[1] Accounts of the Rev. James Round of Colchester, 1857: 'Cotton braces, 8d. A pair of India Rubber braces for Master James, 2/6.'

4. NIGHTSHIRTS

These do not appear to have undergone any striking change. The novelist was chary of describing sleeping garments, lest the susceptibilities of each sex might be disturbed by details of the other's

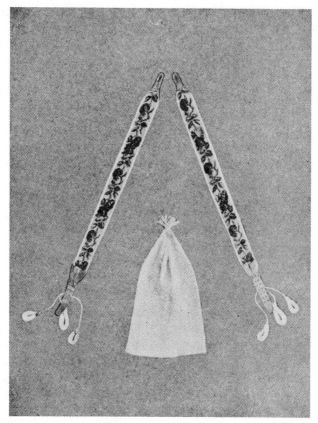

FIG. 70. EMBROIDERED BRACES, *c.* 1850; AND MAN'S NIGHT-CAP, 1800–20

night apparel. All we are told of Mr. Franklin Blake's famous *nightgown* (Wilkie Collins: *The Moonstone*, 1868) is that it was made of longcloth and that it must have been ankle-length.

ॐ WOMEN ॐ

1. THE CHEMISE

The shape remained unaltered. A specimen in the Cunnington collection, dated 1857, is scarcely distinguishable from those of a generation earlier. Longcloth or linen was the usual material, which, by 1864, was sometimes trimmed with scarlet cotton designs.

2. THE CAMISOLE

Continued to be worn over the corsets.

3. THE CORSET

As the waist shortened by 1860 the corset shortened with it.[1] 'The taste for coloured corsets is rapidly increasing' (1862). Scarlet merino corsets cost 10/6 in 1864.

As soon as the crinoline began to diminish tight-lacing returned: 'all efforts tend to make the figure appear as small as possible below the waist' (1864). Stays made in the French pattern consisted of pieces of white silk elastic joined together by narrow strips of white tape forming an open network containing very few bones; they opened in front and were fastened by small straps and buckles, the back being laced. But 'the old-fashioned stays are still too generally worn,' often of red flannel, boned.

Thanks to the new model such phrases as 'her figure magnificently developed, though slender-waisted and lithe as a serpent'[2] became the novelist's standard pattern for a certain type of heroine.

4. THE CRINOLINE

The name has become so associated with the 'artificial crinoline' or 'cage petticoat' that we shall use it to denote any kind of petticoat which was strengthened by metal or whalebone hoops. It appeared in December 1856, as 'the Parisian Eugénie Jupon Skeleton Petticoat, at 6/6 to 25/–.' Early the next year whalebone was discarded for watch-spring. 'It is impossible to make any dress sit well without the hoop petticoat. This should consist of four narrow steels; that nearest the waist should be four nails (1 nail = $2\frac{1}{4}$ in.) from it and

---

[1] Advertisements: 'Stays with patent front fastenings, 8/6 to 15/6; family stays, 8/6 to 21/–' (1857). 'Front fastening corsets, 3/6 to 4/6' (1861).
[2] G. A. Lawrence: *Guy Livingstone*, 1857.

FIG. 71. CRINOLINE HOOPS, 1861

be 1¾ yards long; the other three should be 2½ yards long and placed
—one at six nails from the upper steel, the other two each two nails
from the second steel. None must meet in front by ¼ yard, except the
one nearest the waist.'[1] But 'many ladies of the highest taste and
fashion wear four or five skirts of starched muslin,' flounced or
unflounced, instead of a crinoline (1858). By 1860 the day-crinoline
would have nine hoops of watch-spring and the evening one as many
as eighteen.

All through its career there were innumerable varieties in shape
and material. From 1857 to 1859 the shape was that of a dome;
gradually it became more pyramidal and by 1862 was very distinctly flattened in front, so that by 1866 the bulk of the garment
projected backwards, the front being flat and without springs. The
'Sansflectum' had the hoops covered with gutta-percha and was
washable (*figure* 71); 'Thomson's Crown Crinoline' had very narrow
steels so as to be more flexible, and 'the American cage' of 1862 had
only its lower half encased, the upper being in skeleton form, thus
reducing the weight to half a pound. We are informed that the Crown
variety 'do not cause accidents, do not appear at inquests, are better

[1] Fashion magazine—quoted in *English Women's Clothing in the Nineteenth Century.*

than medicine for the health, are economical, graceful, modest, ladylike and queenly';[1] while in the Ondina waved crinoline of 1863 'so perfect are the wave-like bands that a lady may ascend a steep stair, throw herself into an arm-chair, etc., without inconvenience to herself or provoking the rude remarks of the observers, thus modifying in an important degree all those peculiarities tending to destroy the modesty of English women.'[2] An ingenious device, for evening dress, was to have the front halves of the lowest two hoops hinged at the sides, so that, by means of a concealed string passing up inside the skirt to the waist, it was possible to draw up the front of the crinoline enough to clear the ankles when ascending stairs.

By 1866 many were discarding crinolines for flounced muslin petticoats; or using a crinoline which would fold inwards when the wearer was seated. Examination of some thousands of contemporary

FIG. 72. (*Left to right*) SCARLET FLANNEL CRINOLINE, 1869; SANSFLECTUM CRINOLINE, 1863; CRINOLETTE, 1873

photographs reveals that most Englishwomen never wore the huge 'cage' seen in fashion plates, while many appear not to be wearing a crinoline of any kind.

Contemporary advertisements indicate a wide variety of design and material. Thus 'Woolsey petticoats with patent steel springs and flounced, 10/9' (1858), and in the following year 'The Victoria crinoline lined with flannel, 25/–' would have been for day-wear. The '18 hoop watch-spring petticoat with silk band and tapes, 16/6' (of 1860), and 'Watch-spring skeleton petticoats with 10 to 100 springs, 6/6 to 31/6' (1861) would be light enough and large enough

---

[1] Advertisement.   [2] Advertisement.

FIG. 73. FROM "CUPID AND CRINOLINES," 1858

for ball dresses. The 'Sansflectum Crinolines, the hoops covered with refined gutta-percha, 10/6 to 25/–' served for wet weather, while the 'puffed horsehair jupons, 21/- to 33/-,' of 1864 indicated that the 'cage' was declining in favour.

The quality varied greatly; watch-spring crinolines were preferred to those made of wire as being less liable to break, and those bearing the name of Thomson were considered superior to all others of English make.

5.   OTHER PETTICOATS

The crinoline made the wearing of so many under-petticoats unnecessary, though some used 'the woven woollen petticoat to imitate knitting, in all colours' (1863).

Beneath the skirt over the crinoline was worn an ornamental petticoat, while in summer 'stiff muslin petticoats flounced, set out the dress in a more graceful fashion than does a crinoline; a moderate-sized steel petticoat and a muslin one, with, of course, a plain one over it, make a muslin dress look very nice.' Many white petticoats had a deep hem scalloped or embroidered with broderie anglaise (*figure* 74), and by 1862 they were flounced and trimmed with rows of insertion.

FIG. 74. (*above*) PETTICOAT WITH BRODERIE ANGLAISE BORDER; (*below*) WOMAN'S
DRAWERS, *c.* 1860–70

Day-petticoats (except with light summer dresses) were usually coloured, scarlet being fashionable. 'Linsey petticoats, scarlet, violet and all fashionable colours' (1859). With the looped-up skirt the exposed part of the petticoat was elaborately trimmed with scalloping (often with white wool or scarlet), and with bands of braid or velvet. In 1863 striped plaid petticoats were the mode 'being trimmed almost as much as dresses,' and 'the inevitable flutings are even put round crinoline casings.' In this year also petticoats were being made with gores and attached to a waistband ten inches deep.

Materials used were camlet, cashmere, flannel, taffeta, rep, alpaca and quilted silk;[1] for morning wear alpaca was common.

By 1866 a petticoat of crinoline material was replacing the cage, and 'coloured petticoats in stripes are much worn by day.'

6. VESTS

High in the neck, with long or short sleeves; of merino or flannel.

7. DRAWERS

'If drawers are worn they should be trimmed with frills or insertion' (*figure* 74). In winter coloured flannel knickerbockers were frequently worn, of a brilliant scarlet. 'The knickerbockers are confined just below the knee by elastic; those who are fond of gardening will find these most judicious things to wear.' Such colours were obviously not intended to be entirely hidden from accidental view, and their use may be regarded as an erotic device.

8. THE NIGHTDRESS

'The hem of the nightdress should be 2½ to 3 yards wide.' Usually of longcloth, the collar, cuffs and front trimmed with embroidery.

The night-cap had become old-fashioned.

9. POCKETS

In addition to the pocket in the skirt there were occasions when the old detachable pocket in the shape of a bag with a side slit-opening was suspended round the waist under the crinoline. We find advertised in 1857 'patent safety railway pockets, 1/6,' an article often used by travellers up to the end of the century.

[1] 'Eiderdown petticoats in quilted silk four yards round, 50/– to 63/–' (1863).

IX

1867—1882

THE revolutionary disturbances which had marked the close of the previous period settled down, as happens after revolutions, into apparent stability. The demand for greater physical freedom was grudgingly admitted, provided this was limited to a distinct category of clothing to be worn only in the country. In town, fashion once more exercised a rigid control. This, however, had changed in spirit. Man's costume, resplendent in that play of colours which had transfigured the middle distance, faded into a sombre respectability where social class could only be distinguished by a nice observance of details. Such fragments of his 'linen' as were still visible had subtle significances of which only the gentleman of breeding was fully conscious; the stiff upstanding collar, which held his chin erect above the common herd, was once more the mode, an obvious mark of class, but its exact pattern for each particular occasion would mark the man of birth from him of mere wealth. One observes, too, that as the day shirt-front became obliterated the collar and cuffs grew in importance, stiff with starch, with the wearer entombed in frock coat and monumental trousers. By 1878 we learn, 'it is the correct thing to vote a showily dressed man a snob' (*The Tailor and Cutter*). Only when garbed for sport might his shirt go into mild stripes.

The contrast between the sexes in this respect was immense. Feminine dress exhibited a sensuous combination of colours and curves—the latter mainly based upon the structures concealed beneath. The period presents one of those phases of extreme eroticism, usually lasting some fifteen or twenty years, which often intervene between periods of feminine sobriety. It had succeeded one of dignified expansion, long developing; it was followed by one of prudish austerity destined, in its turn, to be replaced by the notably seductive Edwardian modes. We may suppose that each generation of women is bored by the technique which their mothers found successful, or that after fifteen years of it men at last become dis-illusioned. Then, refreshed by an astringent interlude, they can savour with enthusiasm the alluring curvatures of the couturier's art.

A fashion journal of 1875 explained that 'the reason for the present extraordinary luxury in dress is that the surplus million of women are husband-hunting and resort to extra attractions to that end'; but the pursuit had to be masked in prudery. That frank exhibition of underclothing allowed by the later crinoline was no longer thought decent and was replaced by elaborate concealment made as alluring as possible. In this, underclothing played an important part. The curves of nature, enriched by corset and bustle, became prominent features. 'A well-developed bust, a tapering waist, and large hips are the combination of points recognized as a good figure' (1873), and when the trailing skirt was momentarily raised a fascinating complexity came into view.

Presently the bulk of underclothes became massed at the rear, as though the wearer were about to emerge from its embrace; and then, near the close of the epoch, the encumbrance was discarded and the tightly swathed shape required almost as scanty under-clothing as in the Regency period. 'It would be impossible to make closer drapery; the limit has been reached. The modern gown shews the figure in a way which is certainly most unsuitable for the ordinary British matron.'[1] But she, presumably, was not husband-hunting.

To appreciate the changes exhibited in these fifteen years we have to recollect that it was an epoch of extreme extravagance in dress, and one of growing disharmony between the sexes. From this the lady's refuge was prudery and the gentleman's prostitution; never was the one more studied or the other more cultivated. The erotic attractions of underclothes, of which the professional had made a fine art, became innocently employed by the pure as a ladylike fashion. After all, it was the social duty of a young lady to get married; the pathetic appeal of one to *The Englishwomen's Domestic*

[1] *The Queen,* 1877.

Magazine—'Be good natured, do, and tell us how to look fascinating, or at least good looking'—was being mutely answered by the bustle, the corset, and petticoats that 'are really works of art.' About that complex world of underclothes of the 1870's there seems to cling a faint odour of patchouli.

The use of costly materials such as silk or lace had become permissible, supplying perhaps a kind of narcissus satisfaction. The period saw the introduction of undergarments shaped to the figure in the form of 'combinations,' of coloured silk vests, and nightdresses made discreetly 'attractive.' The fascination of underclothes became so marked, in fact, that by 1875 the dress itself seemed to imitate them, and in the 'cuirasse bodice' mode, the ballroom débutante seemed to be clothed in corset and petticoats, 'suggesting that the wearer has forgotten some portion of her toilet. Few husbands or fathers would allow their wives or daughters to appear in public thus undressed.'[1]

But while the world of fashion was practising the art of sex attraction by such methods, there was the lesser, though perhaps more important, world of progress towards physical freedom. There the walking costume, becoming the 'tailor-made,' was severely chaste, with knickerbockers and 'sanitary underclothing,' hygienically devoid of superfluous charm. It suggested a growing awareness that a woman might have other functions in life than attracting the male or expressing in her clothes the social rank in which he had placed her. In those serge knickerbockers and sex-allergic combinations, mercifully hid from man, woman was revolting—from male supremacy.

ᔆᔆ MEN ᔆᔆ

I. THE SHIRT

For town wear the day-shirt, the curved hem about an inch shorter in front than behind, was of plain white linen, with cuffs and front more starched than formerly, and in 1877 many were 'rounded and fulled into a yoke.' The V opening above the waistcoat varied a good deal, tending however to diminish. At first two studs would be revealed, later only one, except for summer when a deeper cut was allowed. The lounge suit, however, in the form of the

[1] *The Queen*, 1875.

'Oxford and Cambridge (lounge) coats'—'Cambridge coat or jacket as some call them'—was buttoned so high that practically no shirt-front was visible. Gradually other forms of coat adopted this style, so that by 1877 'the waistcoat is so seldom seen,' and the shirt-front still less.

All through the period to expose an inch too much shirt-front (by day) was a social stigma indicating that the wearer was 'not quite.' On the other hand, the summer suit was cut to reveal as much as three studs, so that to appear a gentleman one had to watch the calendar.

The collar for formal day wear became a shallow upright with a small V gap between the points. These points curved slightly outwards, a style of 1870 patronized by Mr. Gladstone, and—later—becoming historical as 'the Gladstone collar' (exaggerated, of course, by the pencil of Harry Furniss).

With the upright collar a bow tie, becoming steadily narrower, was the usual wear. A variation was the satin made-up 'octagon tie.'[1] The knotted scarf tie, often very narrow, was less common than the bow. In 1877 we read there should be 'sufficient opening to display a stand up linen collar and a scarf tied in a sailor's knot, a long scarf for the wearer to tie and fold himself being the most fashionable with stand up collars.'[2] With the deep opening of the summer waistcoat, showing three studs, the small bow tie was *de rigueur*. With the broad cravat, sometimes seen, the horseshoe breast-pin was replaced, in 1870, by a monogram pin.

Linen-faced paper collars and dickeys were being worn by 'unfashionables.'

One learns that in 1877 the sizes of collars ran from 12 to $16\frac{1}{2}$, in stages of half inches; 'very few of the two latter are called for.'

For informal day wear and in the country the double collar continued in use, often the collar and shirt having faint coloured stripes or inconspicuous floral patterns.

The cuffs, now stiffened with starch and closed by links set close to the border, were allowed to protrude half an inch beyond the coat sleeve, though at a third of an inch your social reputation would perhaps be more secure.

The evening dress-shirt was at first made with slightly pleated

[1] 'With a hat all awry and an octagon tie.' W. S. Gilbert: *Bab Ballads.*
[2] *The Tailor and Cutter.*

front, but a perfectly smooth front became usual in the 1870's. It was, of course, starched. Three studs were shown, a fashion which continued in spite of an attempt by the Prince of Wales in 1877 to introduce the single stud front.

With the dress shirt a winged collar, somewhat shallow, was worn, and an extremely narrow white bow. The old frill-fronted shirt had passed to the servants' hall. 'The dress of one generation becomes the livery of the next.'[1]

'From 1860 the French cambric prints were introduced for day shirts. The effect of the American Civil War was to make the price of cotton so high that linen became used for the whole shirt, cotton being dispensed with. In shirts the principal changes (between 1860 and '70) were shown in the breast line being made into 7, 9, 11 and 13 plaits, instead of the 5 as formerly, and for evening wear, the tucks or plaits were greatly worn across the front from centre plait, instead of up and down. The plain front had not yet made its appearance. The shape of the breast was being made similar to the opening of the dress vest . . . it was during this period that separate wrists came into use, also linen and coloured fronts to cover flannel and other shirts at the breast. . . . From 1870 to '80 the principal event was the introduction of the plain breast. It began first by a plain breast with a centre plait, but eventually the centre plait was dispensed with till even the stitching is not shown at the present day. . . . For evening wear a small frill was added to the opening at top side of breast but this fashion lasted only a short time. The cuffs became the shape they are now. Collars changed but slightly. . . . From 1880 to '90 a new feature was having only one stud in the breast instead of three;[2] the using of piqué for the breast instead of linen. . . . Coloured (day) shirts had the pattern and stripes across the breast and up and down the cuffs, instead of the old plan of up and down the breast and round the cuffs. . . . Separate collars changed into a straight collar all round and from that into a collar with a peak or turn-down in front. The turn-down-all-round was still worn and is to the present day.'[3]

---

[1] *The Tailor and Cutter*. A very old observation. Cf. 'The dress of the master of one generation may survive as that of the servant in another.'—W. N. Webb: *The Heritage of Dress*, 1912.

[2] The metal stud with the base cut into a crescent shape for greater ease in insertion appeared in 1869.

[3] *The Tailor and Cutter*, 1895.

2. THE VEST

Usually woollen; hip length, with narrow neck band and centre opening closed by four buttons. The sleeves terminated in woven cuffs.

3. THE DRAWERS

Woollen; ankle length. Closed by four buttons at the front opening. A gusset let in at the back of the waistband, drawn together by cross tapes.

With the knickerbocker suit short woollen drawers were used.

4. NIGHTCLOTHES

Either a nightgown, ankle length, or a nightshirt reaching to the knees.

The night-cap was ceasing to be worn, at least by the younger generation.

ᔕ WOMEN ᔕ

1. THE CHEMISE

Of longcloth, linen or cambric, this usually had a narrow edge of trimming at neck and sleeves, and down the front opening, which was closed by buttons. The front might also have vertical tucking on either side.

The evening chemise was cut very low, sometimes with a back-fastening.

In 1876 'chemises are now made with breast seams shaped to the figure so as not to take up more room than possible beneath the stays.' 'Underclothing has reached a luxury unknown in any age. The most modest lady has now her chemise and drawers trimmed with flounces of real lace alternating with tucks, frills and insertion. A fashionable chemise looks like a baby's christening robe.' 1879 saw 'chemises with pleated gussets on either side of the bust,' and in four types: (1) Like a Princess dress. (2) With three box-pleats in front, and gored back. (3) With a front like a chemisette and much trimmed. (4) Made like a cuirasse with one gore in the centre of the back. The goring was required to diminish the bulk, when the dress had become excessively tight. We must add, however, that many of the surviving specimens are of a much more homely description.

In 1882 cambric, batiste and nainsook, trimmed with lace, were becoming fashionable materials, and the garment was usually gathered at the waist, and sleeveless. The sleeveless *chemise en princesse*, two yards wide, with a flounce at the hem and a deep pointed stomacher, appeared in 1882 for wearing under a trained dress.

FIG. 75. JACONET UNDER-BODICE. FROM 'THE YOUNG ENGLISHWOMAN,' 1876

FIG. 76. RED FLANNEL DRAWERS AND CHEMISE (WITH STOCKINETTE HEM AND WRIST).
MASSACHUSETTS, *c.* 1880

2. DRAWERS

The old form continued, but in 1868 drawers with five or six tucks at the knee and an edging of lace came into use. In 1876 'the new drawers are left open a finger's length up the outer side and the opening closed by three buttons,' a style in which the legs ceased to be entirely separate. Silk or flannel (*figure* 74) was becoming the usual material, and in 1877 'ladies who do not wear foulard wear drawers of flannel under their cambric drawers.'

With the tight dresses the garment 'should barely reach the knee and have a trimming of torchon or insertion with a frill,' while some preferred drawers of chamois leather. Unfortunately no specimen has survived of 'plush drawers, quite tight, with a deep frill of lace at the knee' (1881).

3. COMBINATIONS

In 1877 'the new style of combining chemise and drawers' originated. The garment had either a back or a front opening, and some were made with high neck and long sleeves. Occasionally there were buttons round the hips to which the petticoats were fastened.

Materials used were linen, merino, nainsook, calico, cambric, and washing silks, often pink or cream-coloured. By 1878 'combinations are usually worn,' and to obtain the desirable svelte figure 'chamois leather combinations are worn over the other underclothing; not *on any account* next the skin.'

The function of the garment is betrayed in the comment: 'In the present day the object of dress is no longer to conceal but to display the female form divine.'

4. PETTICOATS

The colours became less aggressive. Whereas in 1867 'we never remember seeing so great a number of red petticoats in the streets,'[1] by the next year 'white petticoats are permissible for day, even in the winter,' though 'fancy alpaca, linseys, cashmere, or quilted silks are more suitable.' The white day petticoat 'should have a pleating nine inches deep; for evening goffered flounces as long as the dress.'

---

[1] 'Scarlet cloth petticoat, the lower 12 inches kilted, 18/–' (1868). 'Coloured quilted silk petticoats from 35/–; satin from 40/–; cashmere, 15/–, of all colours' (1869). 'Camlet petticoats with five flounces, 10/6' (1870).

With the return of the bustle the white petticoat was frequently pulled in just below it with draw-strings. A white petticoat of horsehair or moreen, with the back flounced to the waist, often took the place of the crinolette.

The garment became steadily more complex, with, in 1872, flounces of embroidery or lace reaching above the knees, and could be worn over 'four or five plain white petticoats slightly starched' (*figure* 77). In 1874 the front and sides were gored, and the back, made with tie-backs, had stiffly starched muslin frills to the waist; by 1876 the petticoat might be replaced by a muslin flounce on the inner side of the skirt 'so that the limbs are clearly defined.' Evening petticoats, elaborately trimmed with lace and layers of lace-edged flounces ascending to the waist, with finer flounces over them, were rightly described as 'really works of art,' but for ordinary day wear a cambric petticoat over one of pale blue or pink flannel was a general custom.

In 1877 came the Princess petticoat, buttoned down the back to knee level and made of white material or coloured silk. With it the flannel one was omitted, and instead 'a second narrow skirt fastened to the edge of the stays reaches the knees and is edged with a deep kilting which descends to the ankles, bordered with torchon.' At this date the walking petticoat was $2\frac{1}{2}$ yards wide, while for trained dresses the petticoat, also trained, was four yards wide, the front and sides being gored. The train was sometimes buttoned on at the hem, thus making it detachable. Frequently, for day, short underpetticoats of knitted wool, chamois leather, winsey and serge, were also worn.

By 1882, in addition to the flouncing, steels were inserted at the back, presaging the imminent return of the bustle; while the Princess petticoat, now buttoning down the front, was developing five box-pleats at the back of the waist, which were made to stand out, bustle-wise, by bands or ties attached to the side seams inside. Many evening petticoats, untrained, had at the back five stiff flounces, each made to stand out by means of a draw-string.

5. CRINOLINE, CRINOLETTE AND BUSTLE

While in 1867 horsehair petticoats, gored, and sewn into an elastic waistband, were often substituted for it, yet the crinoline in a small size was not wholly discarded for several years. Frequently it

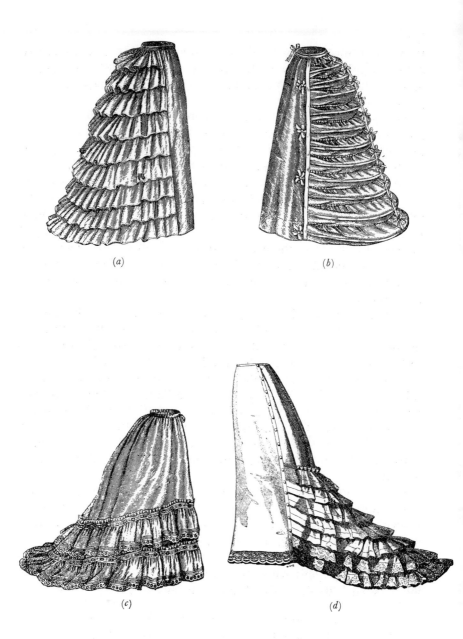

FIG. 77. (a) LONGCLOTH UNDER PETTICOAT, 1873; (b) CRINOLETTE FOR TRAINED DRESS, 1873;
(c) JACONET UNDERSKIRT WITH TRAIN, 1876; (d) UNDERSKIRT, 1879

was not more than a few hoops suspended by bands from the waist, open in front and used to support the bustle. By 1869, hooped only at the back, this became the crinolette 'of steel half hoops with horsehair or crinoline flounces forming a bustle.'

The actual bustle, appearing in 1868, was at first a matter of a few steels or whalebone inserted into the top of the petticoat behind and pulled into half hoops by means of tapes attached on its inner side; the next year it had become a structure of steel half hoops the size of a melon, often fixed permanently on to the top of the crinolette. Early in the 1870's the bustle extended downwards with puffings and flounces of crinoline material, strengthened with a few horizontal steels, the whole reaching to the sides over the hips. 'It rises high above the waist and is of vast dimensions' (1871). By 1873 it had narrowed and lengthened, consisting of a dozen steels encased in material and held in position by elastic bands; under the 'tie-back' skirt it projected backwards without adding to the width; and by the next year 'the bustle is fast disappearing,' though, to judge from contemporary photographs, this was far from being universally true. Then, in 1881, there were rumours that 'tournures are coming back with a vengeance'; at least the petticoat began to develop suspicious signs of its approaching arrival. It was characteristic of the squeamishness of that period that the name 'bustle' was, in the 1880's, considered a little coarse. 'Tournure' or 'dress improver' was a more ladylike appendage to the lower back.

6. THE CORSET

In the late 1860's, and during the phase of tight-lacing, there is abundance of contemporary evidence that a waist measurement of seventeen to twenty-one inches was not merely a fashionable aspiration but a frequent realization, obtainable, in 1867, by Thomson's 'glove fitting corset,' in which the front fastenings were held together by a spring latch; or by the French back-fastening corset with a long steel busk down the front. Prices of these were 12/6 and 21/– respectively.

The corset was comparatively short until 1875, when 'the long corset and tight-lacing to give the long slender figure fashionable' accompanied the change of dress design (*figure* 78). At this period it was discovered to serve a double purpose; in addition to its well-known effect on male susceptibility it had also, it seems, a moral function. 'It is an ever-present monitor indirectly bidding its wearer to exercise self-restraint; it is evidence of a well-disciplined mind and well-regulated feelings.' Thus this ingenious contrivance of whale-bone would inflame the passions of one sex while restraining those of the other, bringing man on to his knees while woman remained stiffly erect.

'The swan-bill corset for wearing under cuirasse bodice, 14/6,'

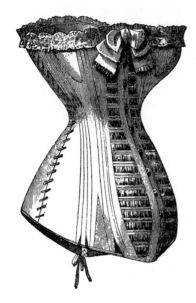

of 1876 and subsequent years had a long front-fastening busk termin-ating below in a powerful curved end, for it seems that figures 'as they advance in years develop un-duly and require a strong busk to keep them down.'

With the sheath-like dresses at the close of this period, back-fasten-ing corsets returned to favour, as the front fastenings interfered with the close fit of the bodice. Such corsets might be covered with black satin and edged with a bertha of lace so that the camisole could be omitted, while, to save space, the over-petticoat was buttoned direct on to the corset.

In 1878 suspenders, attached to the bottom of the corset and clip-ping on to the stockings, began to

FIG. 78. CORSET. FROM 'THE MILLINER AND DRESSMAKER,' 1879

take the place of elastic garters, and by 1882 'the suspender is made of satin and elastic with gilt clips, with a shaped belt fitting the corset.'

7.   THE CAMISOLE

This, often called 'petticoat bodice' became more shaped to the figure, acquiring in 1878 a heart-shaped opening. It was often of calico, though better qualities might be of nainsook edged with a frill or with lace.

8.   THE VEST

From 1875 onwards this was often of washing silk in various

colours, and was made with long or short sleeves. More ordinary materials were merino or flannel, particularly for winter wear.

9. THE NIGHTDRESS

This gradually became more ornamental. In 1867 it developed a stand-up collar and a yoke, the front being tucked (*figure* 80). By 1876 it was 'as much trimmed down the back of the bodice as the

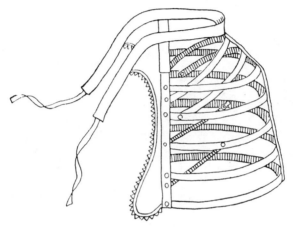

FIG. 79. "CANFIELD" BUSTLE, *c.* 1888

front,' and the next year 'some are made with a Watteau pleat; the front with long pleats down each side of the centre pleat; buttons are no longer put on a flap but in the centre pleat; collars and deep cuffs are usual.'

The usual material was longcloth; more elegant specimens, of foulard, were regarded with some suspicion as being 'very thin,' while some, even, were 'open down the whole of the front and trimmed with a frill.' And by 1880 'the latest idea in nightgowns is to carry the trimming entirely down the front to the hem.'

10. THE NIGHT-CAP

During the 1870's this was revived in a picturesque form as an ornamental mob-cap, which, however, did not survive that decade.

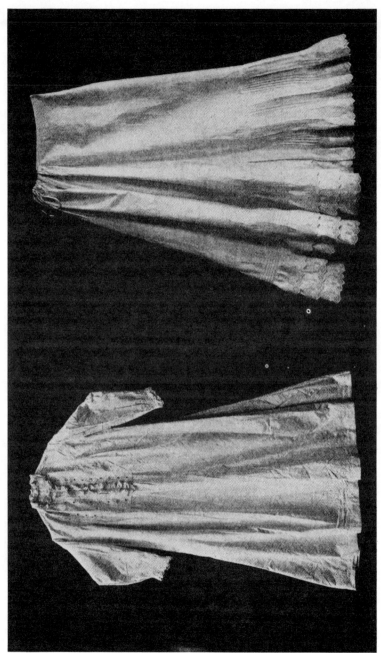

FIG. 80. (*left*) NIGHTDRESS, 1870–80; (*right*) PETTICOAT, c. 1880

It should be noted that although the number of undergarments was, if anything, increased, their texture was becoming progressively thinner and more flimsy; with the tight-fitting dress at the close of the period the actual number was reduced to a minimum.

The amount of underclothes required in a trousseau costing £100 in 1867, included:—

12 Chemises trimmed with insertion, at 15/6; or with real lace at 18/6.
12 Nightdresses at 22/6; 6 at 25/–.
12 longcloth Drawers, trimmed with work, at 10/6; or with lace at 12/6.
4 longcloth Petticoats, tucked and frilled, at 21/–; 3 cambric ditto, embroidered and frilled, at 27/6; 2 French piqué, frilled, at 22/6.
1 dress Petticoat, superbly embroidered, 3 guineas.
6 Camisoles trimmed with lace, at 12/6.
6 patent merino Vests at 7/6; 6 ditto of India gauze, at 6/6.
4 flannel Petticoats at 13/6.
2 pairs of French corsets at 16/6.
2 Crinolines at 15/–.

All garments were machine-sewn (lock-stitch), and generally bought ready-made.

X

1883—1896

THE economic depression which overshadowed most of this
period curbed the extravagance of dress which had been
so conspicuous; new influences were at work. Among them
in a more sober atmosphere was a growing appreciation of
hygiene and a demand for 'sensible' underclothing.

Both sexes were exploring the joys of outdoor sports, for which
appropriate costume was needed. 'At no time in history have the
human nerves suffered as they do now from the wild speed at which
life travels, and the pressure of occupations and amusements,' was
the observation of a contemporary; the spectacle of men riding
'penny-farthings' (described as 'cads on castors') and women
experimenting with Rational Dress meant that new impulses were
stirring.

Innovations in feminine costume, however, were checked by the
prudish dread of arousing unwelcome sex interest; a horror of the
human body seems to have been the hall-mark of gentility. Yet, in
spite of these psychological barriers, there was a fundamental urge
towards greater physical freedom.

With such conflicting impulses, some eager for progress, others
shocked by the signs of the time, the resulting picture was confused;
we see in the fashions a spirit of guarded reticence through which
natural instincts struggled for expression, inhibited by a traditional
attitude of mind. In such circumstances Providence will sometimes
supply an unexpected solution of the problem; a great war, for
example, will release gentility from its intolerable bondage. In the
present instance a less violent event served the purpose, namely the
invention of a bicycle which women could ride. It converted the lady

into a biped, and supplied her with a momentum which carried her headlong into the next century.

The bicycle was, of course, only a stage in the process of physical emancipation which had started in the 1860's with the 'walking costume,' developing into the 'tailor-made' of the 1870's, and the 'tennis costume' of the 1880's. In this progression man led the way, and woman followed. The effect was to produce, with both sexes, a modification of the underclothing adapted to the new activities, while for formal wear the old constrictions persisted. As a result men and women began to require a double wardrobe including two categories of underclothes. The gentleman's 'town' attire still strove to indicate his social position in his shirt and collar; even in his sporting garb there was a curious reluctance to abandon those distinctive features which were apparent in the coloured shirt with attached *white* collar and *white* cuffs. So, too, the lady, playing tennis, shrank from doing so uncorseted or ungloved.

Both sexes accepted the hygienic rule of 'wool next the skin,' and the wearing of underclothes singularly lacking in charm. The scientist rather than the artist was responsible for the garments designed by Dr. Jaeger, early in the 1880's. Illustrations of these models remind us of his German origin, for no mere French brain could have conceived underwear so Teutonic. But, after all, why should the influence of sex attraction be allowed to penetrate into the deeper layers which propriety occluded from vision?

Such at least was the dictate of prudery in the 1880's, when every nice-minded girl was trained to be oblivious of a large area of her body. 'Those are things, my dear,' explained an elder, 'that we don't talk about; indeed, we try not to think of them.' There were physical facts which the shadow of Mrs. Grundy veiled in impenetrable obscurity. We hear of a young lady exclaiming, at the prospect of marriage, 'How awful it must be, to be seen, by one's husband—in—one's petticoats!' But it seems that marriage—at least in the 1880's—might entail more awful shocks even than that. There was a bride who wrote home to her mamma that she was horrified by the sight of her husband's night-*shirts*; and that she was spending the honeymoon 'making him nice long night-*gowns* so that I shan't be able to see any of him.'

Such evidence is valuable; it explains the undergarments of the period and the unconscious attempt to free them from erotic associations, in exactly the same spirit as inspired the tailor-made costume on the surface. Such protective armour, guaranteed to be non-attractive, was a symbol of revolt against the slavery of the sex instinct.

Some, then, would hail the advent of those inauspicious garments as denoting an underground resistance movement against male oppression; others would regard this era of anti-erotic underclothes as evidence of sex repression, or as an interlude between the erotic exploitation of the 1870's and the still more erotic Edwardian period. Whatever view we choose to take of the 1880's—whether we agree with that writer commenting in 1882 on current fashions and suggesting 'is it not possible that forty years hence they may be classified by our successors among the rococo absurdities of a bygone age?'—or whether, at a distance of seventy years, we are now more disposed to regard them as evidence of growth towards light and air through a soil of uncompromising aridity—we shall probably agree that the manifestations of the sexual instinct are never more absurd than when we deny their existence. Technically the period developed some novel features; ideas flowing from across the Atlantic began to modify the Englishman's underwear—especially for less formal occasions—breaking down a number of conventions, together with the more general acceptance of coloured shirts.

But not even America could soften the inflexibility of the starched shirt-front and collar, worn with the frock-coat.

ᔛ MEN ᔛ

Methods of expressing class distinction in costume change more slowly than methods of expressing sex attraction. And as man's clothes tend in the main to be inspired by the former, and woman's by the latter, his 'fashions' appear almost stationary as compared to hers. The difference becomes more marked, of course, as democracy levels out class. As the insignia of social rank depend ultimately on wealth, a period of economic depression hastens their obliteration, while the natural instinct of sex attraction is scarcely affected. In the depression of the 1880's the gentleman's white shirt collar—its exact size and shape—grew in importance, serving to keep the flag flying. Gone for ever were those blissful days when a nobleman could 'jog along on £20,000 a year.'

A social feature of this period was the exquisite, known as 'the masher'; and it is significant that he relied chiefly on his shirt-front, collar and cuffs, to distinguish himself from ordinary mortals.

I. THE SHIRT

The day-shirt for formal wear remained white and starched, with rectangular shaped cuffs. The side slits, by 1890, had a small gusset inserted, and by now the lower border, front and back, was invariably curved. As in the previous period, the amount of shirt-front exposed by the cut of the waistcoat varied with the season; the summer shirt was visible in a V opening deep enough to show one or even two studs, and was generally worn with a butterfly collar, while the winter shirt was only seen in a slight V opening, and had an upright collar presenting a slight V gap between the points.

The height of the collar steadily increased, so that by 1894 it was said 'before long we shall reach the 3-in. standard.' By 1896 the upright collar might have the points overlapping by $\frac{3}{8}$ in., and had a 3-in. front and $2\frac{3}{4}$-in. back; or it might be replaced by a high-band turnover. We learn, in 1890, that 'the Duke of Clarence

FIG. 81. SHIRTS. FROM 'THE TAILOR AND CUTTER,' 1883

is a whale on collars and cuffs, possessing the most elaborate and varied assortment of neckwear that can be found anywhere in the Queen's dominions.'

The nice choice of shirt, collar and tie was a matter of supreme importance, a slightly larger tie being called for in the afternoon than in the morning; a bow-tie for summer wear; the scarf-tie always safe, especially in the striped patterns, and the octagon for men of substance; while in 1890 the 'four-in-hand' tie became fashionable, the ends being knotted and passed through a ring and then drawn under the waistcoat on each side to expose the centre stud or studs. Though we are told in 1894 that 'the laws that govern dress seem fast ceasing to be very irksome,' and that 'the change from the formal made-up bows and ties has given place to a looser and more artistic class of cravat,'[1] the relaxation was only relative, and a gentleman 'to be fashionably dressed must wear his collars and cuffs attached to his shirts.' Actually, however, a democratic innovation was creeping in; not only was there the detachable collar, but detachable cuffs which could be reversed when one edge was soiled. Worse still was the 'cuff protector' which was slipped on over the cuff to protect it for office work. And the false shirt-front or 'dickey' was becoming popular in the commercial world. 'Shirt fronts with collars attached are still a feature of the lower and middle class trade'[1] (1895), where they were, unofficially, known as 'cheats.'

The social status of the white shirt was further threatened by fancy coloured shirts 'with stiff bosom and cuffs, for day—drab and wood shades in medium vertical stripes; with them a white collar is often worn'[1] (1894). And in hot weather 'coloured shirts in pale pink or blue stripes with soft front but stiff white collar and cuffs.'[1] Such innovations emanating from America were accompanied with the challenge that 'coloured shirts are now held to be perfectly good form even with frock coats. Solid colours are barred; neat stripes in pink and blue are favourites'[1] (1894). It seemed a threat to the very citadel of class distinction.

The hot summer of 1893 introduced the cummerbund in lieu of a waistcoat with 'an amazing display of shirt-front'; City gentlemen were driven 'to dispense with braces and wear sash or even belt, and some venture to wear soft striped flannel shirt and white silk tie,' while others indulged in low-cut flowered waistcoats displaying almost as much shirt-front; but we are warned that 'gentlemen endowed with abdominal convexity should avoid' these modes.

The relaxation affected 'sports' shirts, the tennis shirt of 1887–88 having a starched turned-down collar (the 'polo collar'), which, by 1890, became soft, worn, of course, with an Oxford tie. By 1896 the

[1] *The Tailor and Cutter.*

cricketing shirt, the front fastened with pearl buttons, had a Shakes-peare collar, also worn with a tie. Oxford shirting, a heavy cotton fabric, in coloured stripes, was becoming popular, together with 'regatta shirts,' of cambric, in vertical stripes, sold with two detach-able collars, and these flourished profusely on the esplanade in summer.

The Dress-Shirt. While 'the masher's dress coat shews an immense amount of shirt front with large diamond in centre of same'[1] (1885), ordinary folk were content to display much less, showing one or two studs. The dress 'smoking jacket' of 1888 re-quired two studs and these in 1896 were often black. The front remained plain until the pleated front came from America in 1889 as a rival. In 1896 the one-stud front became the more correct, and at this date some dress-shirts were made to button behind. By the close of this period the American influence (which had been affecting English costume of both sexes since the early 1880's) introduced the 'coat-shirt' buttoned down the front so as to obviate having to slip it over the head; the method was accepted for the dress-shirt, but hardly as yet for the day. The tab at the base of the shirt-front, to button on to the drawers, was becoming usual (*figure* 82).

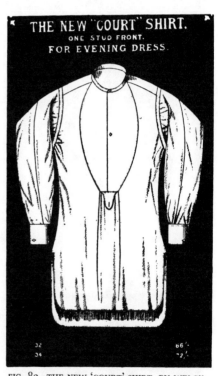

FIG. 82. THE NEW 'COURT' SHIRT, BY WELCH, MARGETSON AND CO., 1883

The butterfly collar with narrow bow continued, the tie of lawn or piqué being $1\frac{1}{8}$ in. wide, 'somewhat broader at the ends than the middle and brought into the butterfly shape by the hands of the wearer' (1894).

[1] *The Tailor and Cutter.*

FIG. 83. SHIRT FORMS. FROM 'THE TAILOR AND CUTTER,' 1889
MR. JOSEPH CHAMBERLAIN AND MADAME ADELINA PATTI.

The material of the dress-shirt was white linen or fine piqué.

The period, it will be seen, introduced an expanding variety of types of shirts, collars and neckties, and a relaxing of the stricter rules of etiquette as to the wearing of them. In the main this may be attributed to American influence.

2. THE VEST

Often described as the 'undershirt.' By 1894 'ventilated undershirts of lambs' wool, with perforations in the armpits,' silk undershirts (at 40/– a dozen whole-sale), and vests in natural wool were usual. 'Scarlet flannel vests lined with perforated chamois leather' were under-waistcoats worn over the under-vests (*figure* 84).

FIG. 84. MAN'S SCARLET VEST, BY WELCH, MARGETSON AND CO., 1883

3. DRAWERS

In natural wool and lambs' wool. The loop of tape outside the waistband, through which the tongues of the braces were passed, became general towards the close of this period. Short pants of absorbent stockinette were worn for bicycling. 'The various kinds of sanitary underwear have steadily gained in popularity . . . there are tastes, however, that only delicate colour effects can satisfy, and flesh tint, heliotrope, lavender, and light blue and other delicate shades have been provided to satisfy their wants. . . . Lightweight woollens will be worn more than ever before'(1895).

4. BRACES

A number of variations appeared in the 1890's such as 'the patent adjustable brace with crosstree at the back,' while some were dispensing with the article altogether.

FIG. 85. MAN'S JAEGER NIGHTGOWN, EARLY 1880's

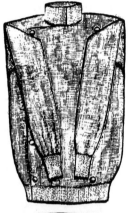

FIG. 86. JAEGER COMPLETE
SLEEPING SUIT, 1885

'Americans, French and Germans have been trained to dispense with braces from childhood' (1889).[1]

5. NIGHTCLOTHES

Pyjamas, in the 1890's, were steadily replacing the nightshirt which, in fact, was being far less advertised. 'Pyjamas in wool and silk stripes, 42/– a dozen, wholesale,' must stir envious thoughts in the minds of to-day.

6. CORSETS

The statement that 'the corset is worn by thousands of men. This is really a stiff band with ribs and is fastened to the pants,' must be accepted with a certain degree of doubt, though the article was certainly advertised and presumably often bought; perhaps chiefly by figures of a certain social prominence.

7. DRESS ACCESSORIES

'Flannel and chamois leather chest protectors, 9/– to 21/– a dozen, wholesale' (1883).

The 1890's saw the general use of sock suspenders, tie clips, metallic devices for holding down the tie round the upright collar, ingenious varieties of studs and cufflinks, etc., designed to simplify the task of dressing.

*   *   *   *

It may be convenient to mention here the principal forms of necktie worn during the second half of the nineteenth century.

[1] *The Tailor and Cutter.*

1. Napoleons

These, usually of black silk or satin, resembled the earlier stock, being a deep swathing band round the neck, the narrow ends coming to the front and there tied into a flat bow. They were fashionable in the 1850's and survived until near the end of the century.

2. Twice-round Scarf

Usually of fancy silk. Fashionable in the 1870's.

3. Derbys

Neckties with straight sides but with one end shorter than the other, the centre being slightly narrower than the ends.

4. Oxfords

Narrow straight ties throughout, the ends indistinguishable.

5. Ascots

The ends expand gradually to a width of some three inches; both ends are of equal width and length, and reversible. Can be tied either flat or 'puffed.'

6. Batswing

Both ends are equal in length, but the wide portions are short; for tying into a bow with 'butterfly' ends.

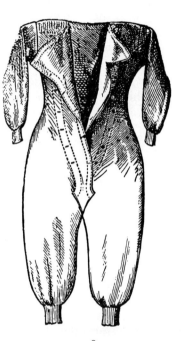

FIG. 87.
WOMEN'S JAEGER SANITARY COMBINA-
TIONS, 1885

7. Made-up Cravats and Octagons

Of silk or satin. The narrow end is armed with a stiffener which is slipped through the back of the cravat when in position, and held by a pin or other fastener.

All forms of necktie also appeared as 'made-up' shapes.

*   *   *   *

Very little has been recorded about the underclothing worn by the 'working man' of last century. The following information has kindly been supplied us by a number of correspondents:

1. A sleeveless vest, usually of white flannel.
2. A flannel body-belt 'about half a yard wide and stitched across from end to end and tied round with tapes.'
3. A flannel shirt of 'about three yards of material with sleeves down to the elbows.'
4. Above this was worn 'a top shirt made of fine striped flannel or flannelette, and in winter a waistcoat lined with red flannel.'

The shirt was made 'on a similar pattern to what sailors now wear,' and with gussets under the armpits. Some had feather-stitching down the tucked fronts.

Coloured shirts and drawers for working days, and white for Sundays.

5. Drawers, known as 'linings,' of flannel or twilled calico, made with a wide waistband, and tied round the ankles with tapes.
6. Garters were a strip ¾ yard long of knitted material wound round the top of the stockings, which reached nearly up to the knee.

∽ WOMEN ∽

The prosaic wearing of 'wool next the skin' was described as necessary 'to absorb perspiration.' 'But surely,' complained one writing in 1885, 'a gentlewoman rarely does anything to cause such an unpleasant thing!' Nevertheless the more progressive woman was advancing so rapidly that she frequently perspired. Active outdoor exercise tended to reduce the bulk of underclothing, and combinations were a convenient substitute for some of the petticoats. Enterprising young women were indulging in such daring adventures as walking holidays, for which 'a companion is highly desirable, not so much as a defence against that bugbear to most women, "a man," but in case of mishap. For clothing "Flannel next the skin" should be the rule; beneath a dust-coloured woollen dress the woollen undergarment must come up to the neck and down to the middle of the thighs, with long sleeves to the wrists; this, with flannel drawers and a light-coloured petticoat is all that is needed for underclothing.' While for bicycling, in the 1890's, 'the simplest and best costume consists of warm combinations, a thick woollen vest or knitted bodice, and a pair of tweed or cloth knickerbockers, with a skirt of waterproofed cloth made close fitting and rather long in front so as to display not a too liberal allowance of ankle. . . .'

In the fashionable world, however, the hygienic gloom gradually lifted, and by the 1890's underclothes once more essayed the art of being 'attractive,' with 'bewitching silk petticoats' (1895), and the lavish use of coloured ribbons; the new note was implied in the statement that 'there is a decidedly fussy element in all good underclothing' (1896). The New Woman is gently reminded of the old technique so successful in the past; of 'the petticoat, foamingly soft, adored by Man,' which skilful prudery could make so effective 'if Woman is to be that soft, sweet, tender bit of humanity which Heaven distinctly intended her to be.' Such, at least, was the advice of a woman's magazine.

I. THE CHEMISE

This continued as in the previous period until the end of the 1880's when the 'Empire chemise' appeared, with a high waist and puffed shoulder sleeves, sometimes also with a frill of lace round the hem.

Early in the 1890's longcloth was said to have become quite *démodé*, and the chemise itself was frequently replaced by combinations.

2. COMBINATIONS

Usually of woollen material, Dr. Jaeger's models being of 'natural wool' (*figure* 85); later, more fashionable forms were made of silk, nainsook, or surah, trimmed with lace insertion, the neck being drawn in with coloured 'baby-ribbons.' With these 'no chemise is needed but a short white petticoat buttoned round the stays and worn under the flannel one.' 'The new cellular cloth of cotton, wool or silk' appeared in 1888.

A 'new undergarment of fine muslin edged with lace combining low bodice, petticoat and drawers, worn over the corset which is worn over the vest,' was introduced by Marshall and Snelgrove in 1892. And in 1895 'charming pale pink llamé combinations with frills of torchon lace at the neck and knee' provided a pleasing prospect for those fortunate enough to see them.

3. DRAWERS

These, worn over the combinations, were frilled at the knees, becoming extremely wide in the leg, so that by 1895 the garment was as wide as the petticoat itself. A picturesque affair some twenty inches round the knee with a 10-in. lace frill, was regarded by many with moral apprehension as savouring of the demi-monde. Prosaic serge knickerbockers gathered just below the knee was an alternative, while 'coloured silk knickerbockers, some two yards wide, often lined with flannel' sought to make the best of both worlds. The knickerbocker form was made with a buttoned flap at the back, which was beginning to replace the old 'open' pattern.

Oddities such as plush drawers edged with lace, or complete sets of underclothing in black surah, were perhaps symptomatic of individual taste ignoring the conventions.

4. PETTICOATS

During the revival of the bustle, from 1883 to near the end of that decade, the petticoat projected in sympathy. The box pleats and flounces at the back developed, in 1883, into the 'crinolette petticoat,' the plain front breadths of which buttoned on to the corset, while the flounced back breadth was tied round the waist outside it. Its length ranged from 19 to 39 in., and steels were inserted round the lower part. The crinolette in its turn gave way, in 1885, to a revived bustle.

Two petticoats were still generally worn, or one with combinations; in winter the usual one of coloured flannel, or one of quilted satin or sateen edged with lace.

By the 1890's coloured shot silk petticoats were in fashion, some being accordion pleated, or with scalloped edge trimmed with lace. In 1891 'petticoats are $2\frac{1}{2}$ yards wide at the hem, close gored at the top, with a drawing-string behind; trimmed with one or two scanty frills of scalloped embroidery with insertion.'

The white petticoat, which had been temporarily eclipsed by the coloured, recovered its supremacy in 1894, enriched with accordion-pleated frills and coloured baby-ribbons. And the next year this elaborate affair 'now at the zenith of its glory,' might be 'of spotted net with endless rows of tucks, lace insertions, frillings and puffings.' By this date it was becoming very much gored at the top and wide at the hem, where it was often edged with ruching.

A petticoat guaranteed to produce an intriguing rustle as the wearer moved was made of moreen.

5. THE BUSTLE

This, as a separate article from the petticoat with back flouncing, began to return in 1883, in a short form for the walking dress and longer for the evening. By the next year it was either attached to the bodice or the petticoat, or it might be in the form of crescentic steels introduced into the back of the dress itself. By 1885 a horsehair pad, some six inches square and often called a 'mattress,' was added; the American kind, of wire—'which answers the purpose much better' —was but one of many other varieties. Unlike that used in the 1870's, the bustle of the 1880's produced a prominence almost at right angles so that it was popularly declared a tea-tray could be comfortably rested upon it.

It declined in 1888 and disappeared the following year.

6. THE CORSET

This continued to be long-waisted during the 1880's, and was often of elegant materials such as silk, satin and brocade, and of a great variety of colours. An evening corset 'in apricot and peacock-blue satin' (1886) was perhaps a specially choice example. In the 1890's yellow was a favourite colour.

By 1890 'the corset is now always worn over the petticoat,' and was elaborately decorated with lace frills and rosettes in colour.

The 1890's saw a somewhat shortened form, with a considerable degree of tight-lacing. It was a girl's ambition to have, at marriage, a waist-measurement not exceeding the number of years of her age—and to

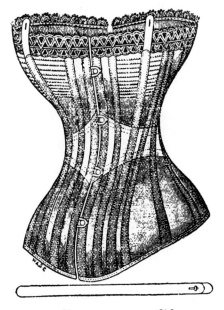

FIG. 88. JAEGER CORSET, 1886

marry before she was twenty-one. The huge sleeves helped to create the illusion. 'Nothing could be more becoming to the figure; the waist looks infinitesimal' (1892); and in spite of the bicycle 'girls pull themselves in while they pad their hips and the side lines of the bust to make themselves look as much like an hourglass as possible' (1896).

7. THE VEST

The usual material was merino, though silk was favoured by the smart world. Though colours were, by many, considered 'not quite nice,' there was a growing liking for them. A specimen of plum-coloured silk stockinette (Platt Hall, Cunnington collection) belongs to this period.

8. THE BUST BODICE

A device to support the breasts introduced in 1889, and worn above the corset. Usually it was made of white coutil, with side bones, and laced front and back.

9. BUST IMPROVERS

These were commonly used all through the period. In 1887 they were in the form of cup-shaped wire structures. Early in the 1890's appliances of flexible celluloid were advertised. A simpler type consisted in a shaped piece of material with circular 'pockets,' each with a slit behind in which a pad could be inserted. A specimen of this kind (Cunnington collection) has pads of assorted sizes; the original wearer explained that at a

FIG. 89. BUST IMPROVER, c. 1896

dance the size she would select 'would depend on who my partner was to be' (*figure* 89).

10. THE CAMISOLE

High and close-fitting for day wear, and with a low V neck for evening; either plain or trimmed with lace edging. In 1891 it was sometimes made without fastenings, the fronts, cut on the cross, crossing over and tucking under the petticoat band.

II. THE NIGHTGOWN

In the 1880's, gauging and frilling round the neck, with lace ruffles and jabot, added to the effectiveness of this garment; while in 1883 'white silk is used for nightdresses and pajama suits.'

'The combination nightgown or lady's Pyjama' of 1886 required 4½ yards of calico or flannel, and was made as combinations, with frills at the knees and wrists, and a high collar, and was buttoned down the front.

By 1887 'nightgowns are no longer simple garments but pretty and becoming; for example, made of soft pink silk with a Watteau pleat, a tucked yoke, lace frill down the front and lace ruffles.'[1] 'Coloured zephyr nightgowns (blue and pink) are superseding white ones.' And as the 1890's dawned 'delightfully cosy winter nightgowns of cream and pink flannel trimmed with lace and ribbons,' and others in the Empire style, composed of pink nun's veiling, with gathered waist and puffed shoulder sleeves, frilled all down the front and lavishly trimmed with baby-ribbons, were a feature in the bridal trousseau.

The garment became even more decorative, with a lace yoke and Toby frill, and full bishop sleeves ending in ruffles; or with a cape-like collar, or a frilled plastron and tucked front (1894). And 'the copious use of pink baby ribbons,' commented on in 1895, was perhaps inspired by the subconscious rather than the aesthetic sense. 'Ladies' pyjamas in pale blue and white silk mixture, tied round the waist with an encased ribbon and finished at the wrist, ankles and throat with lace; large bishop sleeves; a cascade of lace down the bodice.'[1] seem to suggest an expression of sex distraction. In fact, the garment of this period, in its various forms, supplied abundant material on which the modern psychologist can exercise his imagination.

[1] Fashion journal.

XI

1897—1908

THE enviable Victorian era celebrated its pinnacle of progress in the glitter of the Diamond Jubilee. The top of the world had been reached, and beyond stretched the promised land of luxury spreading smooth and lush, apparently for ever. The spirit of costume, anticipating the actual Edwardian period, changed in character, and we might say that a new epoch began in 1897. Man's clothing was profoundly affected by the growing taste for sports, the influence of which was two-fold. For one thing, it materially broke through the barriers of class; no longer did each social group confine its attention to exclusive games. Cricket, football and even golf were essentially democratic and required for those participating much the same sort of clothing, irrespective of rank. The cricket field, it is true, still distinguished 'gentlemen' from 'players,' but not by their dress.

The other influence of sport was to spread a taste for more comfortable clothes in daily life, and 'the top hat and frock coat' were gradually becoming a specialized uniform for particular occasions. The 'high collar' fetish saw a growing resistance to its iron rule and the very fact that the 'boiled shirt' earned that contemptuous title was in itself significant of its decline from power. The rule of starch was tottering, and when the dickey and detachable cuffs—to say nothing of the washable rubber collar—aped gentility, it was becoming clear that the genuine article was ceasing to mean what it once did.

The Edwardian gentleman shut his eyes, of course, to these encroachments creeping in from the ranks below; all he could do was to be, if possible, even more precise as to the exact shape of such items as collar and tie, and the proper moments when a little relaxation was permissible. An error meant a social disaster. Thus, in 1900 it was comforting to be assured that 'the striped, coloured or piqué collar almost invariably bespeaks the bounder.' But alas! only six years later we read, 'Mr. George Alexander has just adopted the woollen collar.'[1] When so eminent a leader of gentlemanly modes went over to the enemy in this way, what hopes were there of holding the fort? The fact is, the Edwardian period, seen from a distance of nearly half a century, may look to us like a luxuriant plain, but it was in reality a declivity; its surface becoming rougher and more barren as it approached the abyss. The economic burden was growing more oppressive, and the common man was treading on the gentleman's heels. Even underclothes were bearing marks of democracy.

Feminine fashions, however, seemed oblivious of these threatening changes. Having suppressed, for the time being, the aggressive new woman, the mood reverted to one of picturesque, nebulous mystery, while Edwardian underclothes developed a degree of eroticism never previously attempted. The technique was distinctive; women had learnt much, since the 1870's, of the art of suggestion. Instead of caricaturing the physical outlines of nature they invented a silhouette of fictitious curves, massive above, with rivulets of lacy embroidery trickling over the surface down to a whirlpool of froth at the foot.

The ideal model was the mature woman; her weapons were the straight-fronted corset and the flounced petticoat, which, in experienced hands, were highly effective, though very expensive. A woman of breeding and affluence was thereby distinguished from vulgar imitators. When petticoats were advertised at fifty guineas we may assume they were of a quality fit only for the Best People.

Although, no doubt, prudery would have been shocked by the suggestion, it is apparent that Edwardian underclothes were designed to be erotic, in keeping with the rest of the attire. They were given a more lyrical title—'lingerie'—while 'drawers' became 'knickers.' The crudity of the Victorian garments was obliterated, but there was, as yet, no flippancy and no 'undies.' The purpose of those garments was far too serious for that. Never had man been quite so susceptible to amorphous masses of mere textiles; never had underwear occupied so much attention in the fashion journals where

[1] *The Tailor and Cutter.*

'garments not destined for a public career' are described with enthusiasm. 'There is something very attractive,' writes one in 1901, 'about the elaborate petticoat and its frou-frouing mysteries. Our countrywomen realize at last that dainty undergarments are not necessarily a sign of depravity.'[1] Another, in 1903, declares, 'lingerie is an enthralling subject'; and presently the descriptions become positively rapturous. Beneath 'Simple Evening Seductions' are worn 'these beautiful persuasions,' while 'petticoats of an affectionate character' support 'Temptations in Teagowns.' The appeal of these seductive undergarments even became audible with their mysterious 'frou-frou,' and we are told 'we must all frou-frou till we can't frou-frou any more.' Man's ear could scarcely escape the music of these sirens.

The craving to be alluring under all circumstances affected the more intimate garments to a degree which shocked the elders. Evangeline's nightdress, for example, of embroidered cambric with short sleeves and Valenciennes ruffles, provoked the comment: 'I consider this garment not in any way fit for a girl—or for any good woman, for that matter,'[2] for the cobweb was positively transparent.

Those diaphanous garments were indeed revealing. They exposed —as did most of the undergarments of the period—a new and remarkable attitude of mind, very remote from the Victorian. It was a kind of highly artificial, highly refined and probably unconscious, sensuality. Perhaps it served as a substitute for the purely physical attractions which were prudishly concealed. To a more realistic generation it would seem to have been the ultimate illusion of an unreal world, floating blissfully towards—1914.

✍ MEN ✍

Already in 1898 it was remarked that 'there never was a time in history when everybody was dressed so nearly alike'; and that whereas the coloured shirt had been 'the distinct badge of the working man as the white shirt was of the middle and professional classes,' this, at the time of the Diamond Jubilee, no longer applied. Uniformity was creeping in, in spite of the desperate efforts of the gentleman to keep his head above the crowd.

[1] *The Lady's Realm.*
[2] Elinor Glyn: *The Vicissitudes of Evangeline*, 1904.

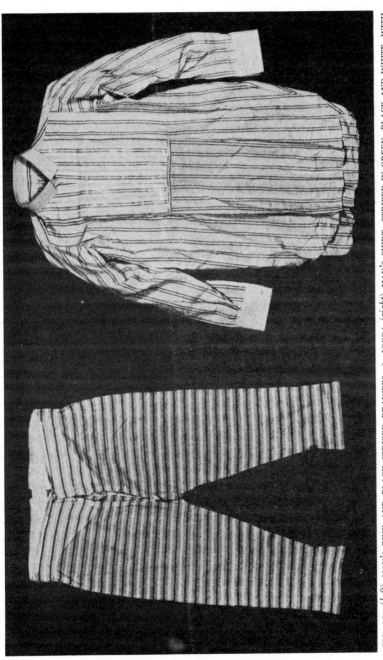

FIG. 90. (*left*). MAN'S PINK AND BLACK STRIPED DRAWERS, *c.* 1900; (*right*) MAN'S SHIRT, STRIPED IN GREEN, BLACK AND WHITE, WITH ATTACHED COLLAR, *c.* 1900

I. THE SHIRT

By day the white shirt was usually made with longcloth body and linen cuffs and front; the attached collar was giving place to the detachable, and, by 1900, the coloured shirt for day wear was becoming accepted.

Thus the correct wear for various occasions was given as: For morning or business, coloured shirt and cuffs to match, white collar, fancy silk tie. For a wedding, white shirt and high white collar, with black satin or light-coloured tie or scarf. For church and Sunday, white shirt, collar and cuffs, fancy silk Ascot tie or scarf. For evening dress, white shirt, high collar, broad-end white tie, mother-of-pearl studs and links. For 'sports' a regatta or Oxford stripe or fancy flannel shirt, polo collar or a linen stand-up.

For business men the front of the white shirt was small, and the cuffs had a double-button arrangement at the wristband to permit shortening while at work; alternatively there were the detachable cuffs. Many of these shirts were made to button at the back. But the coloured cambric shirt was steadily encroaching on the domain where formerly the white shirt had reigned supreme. By 1906 the soft-fronted white shirt, for business men, appeared, together with soft-fronted shirts of Oxford or zephyr shirtings, the fronts often tucked; sometimes the collars and cuffs were still of white linen, but this was no longer essential. Indeed flannel collars were popular 'in keeping with the rage for soft-finished shirts.' There were negligée woollen shirts in green stripes,[1] and in 1908 shirts of 'the new unshrinkable flannel,' Viyella, with neckbands of Italian cloth and slightly shaped at the waist.

Throughout the period the double collar, commonly known as a polo collar, or its variation 'the Rosebery,' was the favourite for day wear, its height diminishing from 3 in. to 2 in. by 1906, and even less the year following. But 'the high collar is always connected with ceremonial occasions.' It was observed, in 1907 that 'the double collar has killed the cravat and the large knot.'

Neckties were of necessity small, whether the Oxford tie, $1\frac{1}{2}$ in. wide throughout, or the silk or satin scarf expanding at the ends, or the bow (either made up or to tie), or the small four-in-hand. The knitted silk tie (1903) was acceptable because it could be tied tightly

[1] Striped flannel shirts cost 3/– to 6/–.

FIG. 91. TENNIS SHIRT, 1907. FROM 'THE TAILOR AND CUTTER'

without damaging the material. The 'washing tie' of 1906, and the washable collar, seem to imply economical subterfuges.

The dress-shirt, with or without attached collar, changed but slightly; and the front diminished somewhat in size. Though one-stud fronts were often worn, three studs were usual until towards the close of the period when one or two became more fashionable in a pleated front 9 to 10 in. wide (1908). While the day cuff was rounded, the dress cuff was square.[1]

The dress-collar was generally of the 'masher' or stand-up type which by the end of this period was not deeper than 2 in., when, in fact, it was being rivalled by a return of the winged collar.

The dress-tie was a small plain bow with square ends, and 'it is a canon of good taste that dress bows should be self-tied.'

2. THE DRESS-SHIRT PROTECTOR

This ingenious novelty, popular at the end of the 1890's, though actually it was a revival, was a pad of black satin, often quilted, worn over the dress-shirt front to protect it when the overcoat or evening cloak was worn out of doors.

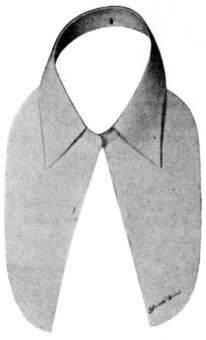

FIG. 92. MAN'S DICKEY WITH 'SHAKESPEARE' COLLAR, c. 1905

3. THE UNDERVEST

Of natural coloured wool, or, in summer, of spun silk or cellular cotton. 'The vast majority of gentlemen dispense with underwear altogether during the summer months' (1906).

4. DRAWERS AND PANTS

Of similar materials to the undervest. The distinction between the

[1] The evening dress-shirt cost 4/– or 5/–.

FIG. 93. (*left and right*) MAN'S PYJAMAS. JAEGER, 1899; (*centre*) MAN'S PYJAMAS IN PURE STRIPED SILK. PETER ROBINSON, 1902

two was becoming recognized; 'pants' were either ankle-length or to mid-calf; drawers were either just below the knee or just above (when they became known as 'knicker drawers,' which by further shortening later became 'trunks').

5. COMBINATIONS

A considerable number of men preferred to have vest and pants in one as a combined garment, a mode which was not yet obsolete, and in design extremely conservative. Even in 1898 they had been 'year after year exactly the same.'

6. PYJAMAS

These had become generally accepted in place of the nightshirt,[1] though the pure-minded clung to the belief that any garment worn in bed must of necessity have improper implications, and 'the advent of a leading actor on the stage clothed in the convenient pyjamas seemed to have shocked the super-latively sensitive ladies in the audience' (1906).[2]

FIG. 94. MAN'S VEST AND DRAWERS. AERTEX, 1906

∽ WOMEN ∽

'Among the lower-class Englishwoman there still lingers a desire for heavy durable longcloth, but we do not call that *lingerie*. A wish for dainty underwear is generally actuated by a desire for cleanliness. The lingerie of the moment is as luxurious as ever, in fact, even more so' (1901).[3] On that note the new reign started. 'There is an immense fancy again for black washing silk for lingerie but the fancy for coloured underclothing has somewhat gone out'[3] (1901). And by 1905 'in the matter of lingerie the present-day modes show exquisite taste and simplicity. Nearly everything is of finest lawn or cambric, and white reigns supreme.'[3] 'Undergarments are lovelier than ever trimmed with Madeira work.... For day wear lingerie is often

[1] All-wool pyjamas cost from 10/6 to 15/-; in zephyr from 4/3 to 8/3.
[2] *The Tailor and Cutter.*   [3] *The Lady's Realm.*

finished with fine buttonhole stitching and dots of different sizes, and the monogram simply but artistically embroidered. For evening wear it is of course more elaborate.'[1] 'Of recent years there has grown up an ultra-fastidiousness in the matter of underclothing . . . now beladed with baby ribbon.'[1] (1906).

This gives us a measure of Edwardian 'simplicity,' and the statement that 'lingerie is by far the most important part of a trousseau' implies its purpose.

1. THE CHEMISE

For day, of fine linen, batiste, or lawn; for evening of lawn or silk. 'The days of combinations are certainly past and we all wear chemises, Empire pattern, sloped at the waist and tied with coloured bows at the shoulders. Evening chemises of kilted gauze, practically sleeveless. . . .'[1] (1901).

Within a few years, however, the chemise found its status once more threatened by its old rival, combinations having the advantage of giving a closer fit over the hips which loomed so largely in Edwardian modes.

2. COMBINATIONS

'Handmade knicker and camisole combinations in nainsook, trimmed with Valenciennes lace, 10/9–21/6' (1903). The next year we are told, 'nearly every woman, I presume, wears combinations of wool or silk and wool.'

For the modest purse there were 'pink flannelette combinations at 1/11½' (1900), but we must not call these lingerie. 'Combinations trimmed with imitation torchon lace, at 5/11½' (1905), or 'combination suit with lace insertion and baby ribbon, 13/11' (1906), indicated degrees of loveliness. In 1908, however, 'combinations are slowly but surely disappearing; replaced by skirt-knickers which are seductive little garments mounted on a deep band.' At the same time the chemise was rendered superfluous by 'the cami-skirt, worn over the corsets and the skirt portion usually divided into two.' Nevertheless both the chemise and combinations were by no means defunct, continuing their useful functions in the middle section of the community.

[1] *The Lady's Realm.*

FIG. 95. UNDERSKIRTS AND CORSETS. FROM 'NEW ALBUM,' 1906

3. THE CORSET

'Fashion decrees that very large hips and great splendour of figure should prevail but also superimposes a distinctly diminutive waist' (1900). 'The stays are of course straight-fronted, giving support but leaving the figure graceful and supple; whilst narrowing the back in a most surprising manner. It keeps English-women in the right place and allows their chest to expand' (1901).

For Edwardian modes the new straight-fronted corset was essential, supplying that 'solidity of figure' which was so admired. 'It is the feature of these stays that while they flatten the figure below they lend fullness to the chest thereby immensely improving the charm of the silhouette. A good waistline is after all very much a matter of one's corset.'[1]

In 1902 the new look, which had been immortalized by the American artist, Dana Gibson, presented 'an upright poise of the shoulders, long sloping bust with straight front line and a graceful curve over the hips. The waist held in well below the figure; the chest carried well forward and the shoulders down; the waist long in front and short behind.'[1] 'Everyone has rushed into the straight-fronted corsets, often with deplorable results.'

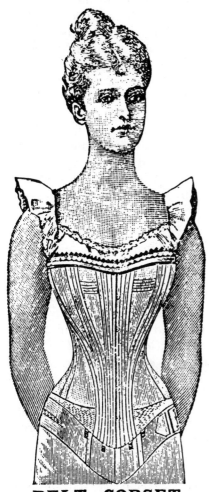

BELT CORSET

FIG. 96. JAEGER, 1899

[1] *The Lady's Realm.*

In 1905 'the Gibson Girl,' as portrayed by Miss Camille Clifford, established an ideal, and with it 'corsets are getting longer and longer below the waist and shorter and shorter above it. The corsetières of Paris bring the corset nearly halfway to the knees.'[1] As a result 'the hips at the back have taken a fresh development. Everyone looks the better for having visible hips and a good shaped bust.' 'You can face the world if you know you are all right behind.' 'For the usual height to-day, between 5 foot 6 and 6 foot in shoes, corsets between 20 and 25 in. will do quite nicely. It is the roundness of the waist and the curves of the hips, the way the figure is held in below it and carried up above it, that tells' (1906).

But alas! fashions are inconstant in their favours and the very next year, 1907, a willowy shape was dawning, so that 'the hips are often a thorn in the minds of women who would fain dress well.' The corset of 1908 was 'cut so deep that to sit down would appear an impossible feat,' and as hips sank into obscurity the famous corset disappeared.[2]

4. THE PETTICOAT

The Edwardian petticoat was always flimsy; not more than two were worn, the top one, particularly when coloured, often being referred to as an underskirt.

It grew steadily more flared and fluffy and frilly. 'Though cut very plain and tight-fitting round the hips, the amount of frou-frou from the knees downwards is immense,' and the correct management of 'frillies' became a preoccupation. We learn from *The Visits of Elizabeth*[3] their uses in a hammock. 'As I knew my frillies were all right I hammocked—and it was *lovely*.' The 'moirette silk petticoat with all the advantage of a rustling silk,' often with accordion-pleated flounce, was available from 12/9 to 21/9 (1900). With the yoked and much-gored day-skirt of 1903 a flounced petticoat served as a foundation, its border sometimes 'stiffened with horsehair or even steel.'

It was, of course, the evening petticoat that became specially exuberant. 'Evening petticoats are far more elaborate than the skirt without, and are cut with a train' (1901). A 'glacé silk petticoat with deep shaped flounce; trimmed with frills, ruchings and pin tucks, 31/11' (1903) would be a very ordinary example. The

---

[1] *The Lady's Realm.*
[2] 'Elastic corsets for special circumstances, 22/6' (1903).   [3] Elinor Glyn, 1900.

FIG. 97. SILK TRICOT CORSET. LONDON CORSET CO., 1904

petticoat of that year was distinguished by a pocket at the foot just above the flounce.

'Not so very long ago to wear lace on one's flannel petticoat and lace frills on other articles of underwear, was simply to be considered quite immoral. Now, however, underclothing with double frills of white spotted net, either tucked or with satin ribbon stitched in rows, and deep flounces of this net round the hem of petticoats are quite fascinating' (1904). Petticoat flounces of broderie anglaise require 5 to 6 yards, while 'detachable glacé frills for underskirts' cost 6/11 for 2½ yards (1905).

We learn that in 1906 'petticoats are peculiarly persuasive just now'—but their peculiar magic was beginning to fade. For though at the beginning of 1907 'these beautiful persuasions have an extravagant frou-frou of frills,' by the autumn 'petticoats are obviously on the decrease, the befrilled and laced jupon already carrying a démodé air when placed in close proximity with the soft falling, clinging skirts that, on being raised, reveal petticoats of an equally affectionate character.'[1] But 'one of the most disastrous aspects of the raised skirts is when the silk underslip is caught higher than the transparency, and reveals—well—anything there is to be seen.'

With the new Empire mode revival there was little room for elaborate petticoats, and although ones of rose-tinted glacé silk or of charmeuse satin with soft kilted flounce were often worn 'some dispense with petticoats and wear maillots instead,' while with semi-transparent summer dresses it was often apparent that directoire knickers were all-sufficing. By 1908 a petticoat was necessarily extremely narrow so that 'the large thick-through woman arrayed in attenuated petticoats surmounted by a waistline of gigantic girth' presented a lamentable spectacle of putting a quart into a pint pot. 'The present figure aimed at is calculated to drive despair to the heart of the irretrievably buxom.'

The materials used were cambric, lawn, batiste, glacé silk, moirette, and in fact any fabric that was flimsy and flounce-able.

5. DRAWERS

'Nainsook knickers with frills of muslin embroidery, 5/6' were advertised in 1900, while 'French drawers of mull muslin or washing

[1] Fashion journal.

silk, with flounce and three rows of insertion, threaded with baby ribbon, worn under lace or silk petticoat, for those who like a froth of frillies beneath their dress skirts'[1] (1904), supplied an exhilarating alternative to the combinations.

'Knickers of fine flannel or alpaca with detachable nainsook linings are an economy but to my mind lack daintiness' (1904). 'Even our knickers which we don for athletic purposes are constructed upon a sound and becoming basis' (1904). 'Wide-leg knickers of India longcloth and Valenciennes lace, 3/–' (1906). The same year we are told, 'the divided skirt is the name for knickers with wide "skirt legs".'

As the period drew to a close the revival of the Empire style of dress required 'directoire' knickers or satin pantalettes, close fitting, or 'the skirt-knickers which the up-to-date maiden delights in' (1908).

6. THE CAMISOLE

'Petticoat bodices, or as we now call them "corset covers," are made of thin silk *en princesse* with no sleeves. Underclothing becomes thinner and thinner' (1906). They replaced the 'slip bodice' of the 1890's, which usually buttoned down the front to hip level.

7. BUST IMPROVERS

'The patent bust improver, placing the possession of a bust modelled on that of the famous Venus de Milo at the disposal of every lady; of flesh-coloured material and less than 2 oz. at 7/6 a pair'[2] (1902).

'The Neena bust improver, cup-shaped perforated metal discs, weight ¾ oz. the pair' (1905).

8. THE BUST BODICE

'Patent bust bodice worn above the corset, with centre lacing; in coutille, 3/6' (1903). 'With the prevailing fashion of corsets bust-bodices are essential' (1904). 'I look so nice in my bust bodice that I contemplate wearing Empire clothes for ever' (1904). Jaeger's 'bust girdle' (1904) was the forerunner of the brassière.

[1] Fashion journal.   [2] Advertisement.

FIG. 98. PRINCESS PETTICOAT BY CHARLES LEE, 1907

9. NIGHTCLOTHES

The nightdress was becoming more and more elaborately trimmed and of flimsier materials. 'Viyella nightdress, cream or pink, 16/9 to 21/-; of nun's veiling, 10/6 to 21/–' (1900). 'Some have large falling collars of exquisite lace with lace trimming in the deep frill at the hem and also forming a frill at the elbow' (1901). 'Nightgown, the square front and back with alternate bands of torchon and embroidery, ribbon-threaded throughout; short sleeves with ruffles, hand-sewn, 33/6' (1903), with garments of a more diaphanous nature, such as shocked Evangeline's friends. 'The craze for Empire nightgowns still continues' (1904).

The garment described in 1906 as 'sleeveless with hanging ruffles at the shoulders, and quite a trousseau item though not outside the requirements of an ordinary woman,' leaves a good deal to the imagination.

Although pyjamas were recognized as permissible, they do not seem, as yet, to have become popular. For one thing, they were not in keeping with the general impulse to have all 'intimate garments' fussily trimmed with lace, etc. Everything had to appear very 'feminine,' and garments having masculine associations were therefore unfashionable. To wear such would incur the risk of being thought a suffragette. As a daring novelty of 1906 the appearance on the stage of chorus girls in pyjamas, singing 'We won't wear a nightie any more!' deserves to be recorded, as evidence of Edwardian progress.

10. TROUSSEAUX[1]

The following is the advice on choosing a trousseau given by *The Lady's Realm*, 1903: 'Some form of combination, that very homely garment which can never be very attractive—two dozen will not be too many, twelve of fairly thick silk and wool mixture for winter and twelve of fine silk or gauze for warmer weather. These to-day are beautifully woven and fashioned at the waist so as to prevent any undue superfluity of fabric; they are mostly worn low and sleeveless.

[1] Advertisement (1897):
'Trousseau set, nightdress, chemise and knickers of exquisite cambric profusely trimmed with billowy frills, hem-stitched, 10/3.'
'Corset, extra long waist, six fastenings, black Italian cloth, 14/11; in white coutil, 12/11.'
'Princess slip bodice, in cashmere or silk, with high or low neck, short sleeves or trimmed armholes; fits the figure like a glove.'

'Pretty chemises and knickers are attractive features of a trousseau. For evening there is nothing prettier than the "Empire" chemise in silk, muslin, lawn or even gauze. For day wear, in silk or lawn, cut square and decolleté with a broad band of contrasting colour across the bust through which is run a coloured ribbon.

'Knickers are wider than ever and trimmed with a goodly amount of frills and ribbons. They are charming in silk with a wide frill of the same edged with narrow lace. The smallest number of chemises and knickers in a trousseau should be two dozen of each. If pink, blue and yellow suit you best by all means adopt them. Pink is a splendid washing colour and a generally becoming one.

'You cannot do with less than three or four pairs of corsets. Black silk batiste is charming to wear with dark dresses. Then you must have two pretty brocaded pairs for summer and evening wear.

'Besides your silk and brocaded petticoats you will require about a dozen in cambric.

'There is nothing more charming, dainty and comfortable than the *robe de nuit* of the moment. Surely a touch of illusion in such a matter as a *robe de nuit* with an underlying current of coquetry is permissible in a young and charming bride. Two or three dozen nightdresses are not too many. . . . Americans and other ultra-smart folk are very fond of black silk or gauze nightgowns; but I do not think they should have a place in bridal trousseaux; I confess to a predilection for the purest white. Silk, fine French lawn, muslin and cambric are charming for night wear. . . . You should spend a large portion of your trousseau money on these important garments.'

XII

1909—1918

THE outstanding event of this period was, of course, the first World War. Its effect on the clothing of both men and women was certainly great, but it is scarcely sufficiently realized, perhaps, that these changes had already begun before 1914 and that the war merely hastened and developed them. The impulse was in being; the war gave it impetus towards a simplification, which enabled fashions to reach a still larger section of the community, at least in their cheaper forms. Such distinctions as remained were based more on wealth than on social status.

Underclothes were permitting freer movement, but what was still more significant was the growing inclination to reduce the layers which covered the body. It was being slowly realized that in the active life of the modern world so much clothing was unnecessary and a relic of obsolete ideas. A new conception of decency began to appear which has characterized the underclothing of the last forty years.

In men's underclothing the symbols of social rank, except for formal occasions, were declining; the gentleman's shirt and collar were no longer distinctive; the fashionable collar, or a good imitation of it, could be bought for 6½d. or less, the reign of the soft shirt was established, and the frock-coat and top hat were tottering to their doom. In 1911 Mr. Seymour Lucas, R.A., lamented the growing uniformity of masculine apparel, sighing 'for the time when a duke could be recognized by his garb.' Beneath the surface democratic novelties from America were coming into play in the direction of reducing the weight and substance of male underwear, as though we were no longer so fearful of our climate; or was it that we were discovering that, after all, it is admirably suited for an active life?

As a result of these changes man's underclothing became more rational and therefore ceased to be interesting. Being scarcely more than a detachable lining to his suit, its only trace of class distinction was the frequency with which it could be sent to the wash.

Happily feminine underclothing has never for long surrendered to the dictates of reason, and in spite of two great wars clings for inspiration to the promptings of instinct. In 1909, however, fashion became abruptly serious; the prospects of war and the growing burden of taxation called a stop to the frivolous extravagance of Edwardian modes; underclothing was reduced in amount and much simplified. The new classical line was severe, and its attractive power did not depend on the mystery of suggestion. The actual outlines of the body itself were no longer disguised through the intermediary of complex lingerie.

The 'hobble skirt' mode preceding the war no longer presented a built-up area on an expensive foundation; with the reduction in the amount of underclothing here was a style which offered equal opportunities to all.

The first two years of the war, when most women were but spectators, revived the romantic appeal of flounces and frillies, but as increasing numbers became active participants that exuberance disappeared. Those in uniform learnt to accept patterns of garments from which traces of glamour had been officially banned.

Underclothing became, of necessity, more 'practical.' Shortage of labour and laundrywork meant that lingerie needing elaborate washing and ironing became an impossible luxury. Gone for ever were those lacy white allurements; the realism of war demanded muscular legs.

A natural urge to maintain femininity produced in 1916 a daintier version of combinations, which received the name of 'cami-knickers,' and helped to preserve the wearer's self-respect, however austere might be her outward appearance.

But by the end of those disruptive years woman was arranging for herself an entirely new shape, with—in the phrase of a fashion writer—'the careful avoidance of what used to be known as a figure.' By the aid of long cylindrical corsets every curve was suppressed.

Underclothing no longer functioned to emphasize hetero-sexual features but, on the contrary, to obliterate them. The ideal model was not Venus but Ganymede. For this, 'lingerie' would have been quite inappropriate; a new name was needed for garments which by attenuation were becoming slightly absurd, though still preserving a traditional power of charm clinging to their wispy filaments. A kind of playful pet-name was obviously required, and woman's innate genius immediately supplied it. Lingerie became undies. The change marked more than just the end of a war; it betokened the end of an ancient attitude of mind, of a defensive taboo, and—perhaps—of a means of attack.

ல MEN ல

An examination of catalogues issued by firms supplying men's underwear during the years preceding the first war shows a progressive increase in the variety of articles available. The orthodox pattern of each appears in a dozen different forms, each, no doubt, to suit individual tastes and purposes as well as purses. Evidently the customer was in the happy position of being able to dictate to the trade his personal requirements. The refinements of civilized life—so far as clothing is a test—had reached a high level. 'Fashions' had become available for the many in a wide range of quality.

During the pre-war years the gentleman still clung desperately to the principle that his clothing must be uncomfortable to distinguish him from the rest, while a new version of the semi-gentleman—known as the 'knut'—burst into view, resplendent 'in pink shirts, orange ties and purple socks.'

I. THE SHIRT

'The long-fronted white or printed shirt is now obsolete' (1909).

The 'business shirt' had a stiff front of 10 in., and usually detachable cuffs, but for day the white shirt was being steadily displaced by the soft-fronted, made of flannel in winter and of negligée French print (at 4/6) or cambric in summer. These often had pleated fronts, the pleats varying from 1 in. wide to narrow tucks, and were commonly in shades of green or heliotrope with ties to match (1909). They were worn with a white double collar. The day-shirt of soft crêpe de Chine with soft double collar and cuffs was a luxury form.

The soft-fronted tunic shirt, with soft collar, became a feature of the pre-war years, especially in summer, while for formal wear the starched white shirt with shortened front and double or winged collar not exceeding 2 in. deep, remained the correct wear.

It was observed with regret, in 1912, that Eton boys had taken to wearing dickeys. 'Can a gentleman wear anything that is unreal, a cheat, a sham and a substitute? Taxation must have hit the aristocratic papa very hard.' (*The Tailor and Cutter.*) Worse still, gentlemen were observed playing golf in shirt-sleeves, which 'we have always regarded as against the etiquette of the game.' Tradition still claimed that man's shirt was essentially an *under*-garment not to be freely exposed, except for its specially prepared front, to the eyes of ladies; and a gentleman accidentally caught in his shirt-sleeves by them would be apologetic.

The day-tie was generally the scarf in a narrow knot, though the made-up 'four-in-hand' or the bow knot were also popular. A curiosity of 1913 was the hand-painted poplin tie, at 1/6. The war years rapidly swept these refinements away. 'Stiff white collars are disappearing and soft collars are worn by all classes.'(*The Manchester Guardian*, 1917.)

The dress-shirt saw a revival of the pleated front with four to eight pleats on each side. 'Even waiters are taking up the pleated shirt' (1909). With it the winged collar was usually worn.

2. VESTS

With long or short sleeves; made of unbleached cotton, white gauze or net for summer, and of merino, llama and flannel for winter (*figure* 99.)

Summer merino vests, 3/6–4/9. Natural summer viyella, 4/9–5/3. China spun silk vests, 6/6–7/6. (Prices of 1914.)

3. DRAWERS AND PANTS

Of unbleached cotton, calico, gauze, merino, llama and flannel. Trunks are advertised.

Summer merino pants, white, 3/9–5/–. Gauze merino, 2/9–4/–. China silk, 7/9–9/–. (1914 prices.)

4. COMBINATIONS

These were still being worn by many men, to judge from the advertisements.

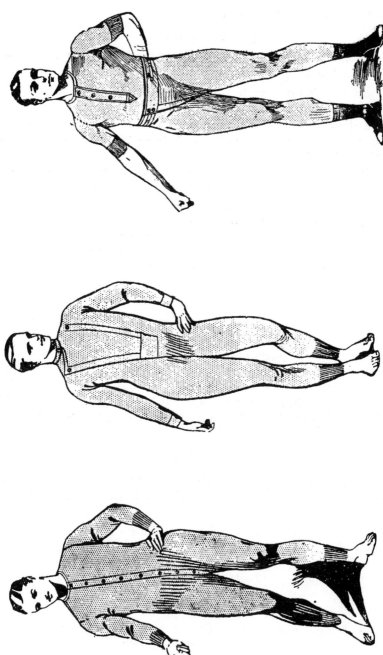

FIG. 99. (*left and centre*) MAN'S UNITED GARMENTS. JAEGER, 1914–15; (*right*) MAN'S UNDER-VEST AND PANTS. JAEGER, 1914–15

5. NIGHT WEAR

Longcloth nightshirts, 2/6–5/6. Of white or coloured silk, 17/6. Of flannel, 6/6–11/6.

Pyjamas: Flannel, 12/6–21/6. Viyella, 18/6–20/6. Silk, 27/6. (1915 prices.)

The effect of the war was to produce a rapidly increasing scarcity of woollen materials, so that by 1918 'the cost of materials is two or three times pre-war.'

By the end of the war the following comparative figures (from *The Tailor and Cutter*, 1918) indicate changes of cost:—

	The Artisan			The City Man		
Shirt	Pre-war 2/11	1918	4/11	Pre-war 4/11	1918	8/11
Underwear	Pre-war 8/11	1918	15/6	Pre-war 12/11	1918	21/-
Collar	Pre-war 6½d.	1918	9d.	Pre-war 6½d.	1918	9d.
Tie	Pre-war 1/-	1918	1/6	Pre-war 2/6	1918	3/6

◌ WOMEN ◌

The new silhouette, with a skirt of 1½ yards round the hem, left little space for expansive underclothing. But this managed, nevertheless, to preserve a somewhat more frivolous note than appeared on the surface. 'All up-to-date lingerie boasts of broad threaded ribbon'[1] (1909), while insertion and lace decorated the borders. A romantic note was struck during the war with 'regimental-crested undies,' and 'what could be more delightfully sentimental than *his* name embroidered on one's garter?' (1918).

1. THE CHEMISE

This was in the Empire style, often square-cut with narrow shoulder straps, and the top enriched with insertion. Nainsook was a popular material.

Although the garment lost favour it by no means disappeared; thus in 1917, 'crêpe de Chine chemise, vandyked edge, ribbon-slotted waist, ribbon shoulder strap, in white, sky, pink and helio, 24/6,' was being advertised.

2. COMBINATIONS

'The fashion is to replace chemise and skirt-knickers by skin-fitting combinations and silk pantalettes; but it is more amusing

[1] *The Lady.*

FIG. 100. NIGHTDRESS, CHEMISE AND DRAWERS, 1911

FIG. 101. 'NUFORM' CORSET. WEINGARTEN BROS., 1911

than words can describe to observe how frequently the fashion is ignored'[1] (1909).

'Summer combinations, low or high neck, short sleeves, some being made to open all down the front. Of pure wool, 4/11' (1911). These, we are told, 'outline the figure with admirable accuracy,' being close-fitting and reaching just below the knees. They were also made of silk.

In the early years of the war 'white mull combinations with wide leg knickers trimmed with lace' had a brief return.

3. THE CORSET

'In all corsets whether back lace or front lace, boning was all-important. The strain on the garment was terrific.'[2] Though whale-bone was still in use an improved method of rust-proof boning was introduced; in 1912 clock-spring steel covered with hard rubber or celluloid was adopted and 'the whalebone industry never recovered from the blow.'[3]

Under the heading 'The Corset Makes the Figure' it was stated, in 1912, that 'the contour of the season's figure gives the effect of the natural waist—which simulates both the Grecian and the Oriental—with long lines and a slightly curved but closely confined hip.'[2]

Throughout the period the corset remained straight-fronted, while steadily shortening above the waist and lengthening below, thus producing 'a sheath of cloth and steel'[3] (*figure* 101).

4. THE PETTICOAT

During the pre-war years the Princess petticoat was in high favour, that of crêpe de Chine being recommended as 'a chic allurement.' For the modes of 1911 'the Princess petticoat is absolutely indispensable,' often with wide border of broderie anglaise surmounted by rows of insertion. As the skirt narrowed the petticoat became almost tubular; some, however, preserved accordion pleating from the knee level.

With the wider skirts of 1915 and 1916, the garment had a brief return of its ancient glory. Yoked and fitting close at the hips, it

---

[1] *The Lady.*   [2] Fashion journal.
[3] Information kindly supplied by Messrs. Warner Brothers.

FIG. 102. (*left*) CORSET WITH SHOULDER STRAPS AND SUSPENDERS, 1918; (*right*) BOUDOIR CAP AND LINGERIE, 1918

became wide at the hem and much flounced and frilled. 'The petticoat is a truly exuberant tempestuous affair' (1916). 'Not a few are set out with a line or two of wire,' and there were fears of the crinoline returning in the midst of a world war.

Washing silk was a popular material, or 'the new petticoat in triple ninon, knife pleated with picot edges and finished with ruching, 29/6,' while some were made with detachable frills of moirette, taffeta, etc. 'Some petticoats are cut with a flare, others triangular, some almost equilateral triangle in shape, to give the required swish of the present fashion.'[1] When made of taffeta 'the frou-frou of silk skirts is heard once more in the land' (*figure* 103).

'How our grandmothers would have wondered could they have seen the underwear of the present day, so gossamer. . . . Some people in mourning wear black underwear made of thin black batiste.' Suitable, no doubt, for merry widows.

The grim realism of 1917 and 1918 sobered the petticoat to a simpler form, and by the end of the war it had lengthened slightly with a straight-hanging flounce. 'White cambric petticoat with under flounce, prettily trimmed with Valenciennes, and insertion, embroidery and threaded ribbon, 15/11.' (Summer, 1918.)[2]

5. THE BRASSIÈRE

This appeared under that name in 1916—'the new undergarment which takes the place of the old-fashioned camisole.' 'Gowns of utmost softness and semi-transparency have made a bust support essential' (1916). 'The French and American women all wear them and so must we; a modiste will insist on a brassière to support the figure and give it the proper up-to-date shape.'[3]

6. THE CHEMI-KNICKERS

In 1917 appeared 'the new underslip, worn over the corset, helping to reduce the number of undergarments; a button and loop can be put at the lowest hem to catch the skirt together in divided skirt fashion.'[4] The garment speedily became known as the 'cami-knickers.'

7. THE KNICKERS

Of two types—the French, with wide frilled legs (*figure* 106); and the close-fitting directoire type, often of woven materials. These

[1] *The Lady*, 1916   [2] *The Lady*.   [3] *The Queen*, 1916.   [4] *The Lady*.

FIG. 103. UNDERSKIRT, 1916

were sometimes known as 'culottes,' e.g., 'fine stockinette culottes with ribbon bow at the knee and elastic at waist and knee, 3/3' (1911), which appealed to those who preferred to be clad in French words.

In 1913 'the tango and the peg-top fashion between them are

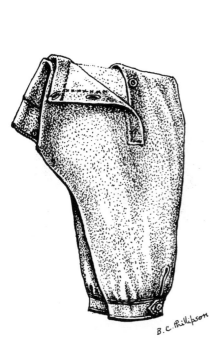

FIG. 104. FLEECY-LINED KNICKER.
MORLEY, 1912

FIG. 105. 'SHOT' KNICKER.
MORLEY, 1912

responsible for a completely new form of skirt-knickers. The characteristic of the new garment is that it is formed entirely of one length of material falling from the waist in front to the knees, and up again to the waist at the back, with slits at the sides for the legs.'[1]

With the wider skirts of 1915 'some petticoats are divided into two wide legs and covered with frilling.' 'Skirt knickers trimmed with Valenciennes, 15/–' were announced in 1915.

[1] *The Lady.*

FIG. 106. (*left to right*) COMBINATIONS AND PYJAMAS, 1918; CHEMISE AND DRAWERS, 1918; CAMISOLE AND PETTICOAT, 1918

9. NIGHTCLOTHES

The pre-war years saw the nightdress in the Empire style continuing, the top trimmed with insertion and lace;[1] others were

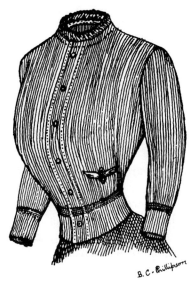

FIG. 107. MERINO FINISH SPENCER. MORLEY, 1912

made with a yoke, the neck square, or round, often with Peter
Pan collar, and with long sleeves frilled at the wrist. In the
'romantic' war years 'low-necked nightgowns with short sleeves are
an extravagant necessity of the hour. Some are absolutely sleeveless'
(1916).

But the pyjama suit was a growing rival. 'In response to a steadily
growing demand' 'pyjama suits in pure zephyr at 7/6 or in silk at
27/6, the jacket fastened with brandenburgs' (1912). War conditions
hastened the change.

Certain less fashionable undergarments, but none the less very
frequently worn, were the woollen vest and the knitted spencer;
these had persisted from early Victorian days among those for whom
extra warmth in winter seemed even more important than following
the increasingly chilly footsteps of fashion.

[1] 'Nightgowns of nun's veiling, square-cut neck and lace insertion, elbow sleeves,
ribbon bows.'—*The Lady*, 1912.

XIII

1919—1939

THE period between the two Great Wars was remarkable for a new attitude of mind towards the function of clothing, and especially towards that of underclothing. It is sometimes assumed that this was but repeating the experience of the Napoleonic wars, when there was an extraordinary reduction in the amount of underclothing worn by women. The resemblance, however, is misleading. Then the aim of costume was to emphasize the bodily shape—in the case of women by flimsy clinging dresses and of men by tight breeches; there was very little actual exposure of the skin. The conspicuous intention was to outline the regions normally sex attractive. But in the period from 1919 onwards it was the actual surface of the body which was to be exploited.

A kind of 'skin worship' became almost a new religion. Devotees tanned their bodies by sunlight, real or artificial, or by stains; women improved their faces by paints, lotions, and skin foods containing —it was hoped—the latest hormones, to say nothing of powders of every conceivable shade. To concentrate attention on the face they cut off their hair and tore out their eyebrows. It was accompanied by an outlook and habits essentially juvenile, and the juvenile shape of body became the feminine ideal, described enthusiastically by a fashion writer as 'such enchanting, sexless, bosomless, hipless, thighless creatures.' It was the glorification of youth.

Several factors contributed to this curious phase. The first war released, like a genie from its bottle, an aggressive spirit opposed to the symbols of class distinction in costume, and there is, after all, no more thoroughly democratic fabric than bare skin, which is entirely free from evidence of class. There was, too, the desire to strip off conventional trammels, especially those associated with the previous generation responsible for the war. A popular longing to return to 'the simple life' is not uncommon when civilization has got into a thorough mess. What more desperate resource than a nudity camp?

The majority of both sexes, however, were content with degrees of denudation, underclothes being reduced in number, extent and thickness. Men shortened their pants into trunks, and 'fight shy of woollen undergarments, at any rate the younger men' (*The Tailor and Cutter*, 1929). The American influence on men's underwear became very noticeable with the gradual introduction of the singlet in place of the buttoned vest and the union combination garment instead of separate vest and drawers, together with the preference for thin materials such as artificial silk. Women's undergarments shrank until a brassière and short panties under a dance frock were considered adequate.

As a result a considerable area of skin was, in both sexes, merely covered by a single layer of fabric—the dress or the suit, as the case might be. Obviously underclothing had lost two of its original functions; it no longer preserved the warmth of the body, nor did it disguise its essential shape. Formerly it would have been thought necessary to have a layer of washable material covering the skin, but perhaps the 'hot bath' habit, becoming so general after the first war, was thought a sufficient substitute, together with the modern development of dry cleaning of clothes. It seems that the skin itself had become less sensitive to changes of external temperature, and more sensitive to contact with textiles which had therefore to be as smooth as possible. For this nothing was more suitable than artificial silk, which had become available to all.

To regard this widespread reduction in the amount of underclothes as primarily erotic in purpose is, we think, to misinterpret the evidence. It is surely significant that in the 1920's young women were at great pains to obliterate the breasts and to reduce the feminine shape of the hips by excessive slimming; while the actual regions which were exposed bare by day were the arms, and the legs below the knee, a kind of display very characteristic of childhood, but which has only slight sex appeal.

Nevertheless, however attenuated feminine underclothing became, it preserved—and still preserves—its old erotic association of ideas.

Undies are not made unimportant by being called 'amusing,' and their importance has become insisted upon by a very significant change affecting, indeed, the underclothes of men as well. It is not the reduction in *amount* but the taste for *colours* that expresses the erotic impulse. Both sexes have discarded the use of white underwear. For centuries 'white' had been recognized as a symbol of the chaste 'pure mind'; it has no emotional tone. It represents the antithesis of erotic colours. That it should have fallen into dissuetude after the first war when there was a marked relaxation of sexual inhibitions is more than a coincidence. The instinctive desire for coloured undergarments was, of course, given a wider scope by the improved methods of dyeing washable fabrics following the war, but the supply was produced by the demand. And the demand meant that underclothes, both for men and women, should be given an emotional background. This was certainly not a move in the direction of making them more 'rational.' Nightwear showed a similar impulse. A girl, we may suppose, was cheered by the thought that beneath her workaday attire she looked 'a perfect peach' in peach-coloured undies, and the bachelor, in pyjamas striped like a tiger, would feel that he, too, in certain circumstances, could simulate a beast of prey.

In the art of costume the use of a brilliant colour always implies a wish—often unconscious—that the garment may be seen and admired; for it to be seen only by the wearer scarcely satisfies the instinct for arresting colours. To say, then, that the taste for these gladsome undergarments was essentially erotic is but to agree that under the surface of a drab world the pulse of Nature was beating hopefully as ever—

> . . . and all unseen
> Romance brought up the Nine-fifteen.

∽ MEN ∽

In the early days after the war was over the first impulse was to try to forget it; for a few years attempts were made to revive the distinguishing marks of the gentleman as they had been just before the vulgar disturbance of 1914–18. Starch had been the gentleman's best friend, but now it failed to restore the *status quo ante*, and by 1928 that popular leader of fashion, the Prince of Wales, publicly condemned 'the boiled shirt' of his ancestors. His personal taste for somewhat garish colours in dress was in the new spirit, and encouraged the break with tradition. He helped to establish the modes of the common man.

I. THE SHIRT

(a) For Day Wear

Although for formal wear the white shirt with starched front and cuffs persisted through the 1920's, it was equally correct to wear with a morning coat a striped shirt with white collar, usually winged, and a bow tie or sailor knot; with the lounge suit, a coloured shirt with double collar. 'Coloured collars to match the shirt are no longer fashionable. The correct shirt for the newly popular white collar should be of some light shade of taffeta or Oxford shirting, with a heavy silk tie of some fairly bright hue, patterned or spotted'[1] (1925).

The next year we are told, 'since white shirts practically disappeared except for formal and evening wear, there is tremendous scope in colour—putty shades, cedars, blue-greys, peach tones . . . ,' and 'coloured collars to match are going strong' (*The Tailor and Cutter*, 1926). 'The new soft collars with detachable supports are a great advance on the sloppy silk ones of a year or two ago.'

The white and the coloured collar were social symbols, each struggling to come to the front in a neck-and-neck race, aided by characteristic ties. 'Reptile ties are so realistic as to be truly startling,' and were shunned by those of sensitive taste. 'A revival of the Ascot would be welcome. It makes a good-looking man handsome and an ordinary man distinguished' (1926).

By now, for formal wear, a striped shirt, winged or double collar, with Ascot bow or knot tie was correct, while for other occasions a striped or coloured shirt, double collar and dark tie were usual. The knitted tie was popular, but not to be worn with a winged collar. During the next four years the Ascot, either as a crossover cravat held in place by a pin, or the broad wrap-over almost filling the V above the waistcoat, effected a brief come-back for formal morning dress, while the informal tie broke out into strongly marked 'fancy' stripes, in which the common man asserted himself in a noisy fashion.

For 'sports,' such as golf, a coloured flannel shirt with soft collar, pinned, could be worn; for weddings the plain white shirt and

[1] *The Tailor and Cutter.*

collar; and for funerals the white shirt with black stripes (and, of course, black tie) was required as late as 1926.

Conventional restraints relaxed as the next decade opened. 'A well-defined tendency is for ties, collars and shirts, worn with morning coats, to display more colour' (*The Tailor and Cutter*, 1929).

Pale blue shirts with morning suits, and shirts of poplin, silk, tussore, and striped zephyrs, with stiff collars to match, worn with open-end neckties of striped foulard became fashionable. And when at Ascot there were seen blue-striped, pink-striped and plain blue shirts and collars, with lavender and blue ties, it was evident that the white shirt for day wear was not only 'dead but damned.' Yet although the collar was usually the colour of the shirt, and often striped, white collars persisted. One firm was showing 'over twenty distinct and separate styles of white stiff collars' (1929)—usually of the double form with pointed fronts. Evidently not all men were willing to move with the times.

Meanwhile the 'tennis shirt' was providing a wide choice of materials—white, matt and cream cotton taffeta, union flannel, twills, silks and lustre weave.

The 1930's saw an increasing preference for the coloured shirt, made with or without attached collar,[1] in silk, taffeta, crêpe and wool taffeta, while collars of the Van Heusen[2] make also became popular. The day-shirt made in the coat style was becoming very general. This form, borrowed from America, enabled the garment to be put on without disarranging the carefully arranged hair-wave or disturbing its buttery surface.

(b)   The Dress-Shirt

Soon after the war the front with two studs became the settled mode, in spite of the Prince of Wales's adoption, in 1926, of the single stud. At the same time the shirt of marcella or piqué with plain semi-stiff double cuffs, or the shirt with pleated front, captured popular taste. The latter, for some reason, might not be worn with dinner jackets.

---

[1] Shirts with attached collars returned to favour about 1933.

[2] The Van Heusen collar, an American invention, came here in 1922. Its fabric is woven on the curve, thus ensuring a better fit; the fold line, instead of being an extra piece of material, is actually woven into the collar, the material itself being multi-ply cloth, giving extra strength. (From information kindly supplied by the editor of *The Outfitter*.)

The winged collar, with wider wings, was worn, with a bow tie of the 'thistle type,' that is, with the ends expanding (*figure* 108).[1]

The stiff front became narrower by 1928, when the soft-fronted shirt became permissible with the dinner jacket. The pleated front had but a short life; the laundry saw to that. And the 1930's found the double collar creeping into use, at least with the dinner jacket, while the fancy materials declined in favour.

(c) *The Sports Shirt*

A novelty of the late 1920's was the combination shirt, of cotton or wool taffeta; the upper part in shirt form with turn-down collar, continued below into knee-length trunks.

2. THE COMBINATION

This garment, derived from America, became increasingly popular after the war, so that by 1929 'a more general adoption of

FIG. 1c8. MAN'S EVENING DRESS-SHIRT, WITH MARCELLA FRONT. AUSTIN REED LTD., 1938

the combination of one-piece suit for underwear in place of a vest and pants' (*The Tailor and Cutter*, 1929) was noted. At first it was mainly for summer wear, in white gauze, merino, Aertex cellular, or natural wool (from a list of 1927)', and was made with 'half sleeves, pant legs, short legs or knicker legs,' but it soon appeared in heavy woollens for winter. The garment tended to become sleeveless, with a V neck and with short trunk legs, even for winter wear.

---

[1] The correct wear (1937) for full evening dress:—White shirt with starched front, one or two studs; starched single cuffs, square cut. Plain gold or pearl links and studs.

With dinner jacket, a soft-fronted piqué shirt permissible, with double cuffs and polo collar. Black tie.

For both, the tie in narrow knot with wide ends.

(From information supplied by Messrs. Austin Reed Ltd.)

FIG. 109. (*left to right*) SINGLET AND SHORTS. JAEGER, 1935–6; MAN'S UNIT-SUIT. JAEGER, 1936–7; MAN'S PYJAMAS. JAEGER, 1929–30

3. SHORTS AND TRUNKS

These, made with Lastex waistbands, became very generally worn in the 1930's.[1]

4. THE SINGLET

Some with jersey necks and quarter sleeves, and others with low neck and sleeveless, were in the 1930's displacing the vest.

5. THE VEST, DRAWERS AND KNICKER-DRAWERS

These still continued to find favour with many, and were more or less on the old models.

Although the above undergarments were very commonly in natural colours, there was a growing taste for something more exhilarating. 'The cult of colour in gentlemen's outfitting grows

[1] In 1938 'jockey shorts' (manufactured under licence by Lyle & Scott, Ltd.), and also cut-sewn shorts in poplin, appeared.

apace' (1929), and we learn of 'even undervests, drawers, and combinations in salmon pink, sky blue, light fawn, peach, etc.' (1929),
in fabrics formerly reserved for feminine underwear.

6. PYJAMAS

These were in fabrics of lighter weight than formerly, and of a
wider choice of materials; silk, artificial silk, cotton mixtures
mercerized to give a smooth surface, with damasked patterns and
coloured designs. By the 1930's they had become man's gayest
garment, except for his dressing-gown (*figure* 109). The practice, which
arose after the war, of pottering about the house in pyjamas and of
both sexes seeing each other strolling to the bathroom, entirely
destroyed the ancient association of nightwear and strict privacy.
After all, this was but a return to the idea of the eighteenth-century
'nightgown,' which had been a kind of informal negligée.

We find that trade catalogues were still listing 'gentlemen's
nightgowns,' reaching the ankle, as late as 1930.

∽ WOMEN ∽

No period in history has presented a greater variety of underclothes, and though so much reduced in bulk, they developed a new
importance and complexity. Familiar names were attached to novel
shapes, and new names to old; composite garments of two or more
parts came and went; items hitherto belonging to the other sex
appeared in feminine guise, with, perhaps, titles jocular or slangy.
The practice of rival manufacturers attaching distinctive trade names
to models not otherwise distinguishable, added to the confusion.
In time to come students of costume, poring over this period, may
well find it the most baffling of any. The task of clarifying is difficult,
and it has seemed better to rely largely on contemporary descriptions,
together with some prices.

Of the many materials employed artificial silk in various forms
predominated, and this was available for all classes. It is also
interesting to note that after the first World War, 'Government
Balloon fabric, for lingerie, men's shirts and pyjamas, 3/– a yard,'
was advertised in 1920.

The garments may be divided under two headings, Single and
Composite.

A. Single

1. THE CHEMISE

Becoming 'the vest,' in 1924, though surviving under its original name until the end of the period. Samples of different dates indicate prices:—

'Lawn chemise and knickers, handmade and tucked, Valenciennes lace and ribbon,' 10/6 each (1919).

Milanese silk chemises, 52/6 (1920).

'The latest backless chemise for evening, in triple ninon and lace, from 35/–' (1926).

The chemi-vest, in art silk, 31 in. long (1928).

'Chemise in silk suzette or chiffon, 18/9' (1938).

2. THE UNDER-VEST

Usually of wool, was an unfashionable garment, but nevertheless worn by many, and appearing in trade catalogues throughout the period. Some were also made in a mixture of silk and wool, for example: 'Milanese silk vest, 15/9' (1924). 'Spun silk vest, 21/9' (1936).

3. COMBINATIONS

A close-fitting woven garment, becoming almost 'tights' during the 1930's.

Merino combinations, short sleeves, 9/11 (1919). Milanese silk combinations edged with lace, in pink or white, 78/6 (Dickins & Jones) (1920). Silk and wool combinations (1932). Combination tights with lace tops; Lastex at waist and knee (1935).

4. THE CAMISOLE

This disappeared as a separate garment towards the end of the 1920's. A late instance is 'For evening dress, camisole of satin beauté, fastening under the arm, trimmed with lace. In ivory, pink, apple, peach, apricot and cyclamen, 73/6' (1927).

5. THE BRASSIÈRE

Becoming known as the 'bra' in 1937. This developed from the bust bodice, and in the 1920's became very tight, compressing the breasts to produce the straight, shapeless form then fashionable

FIG. 110. *(left)* BRASSIÈRE AND DRAWERS, 1927; *(right)* CAMI-KNICKERS, 1926

FIG. III. CORSETS. ROYAL WORCESTER, 1921

(*figure* 110). By 1932 it had shortened considerably and was designed to separate and support the breasts.

'Long brassière in lace and embroidery, coming well over the corset' (1923). The 'no-shoulder strap brassière' (1926). 'Elastic pull-on brassière' (1929).

6. THE CORSET

'Corsets of woven porous elastic, 16 in. deep, 5 guineas' (1923). Wrap-around rubber corsets to compress the buttocks. Rubber corsets with broché panels lacing below the busk, 29/6 (1925). 'Corsets to produce a slenderizing effect on the figure' (1928). 'Corsets define the hips and normal waistline; the waistline of the corset is slightly higher than last year, dipping at the centre of the back.' 'The bust is never compressed or flattened.' 'Low-backed corsets with up-lift brassière, long enough to grip the hips and thighs tightly' (1931).

7. THE BELT

This was a substitute for the corset, which varied from abdominal supports to light suspender belts with or without bones. Some were made of elastic only, and became known as 'roll-ons,' whereas those with a zip fastening were called 'step-ins.' In 1932 the two-way stretch material was introduced by Messrs. Warner Brothers. This was made of Lastex (*figure* 114), a fine elastic thread which could be woven into a fabric. These two-way stretch belts were hailed with enthusiasm, as they gave the wearer perfect freedom of movement without any 'riding-up.'

'Long belt in thread and silk cut low at the back for evening, with elastic top forming brassière, 5 guineas' (1929).

At a mannequin parade in 1933 'each glided past with her suspenders as apparent under her skin-tight skirt as if she were wearing them outside. In many cases the line of her belt was visible.'

'Step-in belt, 14 in. deep, with zip side fastening' (1937).

FIG. 112. BATHING CORSET, 1922

8. KNICKERS

The so-called French drawers with open legs, and the closed directoire knickers persisted throughout the period, though the latter tended to become unfashionable. By 1924 knickers became shortened into 'panties,' and then to 'trunks' in 1930, finally becoming 'pantie briefs,' for sports costume, near the end of the period.

'Woven knickers, various colours, 5/3' (1919). 'Crêpe de Chine knickers, closed shape, elastic waist, 23/6' (1920). Lingerie with coloured hem, e.g. tangerine or lemon, advertised in 1920; and underwear figured with designs of birds and flowers, e.g. black owls embroidered on lawn, in 1921.

'The creaseless perfection can only be acquired by wearing a minimum of clothing beneath. What would our grandmothers have thought of limiting them, with evening dress, to a pair of panties?'[1] (1924). And in 1926 'although the smart world has become accustomed to seeing practically all of a stocking it still considers the knicker an intimate garment.'[1] (In practice, however, strangers sitting opposite would freely exchange such intimacies—in dumb show.) By 1927 knickers were well above the knee. 'Georgette knickers in lovely evening shades, 35/9' (1927). In 1930, 'with the heavier materials for evening dress no petticoat slip is worn. With the very short skirt, knickers confined at the knee were necessary, but now that skirts are longer and slimness just as much admired, the best type of knicker (often yoked) fits close to the leg and ends at the knee without gathers, or if of silk tricot, in a garter band. For sports wear, tricot knickers very like trunks, of the same material as the sports skirt.'[2]

Fine wool vest and knickers. All-wool vest and panties for sports (1932). Very small knickers with elastic net sides, and suspenders hidden under frothy frills. Triangular knickers of pink crêpe chiffon, cream needle-run lace and plissé frills. Tailored panties (1934). For sports, pantie trunks and pantie briefs. Ribbed knicker-briefs (1939).

9. THE PETTICOAT

The original form, attached from the waist, became rare until revived for evening wear at the close of the period, and was replaced by the Princess petticoat, which became known, after the first war, as a 'Princess slip,' and presently as a 'slip.' They varied greatly in design and material, as will be seen.

'Crêpe de Chine petticoat, elastic at waist, 23/6. Striped moirette petticoat, brown, blue or green, 12/6. Soft silk satin petticoat, scalloped at edge, with pleating, 29/6' (1920).

'Princess petticoats with vandyked edge, knee length; or with three

[1] *Vogue.*   [2] *The Lady.*

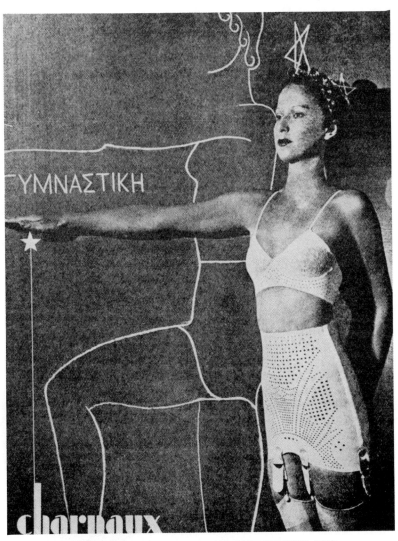

FIG. 113. CHARNAUX CORSET BELT AND CASLIS BRASSIERE, 1933

FIG. 114. THE TWO-WAY STRETCH CORSET AND BRASSIÈRE. WARNER BROS. (CORSETS) LTD.,
1933

rows of petal flounces; in black, navy, flame, castor, 35/9 (1921).
'Fashion denies us petticoats or any underwear that's not of the
flimsiest materials' (1922). 'Princess petticoat in silk milanese,
waistline held in with elastic; length from shoulder 48–51 in.;

FIG. 115. (*left to right*) 'FRILLIES FOR THE TINY LADY'—WAIST PETTICOAT, CAMISOLE AND
KNICKERS, 1939; COMBINATIONS IN SILK AND MERINO, 1934; NIGHTDRESS IN ALL-
SILK SATIN, 1939

shoulder straps' (1923). 'Princess petticoat, round neck, 31–33 in.
long, of georgette, crêpe de Chine, or silk' (1924).

Princess slips with vandyked hem (1927).

'Slips are shaped like the frock, and fit the natural waist. The
straight sacklike slip is wrong. Slips may have brassière top and a
shaped band at the waist to which knickers are attached, thus combining the three garments (especially for evening). Of tricot and
washing satin.' Underslips of heavy silk crêpe in peach or pink, or of
flowered crêpe de Chine, for day; black for black evening frock (1930).
A rustling petticoat was often worn under an evening crinoline dress

in 1931. 'It is important in this season of revealing lines to have a slip that fits like the paper on the wall' (1932).

10. THE KNITTED SPENCER

This was an unfashionable garment, but frequently worn for warmth.

B. COMPOSITE

During this period there was an extraordinary outburst of combination garments, various comprehensive names for which appeared in the trade catalogues. Examples of some of these will be given under their appropriate headings.

1. THE CORSELETTE

A combination of corset and brassière, appearing first in America in 1921, and followed a year later by the 'underbelt corselette,' with added belt for extra abdominal support. This was also known as the 'foundation garment.'

Subsequent variations, with additions, were produced, such as:—

The Corslo-silhouette, a combination of bust bodice, hip belt, jupon and pantalon; of satin (1923).

The Corslo-pantalon-chemise, knickers, corset and camisole in one, with suspenders attached on the inner side (1923).

Corset, bust bodice, detachable knickers and petticoat, stepped into and fastened behind, for evening wear, 'ensures perfect control' (1925).

The combined bodice and hip belt (1929).

' "Scanties" are slim-fitting knickers to replace panties and belt, under beach dress or shorts' (1934). A similar garment is also referred to later as 'pantie trunks,' 'pantie briefs,' and another variation was Charneaux's pantie-belt.

2. CAMI-KNICKERS

Formed by uniting camisole and knickers; occasionally called 'chemise-knickers.' They were at first referred to as 'step-ins,' a term later applied to elastic belts with zipped side fastening. Cami-combinations (1919) was another version.

'Cami-knickers in crêpe de Chine, the skirt falling in points from elastic at the side of the waist' (1922). 'Cami-knickers, step-in, with yoke and shoulder straps; petal skirt' (1923). For evening, with back décolletage, cami-knickers of ninon with apron-front, and backless. Cami-knickers in triple ninon, pleated for the bodice, lace trimmed and hem-stitched, with vandyked edge, 49/6 (1924).

'The tailored maid wears a tailored silk chemise step-in, peach-coloured with orchid folds at the hips; or a silk vest with net yoke and straps, and French drawers'[1] (1925).

'Apricot crêpe de Chine cami-knickers with wide lace yoke; lace trims the knickers and flounce of the skirt which is finely pleated on each side'[2] (1927).

'It is almost impossible to imagine anything more fascinating that the lingerie of to-day. The cami-knicker at its best is a thing of sheer delight in peach-coloured georgette'[3] (*figure* 117) (1928).

'The popular cami-comb. in artificial silk, peach, beige, green, cyclamen or black, 14/11' (1928).

'New suspender cami-knickers in crêpe de Chine, with attached suspenders' (1929).

'Modern cami-knickers conform to the contours of the figure.' 'The slightest lump will betray itself; if you eat a grape it will show; the one-piece garment is the only solution'[1] (1932). 'Enchanting and deliciously feminine cami-knickers in crêpe suzette or satin, of sheath-like fit, pink or peach, 21/9'[2] (1938).

FIG. 116.
CAMI-KNICKERS IN
CRÊPE-DE-CHINE,
1922

3. CAMI-BOCKERS

Comprising camisole and closed directoire knickers. The 'bocker' usually fastened behind with three buttons at the waist, the sides of the flap being closed by 'poppers' (press studs).

'Cami-bockers, two-piece; opera top with shoulder straps. Leg buttons at side; double gusset at fork of pleated knicker. Elastic at knee' (1927).

'Low-backed cami-bocker in rayon; directoire knickers and shoulder straps; in peach, mauve, pink or black, etc., 21/9' (1930). 'Cami-bocker in ladderless rayon, tight fitting lace bodice, 21/9' (1930).

[1] *Vogue.*   [2] Advertisement.   [3] *Eve.*

FIG. 117. WOMAN'S CAMI-KNICKERS IN GEORGETTE. STEINMANN, 1928

Other composite garments were 'skirt-knickers,' 'knicker-petti-coats,' and 'trouser-skirts,' chiefly worn during the second half of the 1920's.

NIGHTCLOTHES

The nightgear between the wars reflected the spirit of the dress of the period. The increasing preference for pyjamas, often tailored, and the frank display of regions of the body which formerly had been so carefully concealed, was characteristic. While the nightdress tended to preserve its traditional qualities the pyjamas, still some-what of a novelty, encouraged many experimental forms. The waistless dress of the late twenties and its emphasis on the boyish figure was echoed in the nightgear, with a vogue for jumper pyjamas and tunic tops which disguised the feminine shape and were not unlike the schoolboy's.

With the growing femininity of the thirties, erotic styles developed to a marked degree. The bias cut of the evening dress was imitated in the nightdress so as to fit the outlines of the body; and the low neck and gaping sides would reveal what was otherwise concealed by semi-transparent materials. With these an additional garment, in the form of a short coat or bolero, became a necessity. One notes, too, that the skirt of the nightgown was lengthened and expanded, often with godet pleats, imitating the design of the evening dress.

At the same time the ill-defined low waistline of the twenties changed in the next decade to a high-waisted Empire style. The somewhat masculine pyjama trousers, previously with narrow legs, now expanded from the knee down so as to simulate, when standing, the outlines of a skirt.

Towards the close of the epoch, however, the threat of war intro-duced a more serious note, and the tailored pyjamas and nightdress with long coats worn over them seemed to presage the possibility of sudden air raids and a dash to the shelter. Even so the more glam-ourous modes were still in demand and continued to function.

The colours employed throughout the epoch were very various, of every shade that might catch the eye; white, however, was con-spicuously absent.

The materials were varieties of artificial washing silk and satin, crêpe de Chine, locknit, shantung and occasionally voile. Trimmings, a noticeable feminine addition in the thirties, were commonly ecru lace, or Valenciennes.

FIG. 118. (*left*) WOMAN'S LUVISCA PYJAMAS, 1924: (*centre and right*) PYJAMAS, 1927

The boudoir cap of the Edwardian period had a revival in the twenties, being then used to protect the shingled hair; the shape of the cap was beehive, of ribbon and lace. Later, in the thirties, as the hair-style changed, it became little more than an elaborate hair net worn on the back of the head.

The following examples, selected from contemporary sources, give an indication of these various changes:—

1920. Jumper pyjamas in crêpe de Chine, 89/–.

1922. Nightgowns with immensely wide sleeves, so as to reveal the body.

1923. Nightdresses, with or without waist ribbon; round or square neck. Sleeves, wing or bell opening, or straps across the upper arm. Deep side opening. Pyjamas with Peter Pan collar or jumper top.

1927. The nightdress with high-waisted lace top was the mode, and some were smocked. Kimono sleeves were popular. Some with V neck and sleeveless. 'Sunset-shade crêpe de Chine nightdress with lace top and shoulder sleeves' would be suitable for a trousseau, while the colours favoured are indicated in the advertisement of 'crêpe de Chine nightgown in Madonna blue, cowslip yellow, turquoise, lilac, melon, tulip-leaf green, coral and rose' at 29/6.

Pyjamas were often tailored, with tunic top, sleeveless or with long close sleeves; the legs somewhat narrow.

The three-piece pyjamas had a short straight coat, as in 'suit in satin beauté, 6½ guineas.'

Lace-wool pyjamas, for greater warmth, were for winter wear.

1928. Pyjamas of a more picturesque nature, and made from patterned materials, indicated a decline of the merely boyish type. Some with jumper top and sleeveless were in floral-patterned crêpe de Chine or in check materials. The V neck was popular.

Something more bizarre was the 'engineer's overall pyjamas in satin and check georgette; an all-in-one suit buttoning down the front, pocket on the leg, shoulder straps.'

1930. The Empire nightgown with little jacket returned to favour.

1931. The design of pyjamas underwent an important change. In place of the tunic top a tucked-in blouse, sleeveless, was worn with trousers immensely wide in the leg and with a flat band across the top of the front.

1933. By now the nightdress, following the mode of the dress, was cut on the bias so as to fit the body more closely, the lower part of its skirt expanding to a great width at the hem, often in godet pleats, sweeping the ground. Many were cut in panels and shaped at the waist. Being often of transparent materials such as mousselaine and lace a sleeveless lace bolero was provided. We read that 'a nightgown of flowered chiffon, with cowl neck, cut on the cross, almost backless, ribbon sash, is a very seducer of stout hearts.'[1]

Pyjamas, with tucked-in jumper tops and short shoulder sleeves, had much narrower trouser legs.

1936. The V neck or square décolletage, and often almost backless nightdress had, as alternative, the two-piece garment in locknit; we find advertised the 'one-piece pyjama-nightie with cross-over front to tie behind, in de lustre locknit, 23/6.'

1937. The 'new coat nightdress, wrapping across and fastened at

[1] *The Bystander.*

the waist,' with V neck, short sleeves and edging of lace, was the chief novelty. Cowl necks and high waists were fashionable. Many were sleeveless.

For travelling 'nightie-pyjamas with lounge wrapper in shantung, the wrapper zips slantwise' introduced the zip fastening to nightwear. The wide-legged pyjamas were still in demand rivalling the narrower type.

1938. The Empire waist was fashionable for nightdresses and many continued in the exotic style, such as 'diaphanous in spirit nightgown, in muted pastel colours, 29/6,' while 'for sweet dreams a maize georgette nightgown, pin-tucked with ecru lace shoulders and sleeves, at 95/–' seems quite suitable.

Others, more conscious perhaps of the approach of war, were turning towards more practical styles.

1939 saw the addition of long coats to nightdresses and to man-tailored pyjamas, both of which now usually had long sleeves. Frequently the pyjama leg was drawn in above the ankle, frilling out below in the mode suggested for defence against gas attack. And as glamour faded from the darkening world the shadow of the siren suit gave the shape of things to come.

EPILOGUE

FROM the foregoing account it will be seen that the history of underclothes has presented a number of curious features, reflecting, sometimes even more clearly than the surface garments, those potent forces which affect social life. In the process of rationalization the undergarments of both sexes have now almost completely discarded evidence of class distinction; what still lingers is the eroticism associated with women's, which had developed slowly until it became so significant during the period of Victorian prudery.

The first stage of psychological release from the thraldom of an inanimate symbol is the recognition of its essential absurdity; women have long considered men's underwear as plain prose, but think of their own as poetical. To men those garments may be 'amusing,' but not yet ridiculous. Did we not read in the war of a bomber crew's mascot—a pair of 'cami-knicks'—symbol of England, home and beauty?

Posterity may wonder how the feminine movement towards nudity, which was such a feature in the late 1920's and early 1930's, was regarded by men. Mr. Bernard Shaw expressed the opinion that 'women have taken a very large step towards nudity, and sex appeal has vanished. Bring back clothes and it would be increased' (1929).

The average masculine judgment may be culled from *The Tailor and Cutter* of that year. 'Never has been seen such an exhibition of feminine limbs as at present. Not all agree that the lifting of the curtain has increased their advantages or added to their charm; better for women if their limbs were wrapped in mystery. The sights that are thrust upon the sons of men are enough to stifle young love and drive romance shuddering away. It was the practice once for young women only to show the best sides of themselves to their lovers.'

We have to reconcile this masculine view with that of a feminine critic in 1935 who remarked 'Nudity is the new hue and cry in fashions. Bodies are just bodies now.'

We have refrained from tracing the history of underclothes down to the present day, partly because it is difficult to view recent fashions in their true perspective, and partly because the second World War seemed to close a chapter of this subject. For some ten years fashion was paralysed. Men and women wore whatever they happened to have, or could get or construct from the oddest sources. Men were shorn of their shirt-tails, and for women the term 'black-out materials for sitting rooms' often had a hidden meaning.

To-day, when a revolution in underclothes seems imminent, it would be more proper to let some future historian pick up the broken threads. From America comes the new synthetic fabric, nylon, possessing the character of being silk-like, easily washable and drying in an hour or so without the need of ironing. Garments made of it can be washed overnight and are ready to wear next morning. And now there are rumours of yet another American invention, the fabric 'orlon,' which has the additional attraction of being waterproof. We understand that both fabrics are likely to become reasonably priced before long, when, presumably, some such material will be the staple for all undergarments of both sexes. Presently we shall all be washing our underwear as easily as we wash our bodies, if indeed we don't have washable cellulose suits and dresses, and underclothing is dispensed with entirely.

Already we are learning from American ingenuity to abandon useless and obsolete traditions which have controlled the design of underwear for so long, and to require in their place greater comfort and convenience. It seems we must look westward for new ideas, and as Canning did after the Napoleonic wars, call the new world to re-dress the old.

BIBLIOGRAPHY

PRIMARY SOURCES

Medieval miniatures and effigies; contemporary poetry, drama, fiction and diaries, the authors of which are mentioned in the text.

Portraits and prints of the respective periods.

Numerous fashion journals of the nineteenth and twentieth centuries, such as *The Beau Monde*, *La Belle Assemblée*, *The World of Fashion*, *The Art of Tying the Cravat* (1828), *The Whole Art of Dress* (1830), *The Tailor and Cutter* (from 1869 to 1930), *The Queen*, *The Lady*, *The Gentlewoman*, *Vogue*, *Eve*, *The Lady's Realm*, *Harper's Bazaar*, etc.

Catalogues of the wholesale and retail firms mentioned under 'Acknowledgments.'

The collection of specimens in those museums similarly mentioned.

A number of old newspapers.

SECONDARY SOURCES

The works of Joseph Strutt, *Dress and Habits of the English; Manners and Customs of the English* (1796).

Fairholt's *Costume in England* (4th ed., 1909).

Shaw's *Dresses of the Middle Ages* (1843).

Planché's *Encyclopaedia of Costume* (1876).

Ernest Léoty's *Le Corset* (c. 1890).

Kelly and Schwabe's *Historic Costume* (2nd ed., 1927) and *History of Costume* (1931).

Leloir's *Histoire du Costume* (1935 *et seq.*).

Adrien Harmand's *Jeanne d'Arc, ses Costumes, son Armure* (Paris, 1929).

Linthicum's *Costume in Elizabethan Drama* (1936).

(To the two last-mentioned we are specially indebted.)

Eva Lundquist's *La Mode et son Vocabulaire* (Göteborg, 1950).

Katherine Esdaile's *The Life and Works of Louis François Roubiliac* (1928).

James Laver's *Taste and Fashion* (1937).

Wright's *Domestic Manners and Sentiment in the Middle Ages* (1862) and *History of Caricature in Art* (1865).

The works of John Ashton and W. C. Sydney on the social life of the seventeenth, eighteenth, and nineteenth centuries (1880 to 1890).

Numerous Memoirs and Lives.

APPENDIX

THE STURE SHIRTS

These famous shirts, four in number, now preserved at Uppsala Cathedral, Sweden, formed part of the clothing of the Sture family, Swedish aristocrats murdered in 1567.

The material is two-thread linen twill; the shirts consist of front-piece and back-piece joined across the shoulders and at the sides by seams. Two have high attached collars ornamented along the top with a plaited frill; the sleeves of one have cuffs similarly ornamented. Two have no collars or cuffs, but instead a broad band in the low neck-opening and at the wrist. These may possibly have been used as nightshirts.

FIG. 119. A STURE SHIRT, 1567

'The linen undergarment prior to about 1350 did not differ in cut from the upper garment, the tunic. When the tunic during the latter part of the fourteenth century was opened in front and provided with a collar, it is probable that the undergarment kept the shape of the old tunic. At the end of the fifteenth century it became fashionable with jackets cut low in front to show the shirt with its many folds and adornments. . . . At the close of the fifteenth century the sleeves had been drawn up towards the low neck and the slit had been moved to the side of the neck along the seam between the front piece and the sleeve. During the earlier half of the sixteenth century the low neck disappears, and high collars again come into fashion. It is in this phase of the evolution of the shirt that we have to place the Sture shirts, Nos. 1 and 2. They represent in relation to the medieval forms a new type with shoulder seam and narrow, reinforcing crosspiece.'

(Extract from *Livrustkammaren*, Vol. IV: 8–9. Stockholm.)

INDEX

A CATALOG OF SELECTED
DOVER BOOKS
IN ALL FIELDS OF INTEREST

A CATALOG OF SELECTED DOVER BOOKS IN ALL FIELDS OF INTEREST

CONCERNING THE SPIRITUAL IN ART, Wassily Kandinsky. Pioneering work by father of abstract art. Thoughts on color theory, nature of art. Analysis of earlier masters. 12 illustrations. 80pp. of text. 5⅜ x 8½. 23411-8 Pa. $4.95

ANIMALS: 1,419 Copyright-Free Illustrations of Mammals, Birds, Fish, Insects, etc., Jim Harter (ed.). Clear wood engravings present, in extremely lifelike poses, over 1,000 species of animals. One of the most extensive pictorial sourcebooks of its kind. Captions. Index. 284pp. 9 x 12. 23766-4 Pa. $14.95

CELTIC ART: The Methods of Construction, George Bain. Simple geometric techniques for making Celtic interlacements, spirals, Kells-type initials, animals, humans, etc. Over 500 illustrations. 160pp. 9 x 12. (USO) 22923-8 Pa. $9.95

AN ATLAS OF ANATOMY FOR ARTISTS, Fritz Schider. Most thorough reference work on art anatomy in the world. Hundreds of illustrations, including selections from works by Vesalius, Leonardo, Goya, Ingres, Michelangelo, others. 593 illustrations. 192pp. 7⅛ x 10¼. 20241-0 Pa. $9.95

CELTIC HAND STROKE-BY-STROKE (Irish Half-Uncial from "The Book of Kells"): An Arthur Baker Calligraphy Manual, Arthur Baker. Complete guide to creating each letter of the alphabet in distinctive Celtic manner. Covers hand position, strokes, pens, inks, paper, more. Illustrated. 48pp. 8¼ x 11. 24336-2 Pa. $3.95

EASY ORIGAMI, John Montroll. Charming collection of 32 projects (hat, cup, pelican, piano, swan, many more) specially designed for the novice origami hobbyist. Clearly illustrated easy-to-follow instructions insure that even beginning papercrafters will achieve successful results. 48pp. 8¼ x 11. 27298-2 Pa. $3.50

THE COMPLETE BOOK OF BIRDHOUSE CONSTRUCTION FOR WOOD-WORKERS, Scott D. Campbell. Detailed instructions, illustrations, tables. Also data on bird habitat and instinct patterns. Bibliography. 3 tables. 63 illustrations in 15 figures. 48pp. 5¼ x 8½. 24407-5 Pa. $2.50

BLOOMINGDALE'S ILLUSTRATED 1886 CATALOG: Fashions, Dry Goods and Housewares, Bloomingdale Brothers. Famed merchants' extremely rare catalog depicting about 1,700 products: clothing, housewares, firearms, dry goods, jewelry, more. Invaluable for dating, identifying vintage items. Also, copyright-free graphics for artists, designers. Co-published with Henry Ford Museum & Greenfield Village. 160pp. 8¼ x 11. 25780-0 Pa. $10.95

HISTORIC COSTUME IN PICTURES, Braun & Schneider. Over 1,450 costumed figures in clearly detailed engravings–from dawn of civilization to end of 19th century. Captions. Many folk costumes. 256pp. 8⅜ x 11¾. 23150-X Pa. $12.95

PIANO TUNING, J. Cree Fischer. Clearest, best book for beginner, amateur. Simple repairs, raising dropped notes, tuning by easy method of flattened fifths. No previous skills needed. 4 illustrations. 201pp. 5⅜ x 8½. 23267-0 Pa. $6.95

A SOURCE BOOK IN THEATRICAL HISTORY, A. M. Nagler. Contemporary observers on acting, directing, make-up, costuming, stage props, machinery, scene design, from Ancient Greece to Chekhov. 611pp. 5⅜ x 8½. 20515-0 Pa. $12.95

THE COMPLETE NONSENSE OF EDWARD LEAR, Edward Lear. All nonsense limericks, zany alphabets, Owl and Pussycat, songs, nonsense botany, etc., illustrated by Lear. Total of 320pp. 5⅜ x 8½. (USO) 20167-8 Pa. $7.95

VICTORIAN PARLOUR POETRY: An Annotated Anthology, Michael R. Turner. 117 gems by Longfellow, Tennyson, Browning, many lesser-known poets. "The Village Blacksmith," "Curfew Must Not Ring Tonight," "Only a Baby Small," dozens more, often difficult to find elsewhere. Index of poets, titles, first lines. xxiii + 325pp. 5⅜ x 8¼. 27044-0 Pa. $8.95

DUBLINERS, James Joyce. Fifteen stories offer vivid, tightly focused observations of the lives of Dublin's poorer classes. At least one, "The Dead," is considered a masterpiece. Reprinted complete and unabridged from standard edition. 160pp. 5$\frac{3}{16}$ x 8¼. 26870-5 Pa. $1.00

THE HAUNTED MONASTERY and THE CHINESE MAZE MURDERS, Robert van Gulik. Two full novels by van Gulik, set in 7th-century China, continue adventures of Judge Dee and his companions. An evil Taoist monastery, seemingly supernatural events; overgrown topiary maze hides strange crimes. 27 illustrations. 328pp. 5⅜ x 8½. 23502-5 Pa. $8.95

THE BOOK OF THE SACRED MAGIC OF ABRAMELIN THE MAGE, translated by S. MacGregor Mathers. Medieval manuscript of ceremonial magic. Basic document in Aleister Crowley, Golden Dawn groups. 268pp. 5⅜ x 8½. 23211-5 Pa. $9.95

NEW RUSSIAN-ENGLISH AND ENGLISH-RUSSIAN DICTIONARY, M. A. O'Brien. This is a remarkably handy Russian dictionary, containing a surprising amount of information, including over 70,000 entries. 366pp. 4½ x 6⅛. 20208-9 Pa. $9.95

HISTORIC HOMES OF THE AMERICAN PRESIDENTS, Second, Revised Edition, Irvin Haas. A traveler's guide to American Presidential homes, most open to the public, depicting and describing homes occupied by every American President from George Washington to George Bush. With visiting hours, admission charges, travel routes. 175 photographs. Index. 160pp. 8¼ x 11. 26751-2 Pa. $11.95

NEW YORK IN THE FORTIES, Andreas Feininger. 162 brilliant photographs by the well-known photographer, formerly with *Life* magazine. Commuters, shoppers, Times Square at night, much else from city at its peak. Captions by John von Hartz. 181pp. 9¼ x 10¾. 23585-8 Pa. $12.95

INDIAN SIGN LANGUAGE, William Tomkins. Over 525 signs developed by Sioux and other tribes. Written instructions and diagrams. Also 290 pictographs. 111pp. 6⅛ x 9¼. 22029-X Pa. $3.95

PHOTOGRAPHIC SKETCHBOOK OF THE CIVIL WAR, Alexander Gardner. 100 photos taken on field during the Civil War. Famous shots of Manassas Harper's Ferry, Lincoln, Richmond, slave pens, etc. 244pp. 10⅝ x 8¼. 22731-6 Pa. $9.95

FIVE ACRES AND INDEPENDENCE, Maurice G. Kains. Great back-to-the-land classic explains basics of self-sufficient farming. The one book to get. 95 illustrations. 397pp. 5⅜ x 8½. 20974-1 Pa. $7.95

SONGS OF EASTERN BIRDS, Dr. Donald J. Borror. Songs and calls of 60 species most common to eastern U.S.: warblers, woodpeckers, flycatchers, thrushes, larks, many more in high-quality recording. Cassette and manual 99912-2 $9.95

A MODERN HERBAL, Margaret Grieve. Much the fullest, most exact, most useful compilation of herbal material. Gigantic alphabetical encyclopedia, from aconite to zedoary, gives botanical information, medical properties, folklore, economic uses, much else. Indispensable to serious reader. 161 illustrations. 888pp. 6½ x 9¼. 2-vol. set. (USO) Vol. I: 22798-7 Pa. $9.95
Vol. II: 22799-5 Pa. $9.95

HIDDEN TREASURE MAZE BOOK, Dave Phillips. Solve 34 challenging mazes accompanied by heroic tales of adventure. Evil dragons, people-eating plants, blood-thirsty giants, many more dangerous adversaries lurk at every twist and turn. 34 mazes, stories, solutions. 48pp. 8¼ x 11. 24566-7 Pa. $2.95

LETTERS OF W. A. MOZART, Wolfgang A. Mozart. Remarkable letters show bawdy wit, humor, imagination, musical insights, contemporary musical world; includes some letters from Leopold Mozart. 276pp. 5⅜ x 8½. 22859-2 Pa. $7.95

BASIC PRINCIPLES OF CLASSICAL BALLET, Agrippina Vaganova. Great Russian theoretician, teacher explains methods for teaching classical ballet. 118 illustrations. 175pp. 5⅜ x 8½. 22036-2 Pa. $5.95

THE JUMPING FROG, Mark Twain. Revenge edition. The original story of The Celebrated Jumping Frog of Calaveras County, a hapless French translation, and Twain's hilarious "retranslation" from the French. 12 illustrations. 66pp. 5⅜ x 8½. 22686-7 Pa. $3.95

BEST REMEMBERED POEMS, Martin Gardner (ed.). The 126 poems in this superb collection of 19th- and 20th-century British and American verse range from Shelley's "To a Skylark" to the impassioned "Renascence" of Edna St. Vincent Millay and to Edward Lear's whimsical "The Owl and the Pussycat." 224pp. 5⅜ x 8½. 27165-X Pa. $5.95

COMPLETE SONNETS, William Shakespeare. Over 150 exquisite poems deal with love, friendship, the tyranny of time, beauty's evanescence, death and other themes in language of remarkable power, precision and beauty. Glossary of archaic terms. 80pp. 5³⁄₁₆ x 8¼. 26686-9 Pa. $1.00

BODIES IN A BOOKSHOP, R. T. Campbell. Challenging mystery of blackmail and murder with ingenious plot and superbly drawn characters. In the best tradition of British suspense fiction. 192pp. 5⅜ x 8½. 24720-1 Pa. $6.95

THE INFLUENCE OF SEA POWER UPON HISTORY, 1660–1783, A. T. Mahan. Influential classic of naval history and tactics still used as text in war colleges. First paperback edition. 4 maps. 24 battle plans. 640pp. 5⅜ x 8½. 25509-3 Pa. $14.95

THE STORY OF THE TITANIC AS TOLD BY ITS SURVIVORS, Jack Winocour (ed.). What it was really like. Panic, despair, shocking inefficiency, and a little heroism. More thrilling than any fictional account. 26 illustrations. 320pp. 5⅜ x 8½. 20610-6 Pa. $8.95

FAIRY AND FOLK TALES OF THE IRISH PEASANTRY, William Butler Yeats (ed.). Treasury of 64 tales from the twilight world of Celtic myth and legend: "The Soul Cages," "The Kildare Pooka," "King O'Toole and his Goose," many more. Introduction and Notes by W. B. Yeats. 352pp. 5⅜ x 8½. 26941-8 Pa. $8.95

BUDDHIST MAHAYANA TEXTS, E. B. Cowell and Others (eds.). Superb, accurate translations of basic documents in Mahayana Buddhism, highly important in history of religions. The Buddha-karita of Asvaghosha, Larger Sukhavativyuha, more. 448pp. 5⅜ x 8½. 25552-2 Pa. $12.95

ONE TWO THREE . . . INFINITY: Facts and Speculations of Science, George Gamow. Great physicist's fascinating, readable overview of contemporary science: number theory, relativity, fourth dimension, entropy, genes, atomic structure, much more. 128 illustrations. Index. 352pp. 5⅜ x 8½. 25664-2 Pa. $8.95

ENGINEERING IN HISTORY, Richard Shelton Kirby, et al. Broad, nontechnical survey of history's major technological advances: birth of Greek science, industrial revolution, electricity and applied science, 20th-century automation, much more. 181 illustrations. ". . . excellent . . ."–*Isis*. Bibliography. vii + 530pp. 5⅜ x 8¼. 26412-2 Pa. $14.95

DALÍ ON MODERN ART: The Cuckolds of Antiquated Modern Art, Salvador Dalí. Influential painter skewers modern art and its practitioners. Outrageous evaluations of Picasso, Cézanne, Turner, more. 15 renderings of paintings discussed. 44 calligraphic decorations by Dalí. 96pp. 5⅜ x 8½. (USO) 29220-7 Pa. $4.95

ANTIQUE PLAYING CARDS: A Pictorial History, Henry René D'Allemagne. Over 900 elaborate, decorative images from rare playing cards (14th–20th centuries): Bacchus, death, dancing dogs, hunting scenes, royal coats of arms, players cheating, much more. 96pp. 9¼ x 12¼. 29265-7 Pa. $12.95

MAKING FURNITURE MASTERPIECES: 30 Projects with Measured Drawings, Franklin H. Gottshall. Step-by-step instructions, illustrations for constructing handsome, useful pieces, among them a Sheraton desk, Chippendale chair, Spanish desk, Queen Anne table and a William and Mary dressing mirror. 224pp. 8⅛ x 11¼. 29338-6 Pa. $13.95

THE FOSSIL BOOK: A Record of Prehistoric Life, Patricia V. Rich et al. Profusely illustrated definitive guide covers everything from single-celled organisms and dinosaurs to birds and mammals and the interplay between climate and man. Over 1,500 illustrations. 760pp. 7½ x 10⅛. 29371-8 Pa. $29.95

Prices subject to change without notice.

Available at your book dealer or write for free catalog to Dept. GI, Dover Publications, Inc., 31 East 2nd St., Mineola, N.Y. 11501. Dover publishes more than 500 books each year on science, elementary and advanced mathematics, biology, music, art, literary history, social sciences and other areas.